CHANGING THE PERFORMANCE

Changing the Performance: A Companion Guide to Arts, Business and Civic Engagement is a manual for arts practitioners concerned with the relationship between business, the arts and wider society, and particularly those engaged in fundraising.

Julia Rowntree gives a fascinating account of her experiences forging the business sponsorship campaign at the London International Festival of Theatre (LIFT). Faced with a funding crisis in the early 1990s, LIFT responded with a radical experiment in business arts relations – the LIFT Business Arts Forum – in which young students and people from private and public sectors are invited to attend the theatre together and imagine how they might do their work differently as a result of this shared experience.

This book proposes that fundraising for the arts is much more than simply a function for generating income. It fulfils an ancient social role of connection across levels of power, expertise, culture, gender and generation. Rowntree describes why these dynamics are vital to society's ability to adapt. Raising intriguing questions about common ground between artistic, social and commercial innovation, this book offers a new model for the theory and practice of financing the arts.

Julia Rowntree led the London International Festival of Theatre's sponsorship campaign from 1986–95 and since then has led three LIFT initiatives in business, arts and civic relations – LIFTING London, the LIFT Business Arts Forum and the Lecture Series *Imagining a Cultural Commons*. Consultant to a range of organizations on civic and arts development issues, she advises and lectures internationally.

'Rowntree's pioneering work conceptualising and realising the LIFT Business Arts Forum is just beginning to be recognised by the arts sponsorship mainstream. She was first in the UK to explore the impact of changing consumer and business values on the world of arts fundraising. Her leadership of the LIFT Business Arts Forum has taken practice in this field in the UK ahead of the game and her story needs to be heard far and wide.'

Clare Cooper, *Co-Director,*
Mission, Models, Money programme

'This inspiring book is about much more than how art engages with business. For any manager in any organization wishing to understand how change really works – and sticks – this book is a must. For anyone taking their first steps in unfamiliar worlds, Julia's story of success and failure offers companionship and much food for thought.'

Sally Bibb, *Director, Group Sales Development,*
The Economist Group

'An intractable and perplexing challenge: to engage arts and business in true learning partnerships. This volume demonstrates how interdependence in the cultural commons not only achieves innovation in both arts and business, but also brings their joint force to bear on public discourse and social adaptation.'

Shirley Brice Heath, *Professor at Large,*
Brown University

CHANGING THE PERFORMANCE

A Companion Guide to Arts, Business and Civic Engagement

JULIA ROWNTREE

nesta
creative investor

Routledge
Taylor & Francis Group

LONDON AND NEW YORK

First published 2006
by Routledge
2 Park Square, Milton Park, Abingdon, Oxon OX14 4RN
Simultaneously published in the USA and Canada
by Routledge
270 Madison Ave, New York, NY 10016

Routledge is an imprint of the Taylor & Francis Group, an informa business

Excerpt from 'East Coker' from FOUR QUARTETS, copyright 1940 by
T.S. Eliot and renewed 1968 by Esme Valerie Eliot, reprinted by
permission of Harcourt, Inc. and by Faber and Faber Ltd.
Quotation from *The Unbearable Lightness of Being* by Milan Kundera
reproduced by permission of the author.
The New Eunuchs by Blair Gibb reprinted by permission of David Barrett.
Excerpt from *Authority* copyright © 1980 by Richard Sennett reprinted
by permission of International Creative Management, Inc.
Excerpts from *Summer Mediations on Politics, Morality and Civility in
a time of transition* [1991] by Vaclar Havel reprinted by permission by
Faber and Faber Ltd.

Writing and research for this book was undertaken with the support of a
Fellowship from NESTA – the National Endowment for Science, Technology
and the Arts. NESTA is a non-departmental public body (NDPB) investing in
innovators and working to improve the climate for creativity in the UK.
www.nesta.org.uk

Typeset in Minion by Florence Production Ltd, Stoodleigh, Devon
Printed and bound in Great Britain by TJ International Ltd, Padstow, Cornwall.

British Library Cataloguing in Publication Data
A catalogue record for this book is available from the British Library

Library of Congress Cataloging in Publication Data
Rowntree, Julia.
Changing the performance: a companion guide to arts, business
and civic engagement/Julia Rowntree.
p. cm.
Includes bibliographical references and index.
1. London International Festival of Theatre.   2. Drama festivals
– England – London.   3. Theater – Economic
aspects – Great Britain.
4. Art fund raising.   I. Title.
PN2596.L6R69 2006
792.079'421–dc22
2005027392

ISBN10: 0–415–37933–4 (hbk)
ISBN10: 0–415–37934–2 (pbk)

ISBN13: 978–0–415–37933–5 (hbk)
ISBN13: 978–0–415–37934–2 (pbk)

To my colleagues,
family and friends
young and old

Without realising it, the individual composes his life according to the laws of beauty even in times of greatest distress.

(Kundera 1984: 49)

CONTENTS

FIGURES

ACKNOWLEDGEMENTS

The people who have helped this book see the light of day are inextricably linked to the practical experience on which it is based. I take this opportunity to acknowledge their support and encouragement.

The vision and openness of Rose Fenton and Lucy Neal made LIFT the inspiration it continues to be. It was Neal and Fenton who backed my journey into uncharted territory. Colleague Tony Fegan shared the responsibility for plotting the routes to learning. To these, my other LIFT colleagues and the many artists who have provided inspiration, my sincerest thanks.

At the outset of my quest for a new way of doing things, in 1994 Brian Eno pointed me in the direction of Global Business Network (GBN) and led me to three people without whom our new business conversations would have foundered. Barbara Heinzen guided every step, stretching ideas of what we were for and reminding us of the importance of neighbours. Arie de Geus and Gerard Fairtlough stood by us helping to shape and reshape what we did and how we did it. Their commitment and generosity expanded our thinking and ways of organizing in fundamental ways. My thanks to you all and to Lisa Fairtlough and Juri de Geus.

Charles and Elizabeth Handy gave endless encouragement, understanding the value of bringing people together around a table and of asking the right questions at the right time. David Bell of the *Financial Times* backed our experiment and risked unconventional theatre visits and proposals; Krishna Guha wrote the first report. Charles Hampden-Turner shone a light on the significance of culture and tragedy. Alain Wouters took thoughts on theatre seriously. Thank you for giving credibility and shape to unformed ideas in their early stages.

Jean Horstman and Paul Askew have been inspiring co-thinkers, facilitators and supporters. Karen Otazo's unfailing generosity helped the struggle through many a thorny briar and pointed me to a Chinese proverb. The late and sorely lamented Blair Gibb alerted me to the role of poets and human rights issues in relation to corporations. Her pioneering work, poetry and international perspective gave confidence to our own ventures.

Three visionary organizations inspired the need to connect across sectors and to particular places in London: Common Purpose, Vision for London and Global Business Network. Thank you to key individuals behind these: Julia Middleton, Esther Caplin and Napier Collyns, Alison Coburn and Pat Brown.

Other friends and colleagues have offered inspiration and pointers along the way. Adelma Roach pointed me to the Santa Fé Mural Project. Randip Basra, Bettina Wohlfarth, Rebecca Dawson, Tiffany Ball, Noriko Ishihara, Erica Campayne and others orchestrated the fine texture of the Forum. Daisy Froud wrote and wrote. Artists Dean Hill, Ewan Marshall, Andrew Siddall, Fabio Santos, Thierry Lawson, Mark Storor, Felix Cross, Greg Thompson, Peter Reder, Bobby Baker, Beverley Randall, Sean Gregory, Julian West and Jan Hendrickse were steady guides into the unknown. Kenny Guthrie, Maylene Catchpole, Chinh Hoang, Honza Noel, Gemma Emmanuel-Waterton, Robert Hutchinson and students at Lewisham College proved that business had much to learn from the talents of a younger generation.

Many business and public sector people have taken part in the LIFT experiment. Particular thanks are due to Sally Bibb, Kate Owen, Cathy Dunn, Janet Ashdown, Rob Moffett and Euan Semple.

Two arts sponsorship colleagues, Russell Taylor and Clare Cooper, have been sounding boards and moral supports beyond compare. Other colleagues have helped me test ideas outside an Anglo-American perspective. Particular thanks are due to Jean-Paul Déru and European Cultural Diploma students from Europe and Africa; Rustom Bharucha, Neelam Chowdhry, Prasad Vanarese, Divya Bhatia and colleagues in India; Blaz Persin and Nevenka

Koprivsek and colleagues in Slovenia; Mahir Namur and colleagues in Istanbul.

Research needs resources. Three imaginative backers came my way. London Arts funded research into the arts learning needs of business; the Winston Churchill Memorial Trust enabled me to look into shifting relations between commerce and communities in the US. Research in South Africa and India was made possible by the miraculous supporter of the untested, NESTA (National Endowment for Science, Technology and the Arts). It is NESTA's support that made the book possible and laid the foundations for LIFT's lecture series 2003–4.

There is, however, one person without whom this book would certainly not have come into being. Shirley Brice Heath's research into learning beyond institutional walls provided a vital piece of the jigsaw. More than this, she has been the skilful midwife of a book that would not have begun or been completed without her guidance, providing as well limitless hospitality and an inspirational place in which to write. Anchor Bay is a little place on the Northwest Pacific Coast of the US where neighbourly relations flourish and backs are never turned to the ocean. Friends have fed and ferried me, and Mar Vista cottages have provided a writing retreat of perfection. To Shirley and friends, thank you.

My thanks also go to Barbara Heimzen for permission to use her diagrams and to Chai Mason who prepared all for publication using Myriad and Illustrator on Macintosh, and to Anna Ledgard for permission to use her writing on LIFT Learning.

Finally my appreciation goes to friends and relations for their patience with a long preoccupation.

ABBREVIATIONS

A&B	Arts and Business (formerly ABSA)
ABSA	Association for Business Sponsorship of the Arts
ACE	Arts Council England
BSIS	Business Sponsorship Incentive Scheme
BT	British Telecom
DCMS	Department for Culture, Media and Sport
DTI	Department for Trade and Industry
EIU	Economist Intelligence Unit
FT	*Financial Times*
GBN	Global Business Network
GDP	gross domestic product
GLA	Greater London Assembly
GLC	Greater London Council
GM	genetic modification
HP	Hewlett Packard
ILEA	Inner London Education Authority
IP	intellectual property
IP	Internet protocols
LAB	London Arts Board
LIFT	London International Festival of Theatre
LWT	London Weekend Television
M&S	Marks and Spencer
NESTA	National Endowment for Science, Technology and the Arts
NYOBC	New York Outward Bound Center
RSA	Royal Society for Arts, Manufactures and Commerce
SADC	Southern African Development Community

STSI	Academy of Music and Dance
UNRISD	United Nations Research Institute for Social Development
UPS	United Parcel Service
VA	Visiting Arts
VfL	Vision for London

INTRODUCTION

Why this book might change
the way you think

*New opinions are always suspected, and usually opposed,
without any other reason but because they are not already
common.*

(Locke 1690)

I live on a wide street. Bordered by a mix of Victorian mansions,
1930s and Arts and Craft houses, local shops, a factory and a petrol
station, the road narrows as it opens out on one side to a park.
For years on my way to work I walked down the same side of the
street leading to the underground station. In the spring of 1994,
I was faced with a mid-career crisis in need of radical solutions.
The question that vexed me was how to build more equitable relationships between the worlds of arts and business. A wholesale
revolution was required, but I had little idea of where to begin. One
morning, mulling over new directions to be taken, I decided to cross
the street to walk to the station on the other side. I found that the
world looked astonishingly different. The morning sun shone on
that side. Unfamiliar plants grew in front gardens – grapes hanging
on a vine and an olive tree – surprising sights in south London. The
more familiar side of the street looked oppressively crowded,
everyone jostling for a place on the narrow pavement. Simply by
striking out towards the local common, several things happened.
The horizon suddenly expanded bringing with it a lightness of spirit.

The difference of perspective seemed out of all proportion to the scale of the move made.

Crossing the street to view the daily round from the other side, from outside the situation, made it look different and a small shift had made a huge one. If a change is needed, I discovered it helped literally to move my feet and disrupt the habitual path. The crowded side of the street may represent the most direct route, but sometimes it is a matter of survival to take a non-direct route to one's destination. The aim of this book is to encourage you too to cross the street in search of a larger horizon and to think about your role and the role of the arts, particularly the theatre, in today's world.

The steps I took that morning deeply affected how I came to approach the work of securing sponsorship from businesses for LIFT, the London International Festival of Theatre. LIFT is a leading contemporary arts organization in the UK and has, since 1981, brought more than 4,000 artists from around 62 countries to perform in theatres and outdoor locations across London. Through bringing new ideas and new kinds of performance to London, LIFT has contributed significantly to opening up new horizons for artists and audiences in Britain. My work at LIFT began in 1986. My role was to find ways in which LIFT could encourage businesses to sponsor performances in the Festival. Within a short space of time, political changes and globalization of the economy forced changes in approach. Conditions over which there was scant control demanded continuous innovation and adaptation. Constant renewal of the values that inspired both LIFT and my own changing role alongside colleagues has been required. This book relates the intertwined stories of an individual, an organization and external events over a near 20-year period.

This book is partly about fundraising, because that was the starting point for my own new departure. It is a historical document about LIFT and my part of the organization's fundraising picture. It is also about more than that. It is about how, through the prism of LIFT, attempts have been made to make sense of complex, interrelated challenges facing the world.

You may question where your own role and practice relate to economic and political issues such as globalization of the economy, growth in privatization, the growing power and impact of multinational corporations – even the future of democracy and life of the planet. You may feel that these topics do not affect you directly in your daily work. On the other hand, it could be that this book changes your mind and that you will find new ways to contribute to wider debate by viewing your role anew.

If you work in an arts organization, you do not need limitless resources to survive, but without adequate funding its potential will never be fully realized. You apply to funding bodies that demand boxes to be ticked. You seek support from businesses that demand short-term promotional advantages. You persist with attempts to retain the interest of individual supporters. You say to yourself: surely there must be a better way to approach this juggling act.

There are no short cuts or quick fixes but I believe that this effort can be different and thus more interesting and fulfilling. I have even come to think that the work of building support for the arts plays a broader role in social survival than when I began work in this field. The thesis here is that the arts fundraising process is not just about raising money but also plays a vital role in social adaptation and resilience. This is because it can open up channels of communication, human connection, reflection and critique across conventional boundaries of power, expertise, culture and generation. I believe that the proximity between arts and business encouraged in the UK over recent decades paradoxically places the arts in a better position from which to critique the commercial values that precipitated that proximity in the first place.

The new way of thinking is not about offering superficial marketing opportunities to businesses, nor is it an opportunistic ploy to meet the demands of public policy. And it is not a patronizing attempt to bring the arts to the unenlightened. Instead it is a wholehearted effort to develop mutual understanding between the arts, the commercial and civic worlds. The aim is to deepen self-understanding in the world of the arts as well as in commerce and communities. It seeks a three-way flow of inspiration, learning and public collaboration.

The money benefits are indirect but nonetheless real.

This book has few easy answers to the ever-heavy burden of raising funds. It is hoped instead that it offers ways out of dark dead ends and courage that the work is worth attempting again and again and again. It is also a reminder that it is only via alliances between those with resources and those with the power, motivation and time to start new conversations that change is possible.

The job of the next generation of those facilitating links between arts, commerce and communities will be to find ways to answer the question as to why all of us need to rediscover routes to public collaboration rather than simply producing art or events for consumption. In so doing, arts organizations will also find routes to their own renewal. But they may need to question their artistic emphasis, organizational ethos and structure. After all, in the words of craftsman, David Pye: 'Art is not a matter of giving people a little pleasure in their time off. It is, in the long run, a matter of holding together a civilization' (Pye 1978: 9).

Perhaps you are an artist, administrator or fundraiser who has been working for some years to keep your arts practice afloat and flourishing. Perhaps you are someone with this role in a large organization with a sense that all is not right with your world. Perhaps you are a policy-maker keen to be responsive to the changing needs of artists and arts organizations. I encourage you to read the whole of this book, which is reasonably short. But you are doubtless extremely busy and may wish to dip into it before reading it all. If you would like to get a sense of the new way of thinking, then I suggest you look at pages 101–38, 151–67, 211–end.

If you are a fundraising veteran you may be looking not for new ways of thinking but to see if your experience chimes with what I have learned over the years. In this case, I suggest you look at pages 25–37, 38–58 and then go to pages 103–38 and 171–end for indications of a different approach.

If you are working in a country where the free market is in its infancy and the only possibility for engaging businesses is on a commercial footing, then pages 25–37 are for you. Nevertheless, a glimpse at new ways of thinking might enable you to be a catalyst for the wider civic conversations outlined in pages 59–86.

Your primary interest may be historical. If you wish to learn more about the interplay of my own story, of LIFT itself, of a new departure the LIFT Business Arts Forum, and how this interplay relates to world events, key parts of the book will be pages 13–37, 38–58, 59–86, 103–38, 139–68, and 216–end, plus the timeline in Appendix one.

Finally, if you are interested in learning more about questions of globalization and the importance of considering the arts fundraising role in this context, then the last section, from page 216 is for you.

Part one, *Opening a Window on the World*, gives a picture of the development of LIFT, the Festival's international and local vision and its engagement with a younger generation of theatre-makers. This part explores how LIFT was resourced, learning the language of business to build a sponsorship programme from scratch. It describes how working principles emerged from engagement with commercial sponsors. It ends with the wider civic partnerships generated in the early 1990s as a result of political changes in London and in response to failures of the market to manage regional questions. Set in an economic era of market fundamentalism, this history gives a flavour of the status quo that came to spark a revolution in approach.

Part two, *Strategic Conversations*, starts with a crisis and embarkation on a journey of discovery as to why the theatre and new forms of civic conversation might be a matter of survival in today's world. It relates the stumbling steps taken towards a new form of relationship with business, one based on co-learning and critique rather than brand promotion. The result was LIFT's invention of the Business Arts Forum, detailed here. Chapter eight describes findings from two periods of research, one in the UK and the second in the US. Both involved a foray into businesses, public sector and community organizations to assess potential for connections to be made across sectors and generations in the Forum. Lastly, this section reveals why, faced with finite natural resources and the resulting need for fundamental structural change in society, culture, values and beliefs may determine survival.

Part three, *Imagining a Cultural Commons*, begins with how LIFT forged ways of collective learning across cultures of many kinds and how this painstaking work informed evolution of the Business Arts Forum and provoked questions as to why diversity of gender and

generation are implicated in the processes of learning and adaptation. This part takes a closer look at a changing economic and
environmental context in which the future is far from certain.
Commercialization of areas of life previously held in common, such
as intellectual copyright, water and genetic material, has pushed
cultural tensions to breaking point worldwide. Speculation is made
about the role of the theatre as a space beyond the market or the
state in which to reflect on and communicate about issues of
common concern both locally and globally.

In the final chapter, qualities of neighbourliness are put centre
stage and attention given to the significance of the LIFT Business
Arts Forum in this context. Social adaptation inevitably spans
generations. Consideration is given here to questions of succession.

Experience of fundraising at LIFT and the search for different
forms of engagement with businesses and public sector organizations provide the basis of this book but it is a useful guide for anyone
needing to structure new alliances across conventional lines. The
majority is written in narrative form. Boxes have been used for
summaries of principle or approach, and quotations and figures
introduced where I have found these useful to my own understanding. Appendix one provides a timeline of LIFT adaptations,
events in London and the wider world. Appendix two gives a
summary of events seen by LIFT's business supporters in the 1995
Festival. Appendix three shows a diagram of key LIFT adaptations
in relation to sponsorship and the Business Arts Forum.

Experience related here has been at a specific time and in a
specific place for a specific aspect of the contemporary performing
arts. You may learn through this book however that when facing
the unknown it is only through looking anew at one's specific
surroundings and learning from the specific experience of others,
that renewal is possible. In the course of my work, I never found a
book that brought together the range of questions I wrestled with
day to day. Rather, this has been a continual process of experiment
and reflection on both failure and success. It is through the theatre
itself that I have learned what does and does not work. This
book will be helpful to others working to support contemporary
performers or visual artists who question established structures and

ways of communicating. It is a personal story offering ideas for shaping partnerships and funding strategy in other fields such as health, youth arts enterprise or social entrepreneurship. It will also be of interest to people in business and policy-making rethinking ways of maintaining long-term trust and connections with the communities they serve.

You may be a lone operator or you may be an individual working for a large organization. You may be a practitioner, producer, development manager, board member, policy-maker or student. Whatever the case, seeing a way clearly to generate support or find fresh inspiration is extremely hard. A formulaic or well-worn approach that reinforces the status quo may run counter to your instincts, background or the culture of your organization, or even undermine your chosen art form or practice. Indeed a sense that things are not right is a signal for steps to be taken in a new direction. Experience shows that the task of securing funds cannot be seen as separate from the artistic practice itself. It is a social, political and aesthetic process needing strong ideas to connect with supporters both inside and outside your organization.

The book is a reminder that money is not necessarily the only thing preventing you from doing what you want to do. The philosophy, ideas and intentions contained in the search for money are ultimately still more important. Paradoxically, by leaving an immediate search for money to one side, on the other side of the street as it were, new possibilities emerge. By focusing on a horizon that is bigger than the direct financial needs of all parties, there is a chance that those needs become lighter, that the search for money itself will change in tone, become more interesting and thus achieve new outcomes. It may not be easier, but it will be less burdensome and more effective in the long term. As Czech political pioneer, Vaclav Havel, advises in his essay, 'The Power of the Powerless', everyday acts of seemingly small significance are the first and most effective way to counter all-pervading regimes from which there appears to be no escape (Havel 1978).

For policy-makers and students of arts administration, cultural enterprise and cultural policy, issues of funding and critique are the focus of wide-ranging study. It is hoped that the experience recounted here will give practical information for studies in a range of fields from the impact of globalization on communities to studies of theatre, cultural policy, organizational learning, social innovation and corporate social responsibility.

You may be reading this in Britain, Europe, the USA, India, Africa or elsewhere. Ways in which resources are secured for the arts differ greatly from country to country, even from city to city. This story comes primarily from London, among the world's richest, most culturally dynamic and best-resourced cities, where access exists to a range of private and public funding sources. It is often assumed that lessons in resourcing the arts are to be learned from the major capital cities. Many ideas in this book have come from places that might be considered as operating far outside the mainstream. Indeed, LIFT's original inspiration was the degree to which Britain could learn from other cultures and cultural perspectives. A belief that fostering Britain's international connections was a matter of survival took me into the world of the theatre. What I hope this book might do is help to foster a confidence in generating support for living arts practice wherever you are based, because, wherever you are, you probably explore the same questions of tradition, modernity, difference, authenticity and survival. Just as many ideas have been borrowed from different sources along the way towards this book, you should find here something to adapt to your particular art form, culture and geographic location. Or you might simply take reassurance from the fact that resourcing the arts is a challenge in London too and that you are not alone.

Underlying the strategic issues of contemporary arts and business are more timeless themes. This dimension of the book encourages you to think beyond your professional role to explore roles and responsibilities that derive from identity, gender and stage in life. Such an examination can help point to new ways of seeing your role and its interplay with the life of any organization in which you are involved. For example, many observers have commented that individuals spanning boundaries of business, arts and communities are predominantly, though of course not exclusively, women. This is not without significance. There is growing evidence from other eras that women have played a role in facilitating connection and experiment across social boundaries at times of great economic and socio-cultural change. Sometimes, by changing the conversation, they have laid the foundations for social innovation. In the story you will read, old and young, men and women have played their part in enabling all involved to learn in different ways.

Behind everyone's work there is a personal story: daily exclusion from nursery school for bad behaviour gave me early experience of seeing the world from an outsider's perspective; being picked on for having red hair made me detest assumptions based on appearance alone; coming from a family of doctors bred an instinct for diagnosis and the dilemmas of public service. A language degree in the 1970s and a passion for the arts led to LIFT after ten years producing animated feature films and commercials. This mix of cultural and commercial experience equipped me to interpret between the worlds of arts and business. Understanding the language and motivations of both fields enabled me to direct the gaze to a rapidly evolving horizon on which both destinies depend.

Few work in the field of contemporary arts simply to make money. Motivation comes from a wish to enable and resource emergent ideas and artistic practice. It comes from a sense that, however small an interaction, the facilitation of new conversations and new ways of seeing is worth undertaking. You are invited to cross the street and, through my experience, see your work in a way that will make the task of securing resources a lighter and more meaningful one. It is my belief that art is a matter of survival, but raising funds for it should not constitute human sacrifice. I hope this book can help you and your art survive and flourish to reinvigorate the public sphere and keep critique and re-creation of reality alive. Broader survival and the rediscovery of public collaboration may just depend on it. Let me begin with where all this began: LIFT.

PART ONE

Opening a Window on the World

The London International Festival of Theatre

*The mind is but a barren soil; a soil which is soon exhausted,
and will produce no crop, or only one, unless it be continually
fertilized and enriched with foreign matter.*

(Reynolds 1774: 99)

ONE

STARTING BY NOT KNOWING

Over the past 20 years, LIFT has radically, and sometimes roguishly, redefined what we think of as theatre and much of the experimentation in this country can be traced to its influence.
(David Benedict, the *Observer*, 2002)

In 1979, it was received wisdom that British theatre was the best in the world. With no international theatre visiting London on a regular basis there was little chance to learn otherwise. When two young women straight out of university, Lucy Neal and Rose Fenton, visited a theatre festival in Portugal, what they saw became the spark for the London International Festival of Theatre – soon to be known as LIFT.[1]

Fenton and Neal had grown up in a tradition where the text was everything, Shakespeare the point of reference for all other theatre. There was nothing to beat Britain where theatre was concerned. When they took their own production to the student drama festival in Portugal, they witnessed cultures and traditions that were more visual, more physical, more musical than their own and with stronger traditions of ensemble working. It dawned that in some parts of the world, theatre is not even called theatre, but is more akin to wordless spectacle or religious ritual. Only in English is the word 'audience' based on auditory perception; in Italian, for example, it is 'spettatore' or spectator; in French it is 'public' or member of the public; in the drama and dance traditions of Africa, the relationship between performer and audience is closer to celebrant, communicant, participant or co-creator (Harding 2002). Fenton and Neal resolved to bring fresh ideas and a greater range of experience and ways of being to audiences in Britain. They would start an international festival in London.

With clipboards for their office, wages from waitressing and bicycles for transport, they set out to discover how they should begin. They admitted they knew virtually nothing, so asked advice from anyone who would give it. More experienced members of the theatre world were generous with their advice if sceptical about the venture. They doubted that such an influx of new ideas could sustain interest; moreover the inexperience of the two young women was palpable. Few believed that contemporary theatre in foreign languages would have an appeal for London audiences – especially not at the height of summer in theatres with no air-conditioning.

In 1981, the first Festival proved the doubters wrong. A dazzling production from Brazil, *Macunaíma*, had the public queuing round the block. The box-office takings for the theatres presenting this and other Festival shows were higher than at other times of the year. The sceptics had to eat their words. London audiences were hungry to have their eyes opened to theatre from elsewhere.

It was *Macunaíma* that got me hooked.

Macunaíma is a legendary hero of the Brazilian Indians. The play told the story of his journey from the Amazon jungle to the sophisticated seductions of São Paolo and Rio de Janeiro. I watched enraptured as a whole city was conjured from newspaper, its sights and sounds brought forth by performers wielding pneumatic drills at one minute to become towering skyscrapers the next. Macunaíma's fear and naivety led him to encounter both danger and magic among the clamour of the streets and markets. The fields and streams beneath the city were brought silently to life as a woman walked across an empty stage holding in her hands a bowl from which fluttering fragments of green paper fell to make a fountain. Macunaíma became lazy, lecherous and wily, his loss of innocence making it difficult to return to the Amazon yet leaving him confused with life in the city. This experience of theatre was so different from a familiar one of text and declamation. It held within it so eloquently the contradictions of contemporary life that I was drawn into another world, through which my own was to change completely.

That first Festival brought around 10 productions from 9 countries and was run entirely on voluntary help from fellow students, subsidized by unemployment benefit, waiting tables and a grant in support of young people from the Manpower Services Commission. In 1981 the biennial Festival budget was £120,000. By 2001 it had grown to a figure over two years of £2.3 million from 87 funding sources and a paid staff that fluctuated from 6 to around 70 including a team of volunteers. LIFT evolved from a four-week Festival every other summer to commission and present performances and learning projects at different times throughout the year. Over two decades, LIFT brought over 4,000 artists from 62 countries to perform in theatres, parks, abandoned buildings and other surprising locations across the UK capital. Changes in the meaning of 'international', of 'festival', of what it was to live in London and in a sense of the role of theatre prompted evolutions in the nature of LIFT. In 2001, the biennial Festival format was abandoned and LIFT embarked on a five-year public Enquiry into the role of theatre for our times worldwide.

Many artists LIFT presented were well known at home, but unknown in Britain. On occasions, these artists found a platform to reach wider audiences in their home countries and around the world. Canadian theatre director, Robert Lepage, was introduced to London through presentation of *The Dragon's Trilogy* in 1987. Chilean writer Ariel Dorfman's *Death and the Maiden* was presented on stage for the first time during LIFT '89. Two years later, it is said that this became the most produced contemporary play in the world. In 1983, a group of performers from Sierra Leone brought their play *Boh Boh Lef*, a comic and satirical view of the insidious influence of missionaries on communities in Africa. The performers came from a range of professional backgrounds, including a PE teacher and an accountant. In common with other theatre companies in Sierra Leone, they created theatre in amateur groups alongside their paid work. As a result of their visit, they became better recognized in their own country. In 1997, De La Guarda arrived with their taut exploration of Argentina's tragic history under the military junta. The show subsequently returned for a commercial run in London's Roundhouse. There are many other stories of theatre practitioners' lives being changed by an appearance at LIFT (Wend Fenton and Neal 2005).

Closer to home, the Festival has been widely recognized for its part in changing the British theatre scene. Even those dyed-in-the-wool conservatives who claimed, when LIFT began, that British theatre was the best in the world, have doubtless been affected in some way by its presentations.

From the outset, it was decided that the Festival be held every two years. This gave breathing space for programming and fund-raising. A wise decision as it also gave LIFT the opportunity to adapt to changes beyond the Festival, not only wider political, cultural and economic change, but also changes in the theatre world that LIFT itself would come to influence. This pace also enabled Neal and Fenton to raise their families.

So how was the biennial Festival programmed? On average between 17 and 22 productions were presented during a three- or four-week Festival each summer from 1981 to 2001. Theatre productions were chosen because they took theatre into a new realm or they said something particularly interesting about the culture from which they came.

No two Festivals were alike although common elements evolved. A typical Festival was launched with a celebratory event, followed by three to four weeks of performances and a closing ceremony. For example, in 1991, British artists Anne Bean and Paul Burwell launched the Festival by animating an unused power station on the Thames at Bankside in central London. This building since became well known as Tate Modern. Bean and Burwell transformed this giant industrial monument, empty for at least 20 years, into a living thing with flames shooting from the 300ft-high chimney and licking into the night sky from paraffin-soaked ropes festooning the gaunt façade. Vast flaming drums were mounted along the parapets and fireworks streamed across the sky fixed to the backs of remote-controlled toy helicopters. Everyone working on the Festival assembled for the celebrations together with visiting artists, LIFT supporters, foreign dignitaries, members of the public and a few unscripted fire engines.

Fire has always been an essential element of the Festival, serving as a reminder that theatre-making has a primordial celebratory and ritual role. Spectacular events incorporating fire have provided an outdoor context for performances taking place in London's theatre venues including: Queen Elizabeth Hall on the South Bank; the Old Vic; the Almeida; the Lyric Theatre, Hammersmith; Riverside Studios; the Tricycle Theatre, Kilburn; Theatre Royal, Stratford East; Waterman's; and the Young Vic. A typical LIFT programme might include new interpretations of classic texts such as Gogol's *The Government Inspector*, performed by the Katona Joszef Theatre Company from Hungary. Or it might include traditional forms such as Peking Opera or the mythical world of Vietnamese water puppetry to express something about the contemporary world from which these performances came. It might include avant-garde theatre companies, The Wooster Group from the US, or Bak-truppen from Norway.

Sometimes whole communities came to LIFT. In Bali there is no word for artist because performance is a way of life and part of religious ceremony and ritual. For the Seka Barong from Singapadu to make its way to London and undertake a UK tour, performers needed months of negotiation with friends and neighbours. Balinese villages are comprised of smaller units called banyars that in turn comprise a number of compounds. Dr I. Wayan Dibia, choreographer, dancer and director at STSI (the Academy of Music and Dance) in Denpasar, led six months of discussions with different compounds and banyars in order to establish who should make up the group and thus best represent the village. Choices were made on the basis of who would most benefit from the opportunity to travel with the group, who would best fill the performance roles required and who might be needed for other reasons, to look after a 12-year-old dancer, for example. Other negotiations were needed. The majority of Seka Barong performers had other occupations. Teachers, farmers and taxi drivers needed to make sure their responsibilities were covered before they could leave home for any length of time. Other communities brought their experiences to London too. Residents of Cabrini Green housing project in Chicago told of the raw experience of their lives via television screens stacked into high-rise towers on the stage of the Theatre Royal, a theatrical haven in the midst of Stratford East's urban landscape.

Sometimes no theatre existed large enough in London to stage productions that were pushing the boundaries of theatre. The solution was to create a theatre from scratch, often securing a public performance licence for spaces that would remain for use by others. Three Mills Studios in east London was converted for the presentation of the Volksbühne Theatre from Berlin. A redundant bus garage at King's Cross was the venue for *Oraculos*. Colombian director, Enrique Vargas, created a labyrinth consisting of 26 chambers filled with encounters of every kind, sounds, textures, evocative smells and strange apparitions. Treats to awaken all the senses dulled by the assaults of urban living.

Alongside the performances, there was always a place for artists and public to meet, a LIFT Club. A series of dialogues and conferences also underpinned the programme and enabled the public to come to find out more about the creative process behind each production. At the Club, a programme provided opportunities for the public to experience the wealth of cabaret and club repertoire to be found in London and for artists to make impromptu artistic connections.

Spoken language was not the only medium for cultural exchange. On occasions, spontaneous collaboration arose between international and UK artists who did not share a language. They stretched and tested each other's musical and performance vocabularies through improvisation. Enjoyment for others came along the way. Jonathan Stone, one of British musical comedy duo, Ralf Ralf, and Regina Orozco of Compañia Divas, who had brought to London from Mexico an all-female version of Mozart's Don Giovanni, experimented in this way one evening, playing the piano and singing. Everyone in the room knew instinctively that they were witnessing the search for shared communication. When it was found, spontaneous applause erupted. The assembled crowd had witnessed artists taking risks in merging cultural perspectives for a moment.

Artistic decisions governing the programme were inevitably tempered by financial considerations needing perfect balance if the Festival was to fulfil its artistic ambitions. Maximum box-office income was secured by the most popular productions with the largest potential audience numbers. If LIFT was to be true to radical developments in theatre, the programme had to achieve a balance across all the productions it presented with some inevitably better attended than others.

Audiences were attracted by marketing and press campaigns combining generic information about the Festival and more detailed information about individual shows. The arts world in London is intensely crowded; people are bombarded with information at every turn. Funds for marketing were inevitably limited. Considerable effort was put into securing editorial and picture coverage of forthcoming shows. The British press is unusually dependent on photographs. Images were essential to attract audiences to little-known shows. Hence photographers would on occasion be commissioned to visit companies abroad, gathering images ahead of the Festival to help reach expectations for ticket sales. Depending on the scale of performances in any one Festival, LIFT audiences have numbered between 10,000 and 70,000 people for a summer's season.

A focus on London and its peoples

When LIFT began in 1981, the Festival simply presented shows from abroad. This was sufficient to satisfy the curiosity of London audiences. Between the early 1980s and 1990s, the meaning of the word international and the dynamics of cultural relations in Britain changed beyond all recognition. Globalization of the economy, cheap air travel, increasing fluidity in world communications and the growing diversity of London's communities meant that experience of other cultures became much more common among theatre-going audiences and London's general public.

The Festival's biennial rhythm gave breathing space to start with a blank sheet of paper and consider fundamental issues. Before each Festival, LIFT was forced to ask: What and whom are we doing this for? And how do we do it better? What is international? What is Festival? What is theatre? And even – What is London?

Clues to adaptation were found partly in productions that LIFT had already presented, and partly in the way that other Festivals were responding to similar challenges. The city itself was a stage of infinite potential through its people, and its physical and historic fabric. It provided outdoor spaces, surprising locations and neglected buildings for artists to explore and to devise large-scale and intimate events in response.

Two early examples of engaging audiences in fresh ways came from Barcelona, Spain and more specifically grew out of the popular performance traditions of Catalonia. Els Comediants recreated *The Devils* in Battersea Park, taking people on an adventure into the underworld. Although the company numbered only a dozen, members of the viewing public felt as if they were surrounded by a multitude of devils leading them into the corners of a flaming, smoking, other universe, beguiled by temptations and distracted at every turn by enchantment and sensuality. Another Catalan genius was Alberto Vidal, who made himself into an exhibit in London Zoo. He ate, slept and lived for two days in an enclosure alongside cages housing other animals. Small children tried to feed him biscuits. Caring adults became concerned for his state of mind and wrote him letters. In turning away from his enclosure, the rest of the zoo was not quite the same. Were the animals watching us, or we them?

The work of many artists LIFT commissioned had evolved from ancient traditions of ritual, carnival and celebration, frequently in climates sunnier than Britain's. Their places of performance were quite naturally in the open air with an ability to attract accidental audiences. This brought a more varied cross-section of the population to experience shows than was found among regular theatregoing audiences.

In the contemporary arts world, productions made in direct response to a particular location came to be called site-specific – a now commonplace term. These site-specific performances aimed to enliven the imagination of audiences, enabling them to see sometimes neglected, sometimes familiar, corners of the city completely differently. The audience was engaged with that space in a more active way than was the norm in a conventional theatre space, altering the way that people saw their own surroundings. These experiences provided a place for new conversations and new perspectives to take shape, influencing any subsequent encounter audience participants have with that particular location.

Urban Sax, a French company of 30 or so white boiler-suited musicians, descended on Covent Garden in 1983. Throngs of people were led through the alleys and squares around the Piazza – a location less well known than it became by the 1990s. Then, the ghosts still lingered of a lost world of traders, their fruit, flowers and vegetables piled up in the heart of the city. From across the neighbouring rooftops of the Opera House and perilously balanced on the parapets of the Floral Hall, the liquid notes of a lone saxophonist were heard followed by another and another. The watching crowd held its collective breath as musicians, still playing, abseiled down the sides of market buildings. There was an expectation that a grand finale would happen, but the music melted away into the buildings as mysteriously as it had appeared. It was as though the music was always there just beneath the surface of the walls and one had only to listen attentively to hear it. The experience moved strangers to converse.

Other site-specific productions came from a deliberate reaction to the constraints of working in the conventional theatre or fine-arts world. For example, Scots-American performance artist Fiona Templeton recreated her urban poem, *You the City*, leading audiences in an exploration of offices, streets, playgrounds, a church and an Indian restaurant around east London's Brick Lane. This participatory theatre enabled an intimate and poetic experience of the most dramatic social and cultural contrasts to be experienced in the city, impossible to achieve via an experience in a gallery or performance space alone.

A change of emphasis

Around the late 1980s, LIFT began to question the context in which shows were staged and commissioned. An instinct grew that adaptation was required in the emphasis of the Festival. Just as LIFT had historically celebrated the variety of theatre that existed in the world beyond Britain, it was becoming clear that there were as many creative possibilities to be explored at home. London is one of the most ethnically diverse cities in the world.[2] It became more and more obvious that the concept 'international' was not only somewhere across the ocean – the world was right here across the street. Fenton and Neal realized that the Festival should respond to the world that is represented in the people of London. They did not just want to present performances that made people think 'Oh, that's strange and exotic.' Rather than being like butterfly hunters out to pin down the bright and the beautiful, they wished to encourage people to have a real exchange with other cultures and to know that they were sharing something – even creating something together – through that engagement. This impulse came to affect how shows were commissioned and resourced. Three productions stand out.

Flying Costumes, Floating Tombs, directed by Keith Khan, was commissioned for LIFT '91 in collaboration with Arnolfini, Bristol. It followed a period of development with another arts commissioning organization, Artangel. A large-scale outdoor event staged beside a canal basin in Paddington, west London, the show drew on traditional and contemporary Indian and African legends and sprang from the Hosay Festival in Trinidad, mourning the death of Hossein and Hassan, grandsons of Muhammed. *Flying Costumes, Floating Tombs* was performed by a combination of professional and amateur artists and participants from the locality. The production required the co-operation of many different people including barge-dwellers, anglers, the nearby school, businesses and the hospital. People came from many different communities and parts of London to take part in the promenade production.

A more extensive international commissioning process laid the foundations for *Zumbi*, a show produced in collaboration with Black Theatre Co-op and Theatre Royal, Stratford East, presented in LIFT '95. Brazilian theatre director, Marcio Meirelles, had visited London two years earlier. His visit was the starting point for discussions leading to a show based on the life of runaway Brazilian slave hero, Zumbi, who led his community of escaped slaves to resist the

Portuguese for 100 years. Working with a team of 15 Brazilian and British performers, Meirelles devised a show combining Zumbi's story of struggle and resistance with that of the British black community. This production pointed the way for subsequent commissions across geographic distance.

Biyi Bandele, a Nigerian writer living in London, proposed LIFT commission him to bring to the stage the African classic, *Things Fall Apart*, by Chinua Achebe (Wend Fenton and Neal 2005). The tragic story of proud leader Okonkwo, the play exposes the cultural confrontations of colonialism and asks who is responsible when things fall apart? The rights negotiated and the stage adaptation completed, questions of theatrical form came to the fore. This play called for a contemporary West African approach, drawing on music and physical performance. African-American Chuck Mike was invited to direct. He was a long-time Nigerian resident and Director of Collective des Artistes in Lagos. The interest of British black artists was sought, of which a number had performed in *Zumbi*. They saw *Things Fall Apart* as an opportunity to give voice to African stories alongside the African-Caribbean stories more often the focus of British black theatre. Rehearsals took place both in Nigeria and Britain and under the auspices of the National Theatre Studio in London. After the play opened at West Yorkshire Playhouse, LIFT's commissioning partner in Leeds, *Things Fall Apart* came to London in LIFT '97 where it enjoyed great success with unusually mixed audiences at the Royal Court Theatre.

With tragic resonance, all of these preparations took place as news unfolded daily of Ken Saro-Wiwa and the Ogoni people's resistance to the combined evils of Sani Abacha's corrupt regime and the environmental degradations of the oil industry. The execution of Saro-Wiwa was announced during rehearsals. This tragedy brought into sharp focus questions of corporate social responsibility worldwide.

A look to LIFT's future and resources

Regard for LIFT's future, its artists and audiences propelled the Festival to adapt once again to find ways of engaging a still younger generation of theatre-makers. The LIFT Education Programme (subsequently called LIFT Learning) is described later in some detail. The principles forged by the Programme came to have a profound influence on the way in which the Festival adapted and particularly how it adapted connections with the business world, the primary focus of this book.

All LIFT's activities needed resourcing, but sources of money were ever changing, reflecting the swirl of wider political and economic changes. In LIFT '81, '83 and '85, the major source of funds was London's city government, the Greater London Council. Other funds came from the local public body responsible for funding the arts, the Greater London Arts Association[3]; a handful of trusts, foundations, sponsors and individual donors; and the cultural funds from governments of some countries whose theatre companies were invited to the Festival.

In 1986 however, a dramatic shift was in store. Dependency on government funds could no longer be relied upon. Arts organizations were encouraged to look to the business world for financial support.

TWO

LIFT LEARNS THE
LANGUAGE OF BUSINESS

*Ours is the age of substitutes: instead of language we have jargon;
instead of principles, slogans; and, instead of genuine ideas,
Bright Ideas.*

(Bentley 1952)

When I began work at LIFT in 1986, the Conservative government
was in power and pressure was put on the arts to become less dependent on public funds. As part of the free market project sweeping
both the US and Britain, the dominant economic model was based
on the primacy of markets, the pursuit of unbridled self-interest,
low taxation and a minimal state. The arts, in common with many
other activities, were called upon to justify their existence in competition with other demands on the public purse. Government funds
for the arts came to a standstill. What's more, as part of a comprehensive shake-up of local government, LIFT's major supporter, the
Greater London Council, was abolished. In this political climate,
the only apparent route to an increase in funds was the private
sector. LIFT decided to embark in earnest on the search for business sponsorship.

This decision coincided with a moment in my own life when a
career change was on the cards. I had known Neal and Fenton for
a long time and they occasionally covered my job during holiday

periods. We worked close to each other in London. The animation studio where I worked was among the many cheaply rented design and photographic studios of Covent Garden, not far from LIFT's borrowed office premises.

After the inspirational experience of *Macunaíma* as part of the first Festival in 1981, each subsequent LIFT was eagerly awaited, and I offered help and advice where possible. My work at the Festival formally began in 1986. The original plan was to work with LIFT for just a brief period. It was to turn out differently.

My commercial experience tuned with what was needed for getting to grips with LIFT's embarkation on the search for sponsorship. From 1976 to 1986 I had worked as a producer of short feature films and television commercials for products such as Guinness and Babycham, Dulux Paint and Vortex Bleach. Expertise in commercials brought with it a familiarity with the language and motivation of people in the worlds of advertising and business. My role as producer of commercials had been to translate the commercial brief to the artists and, while interpreting cost implications, maintain as much freedom for the artists as possible. From the perspective of the artists, producing good commercials was perceived as not simply a question of delivering everything the advertising agents asked for but also stretching what they thought was possible. Awareness of commercial imperatives and practical experience of maintaining artistic principles in this context was good preparation for attempting to translate what LIFT had to offer to the business world.

As a language graduate, I found the complexities of translation were a source of constant fascination. Sometimes the most challenging translation is faced in settings where people apparently speak the same language, but have different agendas and specialized codes. Words exist in every language that are generally deemed to be untranslatable and even translatable words conjure different images in different imaginations. In the world of animated films, I enjoyed the challenge of attempting to reach mutual understanding across these untranslatable aspects of culture and producing something practical and new as a result. These turned out to be the skills needed to explore how LIFT might generate support and resources from worlds other than conventional public funding. If we were to secure sponsorship from businesses, then my job was to tease out all the directly commercial reasons as to why a business might sponsor LIFT, while ensuring to the best of our ability, that we were not endangering LIFT's artistic principles.

Getting down to work – what did we have to offer?

As a first step, we needed to tease out what we had to offer of direct commercial interest to companies and then set out our stall. It was not immediately clear how we did this. LIFT already had a track record of having staged three Festivals, so there was evidence that LIFT was a dynamic and exciting organization. Nevertheless the number of people in the business world who were aware of LIFT was relatively small. To reach potential sponsors, we needed to identify aspects of our activities holding an interest for people beyond those currently involved in LIFT. We also had to establish a language in which to describe them.

We decided our assets were:

- The Festival as a whole, and artists and productions within it.
- A sense of surprise, energy, colour, vitality, wit and communication from the edge.
- International dimension.
- Local community connection.
- Young risk-taking audiences.
- Some supporters with recognizable names.
- Boldness, energy and originality.

Communicating what we had to offer

If people were to support us, we needed to make our assets visible. We also needed to reassure people that they were getting involved with an organization that would deliver. LIFT already had a track record and images of productions from previous Festivals. Importantly, we were also set up as a charity, the UK name for organizations with not-for-profit constitutions, so we could receive donations.

Our first step was to produce a printed document that made visible our credentials and communicated the style and quality of LIFT. We decided to make a major investment in a LIFT brochure, not a programme of Festival events but a publication that described the history of the Festival, its ethos and supporters. The first sponsorship we secured was a corporate logo by the design group Pentagram. They took on this task as a creative challenge for their younger designers. To create the body of the brochure, we worked with graphic designers who had already worked with the Festival.[1]

Though primarily designed for the business community, this brochure also needed to be our calling card in other settings from foreign governments to artists we were inviting to the Festival. Both copy and supporting visuals had to take these mixed audiences into account without using language for one that would alienate another. The brochure also had to last four years over two Festivals, so avoided specific references that would easily become out of date.

Favourable press comments from previous Festivals were included along with images of shows to provoke people's curiosity. We asked people who knew of LIFT's work to provide endorsements for inclusion. On occasion, we wrote to these people suggesting what they might say. The list included the Secretary of State for Foreign and Commonwealth Affairs, the Director General of The British Council, and prominent figures in the theatre world and in education.[2] The process of putting the brochure together provided an opportunity to reinforce our relationships with these influential people, by making an excuse for us to contact them. This first attempt set a model for how we composed subsequent LIFT publications and how this process itself could be used to build support, clarifying and simplifying the way that we spoke about the Festival.

Finding out why businesses might wish to sponsor LIFT

Our next task was to establish why businesses might be interested in sponsoring LIFT. Sponsorship had come to mean paying for, or contributing towards, a performance in exchange for advertising or other benefits. We sought the advice of people more experienced than us as to what those benefits might be. Armed with this advice and our own first steps, we learned that companies sponsored the arts for one or more of the following reasons:

- Corporate philanthropy – support for the artistic activities of the organization without any demand for commercial return.
- Good corporate citizenship – association with a worthy cause to influence opinion about the company.
- Brand recognition or marketing – reaching a larger audience/customer base of a particular profile through printed material and advertising.
- Brand sampling – getting into contact with a particular audience in order to get them to sample products – usually alcohol.
- Networking – gaining access to political or commercial influence.
- Entertainment for clients or employees.

Parcelling up the Festival

Alongside the broad survey of our assets and the motivation of businesses, we needed to devise ways of framing or slicing up the Festival so that anyone, regardless of motivation, could find a way of getting involved. We had to think what contributors would get in exchange, how their contribution would be recognized and how they would be thanked, regardless of their level of donation. We needed to make them feel good about giving to the Festival. In exchange, we could offer tickets, invitations to receptions, access to influence and new friends, connection with audiences and other supporters, corporate publicity or their name in the programme.

We parcelled up the Festival for sponsors in these ways:

1 Regular membership, corporate or individual
Some people would find the Festival a good idea and be motivated by corporate philanthropy – we asked them to be corporate members at £1,500 each. We understood that this was the sum that some senior managers could sign off at their own discretion without calling on colleagues for a lengthy process of approval.

Alongside corporate membership, we also devised an individual membership scheme for friends and supporters at £25 or upwards that came to include friends and relatives of practically everyone working on the Festival. Members were offered tickets to opening nights, invitations to receptions and membership of the LIFT Club. The number and range of benefits were adjusted to the actual costs they represented to the Festival. For example, corporate members were offered eight tickets to the opening nights of shows.[3] Individual friends were not offered tickets, but given membership of the LIFT Club together with a poster and priority booking for shows.

2 Individual production sponsorship

As the first step in seeking sponsorship for individual productions, we needed to be realistic that some shows would not be at all attractive to sponsors. For those that might be, each show would attract a different kind of sponsor and our approach was tailored accordingly. To be specific, these broadly fell into three types: diplomatic work to be done, family fun and cool audiences. None of these definitions was mutually exclusive, but the emphasis changed with each one.

Examples of the first definition 'diplomatic work to be done' were those productions of high status in the country from which they came and that the ambassador might wish to attend. These productions often came from countries with which Britain had delicate diplomatic relations to maintain. We would engage the ambassador's interest as early as possible, working through the cultural attaché at the relevant embassy. The interest of the ambassador and the promise of his or her attendance at the production would help in the search for potential sponsors or groups of sponsors. Sponsorship of the 1993 visit of the Beijing Jing Ju Opera Troupe from China with their production of *The Little Phoenix* was secured in this way. A small percentage of the total budget for the visit was secured through a combination of donations from members of the China Britain Trade Group and from Cable and Wireless, totalling approximately £15,000. This was at a time when Britain was negotiating the return of Hong Kong to the Chinese mainland.

An example of the second category, 'family fun', was *Cirque Plume* from France, sponsored by the cross-Channel train service

Eurostar, in 1995. LIFT presented this show in a tent on Highbury Fields, a well-loved park in Islington, north London. The show appealed across generations with its combination of quirky sophisticated humour, acrobatic and musical virtuosity and dazzling ensemble working. Eurostar wished to promote its new cross-Channel service to arts-lovers and families as a way of connecting with the cultural riches of Europe. It made sense to attach their name to the project. The sponsorship was for £20,000 and included train fares for LIFT staff and journalists to visit the production in France ahead of the company's arrival in London. This support enabled LIFT to prepare technical details, education programmes, marketing campaigns and press coverage.

The third type of show or project attracted a specifically fashionable or 'cool' audience. Marketeers are interested in bringing brand names to the notice of an influential group. In marketing jargon, these are the people described as 'early adopters', those who set the trend. With its programme of cutting-edge cabaret, in 1987 we were able to attract a new brand of beer, Moosehead, to sponsor the LIFT Club for £5,000. Their brand was promoted in a free Festival newspaper sponsored by the *Daily Telegraph* equally interested in reaching a younger readership. In later years, Gordon's Gin sponsored the LIFT Club as part of its effort to change the image of gin from the favoured drink of colonials to a more youthful tipple.

3 Support in kind
There were also forms of support we could search for that did not directly involve a cash donation: printing, provision of flights or accommodation, publicity, free advertising or airtime. Examples here include the Festival newspaper mentioned earlier and free advertising by *Time Out*, London's listings magazine. This advertising was used to reinforce the commercial interest of brand sponsors such as Gordon's.

4 Advice
We also needed to research key people who might offer us their expertise on a *pro bono* basis. Graphic design, photography and

marketing are examples of advice that on occasions have been provided to LIFT free of charge or at reduced rates.

Finding out who to talk to

Every case of successful fundraising ultimately came out of a personal contact. After much trial and error, it became clear that cold mailings to large numbers of people were completely useless. Different ways of doing research and expanding networks developed, thereby building up LIFT's range of personal contacts:

- Business pages of the daily papers were essential reading as well as specialist newspapers such as the *Financial Times* (*FT*), *The Economist* and design and advertising press. News of different companies and specific individuals offered a valuable way of finding reasons to call people about matters that were not immediately about money. Any hook on which to hang a phone call, email or conversation was an essential starting point before plunging in with advocacy for LIFT or enquiring directly whether there might be interest in sponsoring a production.
- Membership of societies and attendance at conferences also enabled us to meet people. Events with participation from different sectors were particularly useful starting points.
- People on aeroplanes, in pubs and cafés, on buses and on holiday provided potential routes to generating support. If individuals themselves were not interested, they sometimes passed on connections to people who were.
- Existing networks of friends and relatives did not escape our search for commitment and support. This was a job with few boundaries.
- In the case of specific countries, contact was made with the relevant desk officer at the Department for Trade and Industry (DTI), the regional desk of the Confederation of British Industry, the commercial attaché at the relevant embassy, the local British Council officer, etc.
- Publicity of other organizations provided credits for foundations and businesses. These offered clues as to supporters who might be interested in us as well.

Making the proposals

Each proposal was tailored specifically for a particular individual and organization. As many facts as possible were incorporated, but descriptive elements were needed too, in order to capture the imagination of the individuals concerned. Very often these individuals needed to convince colleagues, so we had to provide them with ways of talking about a project that inspired them to be advocates too. They needed to convey the sense of excitement and interest that their colleagues might get out of attending a LIFT event. At the same time they also needed hard facts about the commercial benefits they would derive from agreeing to sponsor.

Proposals included:

- Background about LIFT.
- Outline of project with a feel for what an audience member might experience, accompanied with images if available.
- Venue and dates.
- Existing supporters.
- Likely audience, profile and numbers.
- Benefits offered – i.e. number of tickets to which performances, range of receptions offered, etc.
- Cost of sponsorship.

What sponsorship was needed and what was it worth?

Presenting theatre anywhere is a costly exercise. Hosting a large number of visitors and staging a wide range of shows in London is still more so. Public funding only goes so far. The reason for seeking sponsorship is to expand funds for presentation, accommodation and hospitality and, importantly, to preserve ticket prices at a level accessible to people with a range of incomes. If presentation of LIFT's theatre productions relies on revenue generated by box-office income alone, then ticket prices have to be set astronomically high. If the wealthy alone can afford to attend, audience profile runs counter to LIFT's vision of theatre as a way to bring people together across socio-economic boundaries and to inspire UK theatre students and professionals. Hence LIFT has the need to look for sponsorship alongside other revenue streams such as the box office and public subsidy.

We discovered that putting a value on sponsorship was not an exact science. Sponsors could not try out the article before they bought into it. A risk was inevitably involved. As to the worth of any sponsorship, it was hard to find any rules. Research bore little fruit since other organizations did not readily disclose such information. In LIFT's case, a balance was struck between our ideal sum and how much the potential sponsor was willing to pay. Agreeing to this sum was not like buying and selling a product in a shop; it was more akin to dating. An offer was accepted that seemed attractive at the time. Comparisons with other offers could be made, but in the end any organization can only be its own register of value. Before approaching a sponsor, two figures were held in mind. The first was the ideal figure arrived at in consultation with colleagues, and the second, a figure below which we would be seriously underselling what we saw as our value. We found that the sponsorship range for one production averaged around £5,000, sometimes dropping to £2,000 and on rare occasions rising to £20,000 in the case of *Cirque Plume*. This sponsorship represented approximately one-third of the total budget for that show. Growing to an average 13 per cent of total budget in the early 1990s, LIFT's overall sponsorship percentage was considered high at the time in contrast to other arts organizations.

Media coverage

A cornerstone for securing commercial sponsorship, every sponsor wanted as much exposure as possible, and every arts organization did its best to try and secure the maximum. Yet every arts organization faced obstacles. Where the print media was concerned, visibility could be bought through advertising or secured through editorial coverage. Resources had to be dedicated to the staging of shows, not the purchase of advertising, so this route was limited. On occasions, LIFT was able to negotiate free advertising for specific shows or the LIFT Club with *Time Out*, London's listings magazine. In this case, it was possible for us to incorporate the name of a sponsor and thus offer press coverage as a benefit of sponsorship. Purchase of advertising space simply to satisfy the promotional needs of sponsors was counterproductive.

What is more, editorial coverage was by far the most effective way to attract people to buy tickets; this was a priority and LIFT concentrated its efforts here. We had to ensure that we generated the box-office income budgeted. While recognizing that sponsorship was an increasing fact of arts life, as a rule journalists were not interested in sponsors but shows. They were also only too painfully aware that space was extremely limited in most papers. The press shrank from mentioning sponsors in editorial columns, thus inhibiting press coverage for sponsors in the editorial pages. Doubtless newspapers felt that the sponsors should be buying advertising from the newspaper directly. Even if individual journalists were willing to mention involvement of a sponsor in any production, the sub-editor would often delete the sponsor's name before going to print. *FT* was the only newspaper regularly to cover arts sponsorship issues. Moreover, members of the public did not show deep interest in which company sponsored a particular show, unless that company was controversial. In such cases, it was counterproductive for an arts organization to be seen in association with that business.

The only way a business was guaranteed a mention in connection with a particular event was to pay highly enough for its name to be incorporated into the title of the sponsorship or to devise its own arts package. So, for example, in the 1980s the Digital Dance Awards came on the scene. The Booker Prize continues to be a well-resourced literature sponsorship, followed by the Orange Prize for Fiction and others. LIFT was not of sufficiently high profile to attract a sole sponsor in this way. Neither was its format sufficiently certain and under a sponsor's control. Had we been in a position to secure a sole sponsor, other considerations also had to be borne in mind. Care had to be taken that we were not setting up a situation that eliminated other businesses through competition with the sole sponsor. We were also reluctant to put all our eggs in one basket by spending a year's efforts on looking for a sole sponsor when we might end up with none.

Sponsors were interested in television coverage of performances. Securing television coverage, however, was not straightforward. First, in order to get the most out of television coverage, for both a potential sponsor and for promoting the show's presence in London, it was best to film the theatre company ahead of time, so that coverage could serve to promote the show. This meant that coverage of LIFT shows was extremely expensive as they were almost always, by definition, happening in another country, meaning that a television crew would have to take on the costs of flying a crew to film the company.

Often the timing did not work to our advantage either. So, for example, should we wish to gain television coverage of French pyrotechnician Christophe Berthonneau's fireworks, we would have to be persuading a television company to go and film the production he was staging prior to the one due to happen at LIFT. This might be in Australia or India six or eight months before the one planned for London. At this point, we were still concentrating every ounce of energy we had on raising the money from a variety of sources including sponsors, securing the local permissions for venue use, and negotiating with safety and public licensing and with artists and local community groups. Priority could not go to securing television coverage just in case we could get a sponsor who might be interested.

A more general obstacle to securing television coverage of theatre shows was that they simply do not work very well. Shows made for the stage have been successfully transferred to television, but often only when they have been specially adapted. LIFT's priority is to stage shows for live audiences; televising a show can frequently interfere with audience's sightlines and attention.

Deciding on media priorities is a microcosm of the juggling act that went on throughout all of LIFT's activities. Securing sponsorship from businesses was just one aspect of LIFT's overall fundraising effort from trusts, foundations, public funding bodies and individuals. I was nominally responsible for raising money from businesses from 1986 to 1995; in truth, during this time the task of learning how to do this was shared among Fenton, Neal and myself. Fenton and Neal handled all public funding relationships and the majority of trusts and foundations. In 1995, when I began to forge a different style of relationship with business, LIFT still had to pursue business sponsorship. Angela McSherry, Administrative Producer, led this effort, building new contacts and opportunities for the organization.

Presenting LIFT and raising the funds to pull it off involved constantly balancing artistic vision with financial and human resources. It was only possible to secure sponsorship if the whole organization was alert to the implications and demands of this search. Yet, it was counterproductive if sponsorship demands dominated the organization, diverting its vision and purpose. At all times this balance had to be finely maintained, with priority given to presenting performances to the public and engaging artists and audiences with each other. Staffing and organizational structure had to remain centrally committed to these goals as LIFT evolved. Each individual's working principles had to align with the values of the organization too.

THREE

FINESSING THE RULES
OF ENGAGEMENT

*In most trades people plod along steadily . . . thankful to be paid
for doing what they would be happy to do unpaid if they had
the means of survival. Occasionally, though, some bit of information, some discovery changes the shape of the trivial round,
giving it a new aspect. Perhaps because I never had any training
as a cook, this happens to me with a particular force once or
even twice a year if I am lucky.*

(Grigson 1993: 316)

My role at LIFT needed clarification and a name. No specific
training or guidelines existed. As a bridge-builder between the needs
and resources of the business world and those of LIFT, my role was
essentially that of interpreter. 'Fundraiser' seemed too narrow a
definition for I was not solely engaged in the search for funds. The
term 'Development Director' settled on me from 1986–95 when my
role was to be responsible for developing relationships in a range
of ways, rather than simply seeking money.

Nevertheless, my role was primarily to define and articulate what
LIFT was selling to business sponsors and to generate income.
Through experience of engaging with business supporters, ten
principles emerged, highlighted here and drawn together in Box
3.1 on p. 57.

Confident communication of LIFT productions to the outside world meant knowing about the art, but also detailed changes such as dates, times, tour venues and so on. A simultaneous inside and outside sensing was required. Literally sitting close to the people putting the programme together was vital in the early stages so that information was absorbed as a matter of course. Command of the vocabulary, ways of thinking and ethos of the art helped communicate that energy beyond the LIFT office.

Nevertheless, however vivid a picture of each individual production it was possible to paint single-handedly, this was no substitute for sponsors hearing directly from the Festival Directors about a production or commission they were making or had seen. Thus it was important to involve colleagues as advocates and fellow thinkers at sponsor meetings.

Once the language was acquired, it became clear that the job of securing support would not happen overnight, nor was it a linear process. Success lay in strengthening the organization overall, including building Board membership and other strands of support. If outsiders were going to plug into LIFT, we needed to expand the insiders we could rely on. Just like organizing a party, the more popular it is perceived to be, the more newcomers are likely to attend. If newcomers are familiar with or intrigued by some of the people who will be there, they are more likely to come along.

The consistency needed to build these external relationships over time had resource implications. It is difficult for small organizations to commit to paying someone to have a long-term approach that brings no resources into the coffers in at least the medium term. A balance has to be struck and agreement reached about how the work of development was structured and remunerated. We had no idea what level of funds my post might succeed in generating. LIFT had to take a gamble. My contract was part time at three days a week leading up to the Festival. Following each two-year cycle of the Festival, the contract finished and work was found with other organizations for three months or so before re-starting work at LIFT in time to prepare for the next Festival. When the organization reached a comparatively more stable phase, my contract grew to four days a week. The experience gained at LIFT made it possible to offer up-to-date advice and ideas to other organizations. One of these was the contemporary dance theatre, The Place. The experience with these other organizations could then be brought back to LIFT and vice versa.

To begin with, there was a concern that there might be a conflict of interest. In practice, this did not become an issue. Often, sponsors' interests were so specific, for example favouring dance or theatre, that there was no dilemma. At other times, it emerged that sponsors trusted my judgement and it was possible to engage their interest in several projects. As long as one is clear about what motivates and interests people and is sensitive to how often calls are made on them, then these dilemmas resolve themselves. A set of working principles took shape.

1 Build upon every interaction as potential for personal, financial or advisory support. Whatever it is, it can make a difference
Just prior to my joining LIFT, Fenton and Neal were working to strengthen the Board of Directors and secure a new Chairman. The Board were the guardians of LIFT's legal framework as a charitable organization with principles of public and educational benefit. In the early 1980s LIFT had come to recognize that a Chairman was needed to help the organization open doors. A powerful representative of the political and social establishment was needed but someone who understood the value of contemporary theatre at the same time.

Neal and Fenton had had contact with the then Minister of the Arts, Lord (Grey) Gowrie, a well-known lover of the contemporary arts and accomplished poet. LIFT's introduction to Gowrie was unusual. In 1985 the Festival invited the Fourth Peking Opera Troupe to London to perform *The Three Beatings of Tao San Chun* at the Royal Court Theatre as part of LIFT '85. A Sino-British Agreement had recently been signed detailing plans for cultural reciprocity between the two countries. Indeed the theatre company's visit tested the intentions contained in that international agreement and the existence of resources to back them up. The Great Britain–China Centre, an organization promoting understanding between the two countries, regarded the visit of great significance. It had put all its weight behind helping LIFT to navigate the many complex layers of communication required to make the visit a success.

The company arrived in London. Invitations to the opening night had been sent to the relevant dignitaries. Plans were laid for the company to eat after the show. It then emerged that the Chinese restaurant serving the most appropriate cuisine was some distance from the theatre. The acrobats in the company complained of getting headaches and feeling dizzy when they travelled on the underground. There was no budget for alternative transport. Official diplomatic and cultural channels would have to be called upon to help. Fenton and Neal set out to present the situation to the Minister for the Arts, Lord Gowrie, making telephone calls to his office until he responded. Their tenacity paid off and the money was found for a coach enabling LIFT to provide the best care possible to the company. Gowrie attended the opening night performance that evening and met the company.

Impressed with Neal and Fenton's persistence, when Gowrie was approached to become Chairman of the Festival, he accepted. By that time he had left government to become Chairman of the auction house, Sotheby's. In the climate of the 1980s, the support of a prominent public figure was needed to put LIFT on the map. In turn, perhaps Gowrie needed LIFT, in order to stay in touch with people working at the forefront of contemporary arts practice, to retain charitable activity alongside his work for a private arts organization and, possibly, to satisfy his curiosity about how LIFT could develop under Neal and Fenton's leadership.

I also started enlisting people to help. Gowrie's involvement helped engage people's attention. A few early examples demonstrate that relatively modest support can be of immeasurable value in strengthening the organization. The first person we approached was Geoff Howard-Spink, the Director of a large advertising agency whom I had known through my previous work. We asked him to help us write the first LIFT brochure.

Recognizing that we needed to develop the language in which we would speak about the Festival to the business community, Howard-Spink invited me to a seminar about sponsorship held by the Association of Advertisers. This event gave me more clues about the motivations of sponsors. I met at that meeting Jeremy Kane who worked at Mars, a large privately owned company manufacturing confectionery and pet foods. Mars subsequently contributed funds to our ultimately unsuccessful efforts to bring Peter Brook's *Mahabharata* to London.

Another example of support with a long-term benefit to the Festival came through LIFT's graphic designers, Adams and Coke, who were also designers for the Groucho Club, a well-known watering hole of media glitterati. They proposed Fenton, Neal and myself for honorary membership. Simply having a decent place to meet can be a key issue for small-scale arts organizations – often based in premises that are far from comfortable. Membership of the Groucho Club enabled us to invite potential sponsors to meet at a venue with fashionable appeal. Tony Mackintosh, the Club Director, was keen to support the arts and encourage the less moneyed end of London's cultural life on which he knew the vibrancy of central London depended. In those early days, paying our drinks bill at the Club was a challenge. Even a round of coffees was an investment. Sponsors often lack awareness of the vastly different economic scale at which people in the voluntary sector operate. Tricky situations can emerge when you are attempting to build bridges between worlds, when those with more money just assume that a meal can be bought without a thought. Tony Mackintosh's hospitality went to the heart of this issue and helped LIFT to be in a position of equity with those from whom we sought support. The Club went on to host events and receptions for sponsors and visiting artists.

The next step was to build up a team of people to help more directly in forging sponsorship connections. I did not have impeccable contacts in the business world, but could spot someone who had access to networks that might be interesting to us and, in turn, to whom we might have something to offer. We decided to initiate a Development Council whose sole responsibility was to strengthen our business support. The Council was separate from the Board, LIFT's main governing body, and had no legal responsibilities.

The first members of the Council demonstrated the principle of building on every possible interaction and of maintaining continuity of relationships. Members included Geoff Howard-Spink, the advertising executive already mentioned; Paul Askew, who advised companies on brand and marketing strategy; Jeremy Kane from Mars; and Peter Wilkinson, an executive responsible for sponsorship at computer company, IBM, an existing supporter of LIFT. A later member was Andrew Hepburne-Scott, a merchant banker who had contacted us after reading about LIFT's efforts to stage Peter Brook's *Mahabharata* in the *FT*.

Finding people with whom to engage seems at first a daunting challenge. However, engagement and support start with a conversation. The conversation is the thing. Keep it going, finding fresh news and fresh reasons for keeping it alive over time.

2 Manage relationships with brevity, discretion and equity,
combining formal and informal communications
After the initial few meetings of the Development Council, it became obvious that organizing meetings and writing minutes was too labour-intensive. It became more practical to communicate with the members on a one-to-one basis. This path proved more productive as holding full meetings of the Development Council was cumbersome; numerous suggestions would be made but days later those suggestions were already ruled out by events. Yet courtesy demanded that I follow up and report back on suggestions. Communicating on an individual basis gave more flexibility. The title of Development Council Member was useful to use on letters written on LIFT's behalf and a way for new people to be brought on board as official supporters without their being members of the Board. Council Members were always invited to Festival receptions in recognition of their support. These occasions enabled them to bring others into the fold. This combination of flexibility and formality came to be a proven approach to developing new initiatives.

Weaving new connections into a network of long-term supporters and structuring a conversation either individually or in larger groups involves many modes of communication: telephone calls, emails, letters and so on, but also setting meetings to fit busy schedules all round. It is essential to economize on the number of communications and the volume of information given to people and to constantly ask yourself what people need to know to keep engaged and respond to questions.

It goes without saying that discretion and equity are needed to deal with people over a long period. With so many overlapping relationships, attention needs to be paid to private space and individual connections as well as the public space structured in meetings or experienced during performances. A more formal and equitable mode of communication is needed in larger gatherings for newcomers to feel welcome. Some people you will know very well, but if that familiarity is thrust in newcomers' faces, they will feel alienated. If the job of securing support is a social process of connecting people as much as it is the act of securing support, then it is extremely important to give people equal attention regardless of how much money they can give you.

3 Have faith that the art will inspire sources of support
Each project at LIFT is explored and turned like a prism to see how it might fit with concepts currently in the public arena. Practical ways then follow to connect people to these ideas. For example, LIFT worked with British performance group Station House Opera to stage their show *The Bastille Dances* outside the National Theatre in LIFT '89. Eight thousand concrete blocks were used to re-enact the story of the French Revolution and to make visible the power of the individual to change history. The production had different resonances in different countries. London at the time was at the height of the 1980s construction boom with never-ending expansion of the financial services sector. A collective spirit seemed to be in danger of being swept aside by pure greed. The production was an extraordinary prefiguring of the collapse of the Berlin Wall. The show achieved its full resonance with audiences caught up in the historic changes afoot in Europe when performed to thousands in Salzburg.

In response to the last-minute loss of a grant, a special fundraising scheme was devised. *Be a Brick, Buy a Block* built on the idea of the French Revolution, offering concrete blocks at a range of prices: £10 for peasants (sans-culottes), £100 for bourgeoisie and

£1,000 for aristocrats. Purchasers were invited to choose their status and buy accordingly. Identical blocks were differentiated by a spray-painted stencilled motif of a revolutionary bonnet, a three-cornered hat or a crown. Each block had appropriately coloured rope with which to carry it away: red, dark blue and royal blue. Lord (Peter) Palumbo asked for 200 bourgeois blocks in order to escape the symbolic guillotine. After some persuasion, he stuck with two aristocrat blocks at a donation of £2,000. A limousine arrived to pick them up. The realization that people enjoyed acknowledging their status in playful ways alongside others came to inform other schemes to make lighter the raising of support.

Simply through dogged belief and a collective act of faith, projects have been pursued at LIFT against the grain. Many of these have involved unconventional use of spaces originally designed for other purposes. Examples include Director Deborah Warner's animation of the interiors of neglected London landmarks, St Pancras Chambers in 1995 and Euston Tower in 1997. Another is Keith Khan's *Flying Costumes, Floating Tombs*, staged in 1991 in a car park beside the Regent Canal, an area due for major redevelopment. Never before used for theatrical performance, all these locations for this purpose needed negotiation with landlords, community and other interest groups before they could be secured. Frequently we were not only negotiating use of space but were seeking sponsorship from landlords or businesses at the same time. Only when every stone had been turned and every possibility explored did we abandon an idea; examples include: Peter Brook's *Mahabharata*, which we failed to present in a Docklands warehouse; and Matthias Langhoff's production of Eugene O'Neill's *Desire under the Elms*, which we nearly staged over the platforms of the Eurostar Terminal at Waterloo, prior to the building's official opening.

Even with all the ground prepared, new rejection after rejection after rejection came. A weakness of spirit would occasionally surface that a production would not happen but a conversation with colleagues would reinvigorate my faith and provide a fragment of new information with which to be an advocate, giving a new hook on which to hang the umpteenth phone call. And then it happened: the project could go ahead.

You need to have courage and faith that what you are trying to pull off is possible and worthwhile. I drew great inspiration from Japanese artist, Saburo Teshigawara, choreographer, dancer and director who, when asked about his approach to raising money for his projects, says: 'you have to believe in it. The money will come.' Teshigawara's philosophy, rigour and approach to his work is so compelling, people with money find a way to him.

4 Look for a personal reason for saying 'yes'; it is always there.
Think of a community of participants rather than of individual
supporters
Contemporary France has come to be renowned for ground-breaking circus. With good reason, public funds have been invested in its development in recent decades. In 1995, LIFT presented the magical *Cirque Plume.* The cross-Channel tunnel to France had recently been opened and we approached the train company, Eurostar, to sponsor the Circus. Our broad audience profile matched the range of passengers they wished to encourage to travel by Eurostar, and sponsorship of the circus brought with it promotion of the service in 100,000 copies of our Festival brochure. Peter Kendall, responsible for public relations and sponsorship at that time agreed to let us submit a proposal. It soon became clear that the individual we were dealing with was not simply interested in the public relations benefits of the sponsorship: Kendall was passionate about circus. He knew more about it than we did and did all he could to help make the venture a success. Whatever someone's job may be, personal motivations lie behind any decision. After this experience, in any conversation with a potential sponsor, I would always wait for the second reason that someone may be keen to support us. This second reason may be their own personal enthusiasm or that of their child or partner. Where the arts are concerned, the personal and professional are very closely intertwined. If you can provide a channel for other people's own interests, then they are more likely to be an advocate for their own sponsorship choices with colleagues.

There were some instances where a senior manager had made the decision to sponsor LIFT and a colleague was subsequently assigned to run the sponsorship. It was vital to engage these individuals as though they were patrons too, involving them at a personal level beyond their job responsibilities. Otherwise, it was easy for them to feel alienated by a strong sense of belonging in others.

Be a Brick, Buy a Block, the project described earlier, convinced me that, to be successful, fundraising schemes should touch people's sense of the times, sometimes make them laugh, and connect the art to the outside world. People liked to see themselves alongside others in a broader social picture – everyone playing a part in a common associative life, whatever their pocket and whatever their job. The smiles evoked by this particular scheme raised morale at LIFT and Station House Opera at a time when everyone was feeling beleaguered. The scheme as social process was consistent with the ethos of the art, critiquing social hierarchy and yet bringing people together at the same time. The scheme culminated in a party for 'aristocrats' to meet 'bourgeoisie' and 'peasants' in front of the production itself. Social inclusion is not just for those convention-ally thought of as excluded through poverty. The privileged need channels of social connection as much, maybe even more, than people less financially well endowed. Humour and reflections on key historical events help smooth these interactions. LIFT's way of finding equitable ways to make connections across the spectrum of privilege enabled the art to be put at the heart of this process.

5 Always keep your sights on a horizon bigger than your need for money
Paradoxically, if you focus only on your need for funds, or if fundraising works at the periphery of your activities, rather than at its heart, you do not get very far. Focus on an idea that reaches far beyond the money. Bring that vision to life in an illustration, a story of practical experience on the ground. Capturing people's imagin-ations and establishing trust is a vital foundation to put in place before requesting money. Sometimes these conversations have only turned into funds a considerable time after the initial contact was made. In the challenging world of contemporary theatre, if the idea is right, the money will be found. The key thing is to keep a conversation going over time that has as its focus a horizon that is

common to both arts organization and potential supporter. If you only look to conversations to be about money and the needs of the arts organization, the relationship quickly gives the impression the organization is merely a supplicant. Alas, beggars do not command respect. People may give funds, but they will be modest and only to get you to go away. You may then set your organization up to be a begging operation, rather than a place of invitation in which supporters are engaged and giving support over time through inspiration rather than compulsion.

One of the books I most admire is Rohinton Mistry's *A Fine Balance*. Set in India, Mistry describes the sketchbook of one of his characters, the local beggarmaster – something of a rogue, but with his own professional pride. Each page displays the dramaturgy of begging and each example reaches more effective techniques of extracting funds from passers-by. Perfection in his view involves two beggars with specific qualities:

> The blind man will carry the cripple on his shoulders. A living, breathing image of the ancient story about friendship and co-operation. And it will produce a fortune in coins, I am absolutely certain, because people will not give from pity or piety but also from admiration.
>
> (Mistry 1995: 445)

Asking for money is not enough. The request has to communicate a common human experience that is greater than both giver and receiver.

6 Bring the outside inside and the inside outside, balancing communication with colleagues and connections outside

Keeping your sights on a horizon that is beyond the need for money is all very well, but what does it mean? Adjust your antennae to be sensitive to the changing shapes of things; the great challenges facing the world and geographies closer to home; the ways and levels at which other organizations engage with one another; the questions they are asking; and the forms of meeting, encounter, discourse, vocabulary that people use to explore questions. All this brings the outside into the organization. The inside then has to be looked at and assessed for how it might need to evolve to be in harmony with the world outside, yet remain consistent with the values and purpose of the organization. Sometimes you perceive a change as deeply significant but difficult to explain because it will test the form of your organization and force colleagues to think in a different way. In this case, you have to hold the idea in your mind as something towards which the organization might work as a whole in due course. At other times, your organization may have developed a form of working that is ahead of developments in the outside world. In that case it is necessary to find the elements of this way of working that the outside world might perceive it needs and present them in comprehensible form. This inside/outside sensing is first and foremost an aesthetic sense, perception through pattern and shape and gut reaction before it can be explained rationally.

If misunderstandings down the line are to be avoided, regular communication and brainstorming with colleagues is needed to ensure accuracy of offer rather than over-selling or over-committing. Subtle and fast-moving issues do not fall neatly into regular meetings, requiring a way of signalling and discussing changing needs with colleagues. Ideally, colleagues understand this and adopt an entrepreneurial spirit sensitive to the pressures of securing sponsorship and the implications that follow.

7 Consider that 'no' can be as interesting as 'yes'; 'no' is not always negative and 'yes' not always easy
One of the ways to sense changes in the outside world is to grasp the reasons that people are saying 'no' to requests for sponsorship. A refusal can sometimes be as instructive as a positive answer, indicating future directions for the organization. For example, in the late 1980s I was trying to persuade Catherine Graham-Harrison, then Head of Arts and Community Affairs at Citibank, to sponsor the Festival using marketing vocabulary in my talk with her. This approach was not suitable in her case and suggested that what her colleagues really wanted was contact with artists, a greater understanding of the productions and an opportunity to connect behind the scenes, even that they might learn from the experience. It turned out that Citibank was not seeking the directly commercial benefits

desired by so many other companies. At the time, I thought 'Oh, great, if we had time to organize that it would be fine, but we're happy to give you promotional benefits for your money. That's what our organization is now set up to deliver.'

Our emphasis at the time on the dominant culture of marketing sponsorship forced a turn away from developing this relationship further. Nevertheless, this instance of a 'no' stayed with me and formed one of the foundations on which LIFT came to build a different style of relationship with business.

On rare occasions, people say 'yes' to a phone enquiry immediately or, better still, someone rings up to offer support out of the blue in response to a press article or other promotion. In such cases, it is wise to be prepared for the unexpected implications that follow. Have you prepared an outline proposal so that any questions can be answered in principle with confidence? Even if you do not know the exact details of sponsorship benefits, do you at least have an idea of how supporters might connect with the project? These questions might relate to factors as basic as approximate dates and location of performances, other supporters, associated education programmes and so on. It is unlikely that all these details will be in place at the time of any expression of interest on the part of potential supporters. Nevertheless, the confidence and dynamism that meets any request for information may affect whether the potential supporter remains interested in the venture.

Surprises have happened in this way. An article about LIFT's plans to bring Peter Brook's *Mahabharata* to London from the theatre company's base in France appeared in the UK's premier business paper, the *FT*. Andrew Hepburne-Scott, a banker with a great love of theatre, read it and contacted us to see how he could help. Responding with brief details on the telephone, we suggested a meeting and enlisted Hepburne-Scott to be an advocate at a time when, in reality, all the practical details of the venture were yet to be put into place. He became one of the project's main advocates and introduced us to the Baring Foundation, subsequently one of our long-term supporters. Although in the end we failed to bring *Mahabharata* to London, up to the last minute along that road we had to imagine the implications of each step being successful.

Another experience that taught me an uncomfortable lesson about preparation concerned work at one of London's centres for contemporary dance, The Place Theatre. This came in the early stages of raising funds for a commissioning scheme for young choreographers called *The Place Portfolio*. I had prioritized researching a potential sponsor rather than imagining what might happen if someone responded. Having researched one potential sponsor very thoroughly through newspaper articles and contacts who knew him, I rang and suggested our sponsorship idea in outline. Tim Miller of Framlington Investment immediately gave a positive response and began asking for details that I did not have at my fingertips. It was fortunate that he had sufficient imagination to remain interested, but it was clear that I had not done my homework well. This incident became a warning for the future.

8 Monitor your own gut reactions in every contact. If you feel bad or uneasy about the potential relationship, reassess how that might be explained

A frequently asked question in the field of sponsorship is: would your organization take money from a controversial sponsor? LIFT would not seek sponsorship from a company likely to alienate our audiences. But some potential sponsors or patrons may also impose obligations that are beyond the agreed or assumed outcome. Money can be a way to abuse power, subtly or unsubtly.

Sponsors can make you feel bad by taking a long time to decide on their sponsorship. The corporate timetable simply may not fit yours. This is the gamble of any commercial relationship and the risks of cash flow experienced by any organization. How much time can you dedicate to discussions with a potential sponsor in contrast to more favourable prospects elsewhere? Be realistic in your answer and never trust the arrival of funds until the contract or cheque is signed.

Some sponsorship comes with troublesome strings or difficult outcomes. Examples of this might be sponsorship of flights or design and printing. Be alert to the complexities of this kind of deal. Iqbal Wahhab and Maria Muller of London's 1994 Bangladesh Festival recounted a story with serious financial results. The Festival had secured flight sponsorship for a company of 30 performers. The company arrived safely in London but the airline could not organize return flights until ten days later than the Festival had been promised. This meant the Festival had to conjure funds for that period from a non-existent budget line for accommodation, food, transportation and staff. Given the number of artists involved, this derailed the Festival's finances and resulted in Wahhab having to subsidize the Festival from his own pocket to the tune of £50,000, making for 'a nightmare ending to a project we were extremely proud to have staged' (Email 2005).

Print and design sponsorship can be problematic too. Quality of design, timing and quality of print delivery is critical to the ability of an arts organization to attract audiences. If you enter into a sponsorship-in-kind relationship with designers or printers, one in which you do not have a firm contract, it is difficult to put pressure on them to do a good job and to deliver on time. This may come to threaten your core activity. Agree upon time at the outset, and be confident of the aesthetic approach and reliability of the designers offering you support. If you are a small organization just setting out, you may have little choice but these are risks to which you need to be constantly alert.

Political delicacies also need attention. A friend working in the non-profit area once commented that he would take any money however small and whatever its origins, lamenting: 'it may be tainted, but it ain't ever enough.' In our case stark financial dilemmas such as this rarely occurred. It was counterproductive and pointless, for example, even to attempt securing sponsorship from a business for a theatre company visiting from a country where that business's human rights or environmental record was poor. For this reason, we always had to check with the visiting companies whether they had any objection to having certain sponsors attached to the support of their visit. A theatre company from France objected so strongly to the idea of sponsorship being attached to their visit to London, we found ourselves explaining the climate for culture in Britain. The French company knew only their own nation's public subsidy and support from local municipalities, sufficiently generous to make commercial sponsorship unnecessary.

Other ethical issues came into play where alcohol or tobacco companies were concerned. Alcohol sponsorship was clearly inappropriate to seek for any of LIFT's youth programmes but was appropriate for the LIFT Club. We steered clear of tobacco sponsorship altogether as it risked alienating our audience in large numbers.

The most frequently asked questions about sponsorship are the ethical ones above and whether sponsors interfere in the artistic process. Direct interference in the artistic process by sponsors is unknown in my experience. None ever asked us to change the content of a production or to put their brand name on the stage. Nevertheless, the cumulative effect of market-led sponsorship had an indirect and invisible effect on productions we were able to stage and thus a cumulative adverse affect on the variety of theatre on offer in London.

One example was a production of Eugene O'Neill's *Desire under the Elms* directed by Mathias Langhoff. Among London's many theatres none existed of the scale and adaptability required by this and other productions. An alternative space, normally used for other activities, was needed in which to construct a theatre. The venue we found for *Desire under the Elms* was the spectacular new terminal at Waterloo of the cross-Channel rail service, Eurostar. This space was empty for a period prior to the start date of the train service. Constructing a special theatre was an expensive process needing a combination of sponsorship, public funding and advice in kind in order to succeed. Months of negotiation, bringing together all the potential interests, ended in failure. The potential marketing returns for the sponsor were deemed not worth the investment. The assessment of whether or not the sponsorship would have merited the investment is based on inexact science. It is without question that the novelty value of accommodating the theatre in such an unusual venue would have generated plentiful press coverage.

9 Have constant regard to timing and be bold, just ask, take a risk; they can only say no
Heterochronicity is the ability to manage overlapping timetables of different paces. You need this skill to build bridges between your

organization or practice and a range of external partners. Bear in mind at least four timetables: that of potential supporters, both their personal and organizational schedules, that of your organization and, in addition, events in the world. There is a pace throughout the year to be aware of too. It is no good setting dates in the UK for meetings or receptions for the month before or after Christmas or other major religious seasons, too close to other national holidays, or during school half-terms if those you wish to attend have children and may have holidays booked. You only get people to say 'yes' to things when all of these timetables line up. This is a rare occurrence, so, in order to improve one's chances, the solution is to keep private conversations going while you are planning more public occasions. This means that, if you are not able to engage someone's attention this time, perhaps on the next occasion they will be able to connect. If they show interest, keep in touch.

Managing this complexity also forced us to find ways of surviving that were at one remove from the volatility of Festival programming. Such a move would, we thought, give us greater flexibility about when we could organize a fundraising event. It was not just tied to the dates of the Festival but could be held at other times of the year better suited to the timetables of both LIFT and potential sponsors.

We took such a path in 1988. Funds were needed to enable a Russian theatre company to present their work in the Festival the following year. Our Chairman at the time, Lord Gowrie, had offered to host a private dinner for potential supporters. We needed to generate funds for the visit of the Russian theatre company and this set us to thinking how we could make the most of the opportunity we had been offered. A plan was hatched to combine two ideas: to make this dinner exceptional by inviting chefs to come from Russia to prepare it and to make this the first in a long-term venture: a LIFT International Dinner Series. The benefit of this, we hoped, would be to give us something via which to engage sponsors again in the future, adapting each dinner according to the specific fundraising need at the time. By initiating the first dinner, we would have a story to tell on which to base others. It remained to put the idea to Lord Gowrie. He went along with our plan and agreed to move what had at first been an offer to host a dinner at his house, to build more strategic connections between LIFT and the company of which he was Chairman, Sotheby's, as the company had just opened an office in Moscow.

The point to be made here is that it is always worth stretching the ideas of potential supporters. A delicate balancing act has to be accomplished if this route is taken. It is critical to think through what the practical or financial impact might be, so that neither the arts organization nor the potential supporter is exposed financially or in other ways.

It is also vital to have a practical sense of how any proposition is to be followed through. For example, in the section describing how ideas flow from the art, the scheme *Be a Brick, Buy a Block* was mentioned. When potential purchasers were first approached to buy concrete blocks, the proposition appeared cheeky and nonsensical. After all, the blocks were worth nothing in real terms but people were sufficiently amused to pause long enough for practical details about delivery and collection to be articulated. Indeed, the idea that these blocks were real and just the same whatever their price, injected the humour into this scheme and caused people, with a smile, to reach into their pockets.

Once the dinner idea was approved, it was necessary to negotiate the practical details with a great number of people: the chefs, the British Embassy in Moscow, the house manager at Sotheby's, hotel and flight sponsors, neighbouring chefs in London from whom to borrow a trial kitchen and so on. This work laid foundations for two subsequent dinners, a Hungarian one and one cooked by student chefs to celebrate the start of LIFT's Education Programme.

10 Always communicate after an event or project, explore how you can build a relationship for the future
Communicating after an event or at the end of a project can some-times mean listening to people who were not pleased with the event they have sponsored or helped happen. You need to brace yourself and take those comments on board too. It is through this feedback that you learn for the next time.

Such conversation also allows a sponsor or supporter to air views and to acknowledge that supporting an organization such as LIFT inevitably involves a degree of risk. IBM asked to support the 'most innovative' production in the Festival in 1989, in our view, Catalan company La Cubana's version of *The Tempest*. Starting out as a turgid and conventional production on stage, the performance rapidly deconstructed itself to lead audience members out of the auditorium, equipped with plastic mackintoshes, to enter a supposed real storm on the outside of the theatre. The action took place more or less everywhere in the theatre but the stage, with ambulance crews attending to 'casualties' amid the atmosphere of a real disaster. This use of a grand theatre was extremely challenging for a number of people, giving a twist to the idea of corporate entertainment. The sponsors had made a specific request to support a pioneering production, but whether they were quite prepared for what they got was another question. They certainly would never forget the experience.

Letters or messages of thanks finish a project and maintain layers of good relations on which long-term conversation depend. Formal thanks at group meetings for sponsors and supporters are a matter of course, as to those less visible people behind the scenes who put in place the seamless details of hospitality, enabling people to feel at ease with strangers. In the course of preparing any complex project, individuals go out of their way to smooth proceedings beyond the call of duty and deserve personal thanks, both verbal and written, in addition to any formal recognition. LIFT draws on the expertise and energies of a great number of people and has developed various ways of expressing thanks over the years. Beyond formal letter writing, the Festival has postcards on which to send handwritten notes. Bouquets, the traditional first-night offering to performers, have been offered on more unusual occasions. When once we gave bouquets to both men and women who had advised on a project, one of the men acknowledged that his journey home on the underground had been transformed through conversations sparked by the flowers.

Box 3.1 Working principles

1 Build upon every interaction as potential for personal, financial or advisory support. Whatever it is, it can make a difference.

2 Manage relationships with brevity, discretion and equity, combining formal and informal communications over time.

3 Have faith that the art will inspire sources of support.

4 Look for a personal reason for saying 'yes'; it is always there. Think of a community of participants rather than of individual supporters.

5 Always keep your sights on a horizon bigger than your need for money.

6 Bring the outside inside and the inside outside, balancing communication with colleagues and connections outside.

7 Consider that 'no' can be as interesting as 'yes'; 'no' is not always negative and 'yes' not always easy.

8 Monitor your own gut reactions in every contact. If you feel bad or uneasy about the potential relationship, reassess how that might be explained.

9 Have constant regard to timing and be bold, just ask, take a risk; they can only say no.

10 Always communicate after an event or project, explore how you can build a relationship for the future.

Collective courage

Securing support involves the whole organization. No individual or small collective within a larger group can do it alone as there is a constant need to cross-reference opportunities with colleagues, making connections, having conversations, and seeing where links can be made across different fields and social strata to the artistic vision, ethos and practical constraints of the organization. Artistic vision has to combine with entrepreneurial instinct to ground arts organizations.

Friends doing similar work in other organizations often had sole responsibility for raising money or were shut in a room at some remove from the artistic vision as it evolved. Too often I have seen individuals working in an isolated context become the scapegoat for unfulfilled, unrealistic financial hopes of the organization as a whole. If the organization has fundamental flaws that linger unaddressed or a consistently confused artistic vision, fundraising helps expose these, but at high risk. Often a wish to raise funds can stimulate internal re-examination. Whatever way you slice the organization, it should feel the same on the inside and the outside.

Most rules of support-building are those of courtesy and traditional hospitality, making and keeping friends, having a good conversation and melding all these elements together over time. These principles are doubtless the same the world over, and although they can be made routine and 'professionalized' to a degree, ultimately the quality of welcome and discourse will determine your level of success in securing supporters over the long term. Even with business and marketing sponsorship, individuals responsible for negotiating these deals on behalf of their companies usually want to be treated as patrons. There are no short cuts to treating people well and getting the welcome right. Indeed, making these processes formulaic will undermine their quality. It will push people into fixed roles of donor and supplicant and mean that qualities of connection are inauthentic. Arts groups need resources. Donors need those who can work effectively with their resources. Both sides of the equation have to remain evident. The focus of attention for both should be on the project itself, rather than the dynamics of giver and receiver. Antoine de Saint-Exupéry embodies this dynamic for me: 'To love is not to gaze at one another; it is to look together in the same direction'[1] (Saint-Exupéry 1939).

These principles cannot be directly imitated or rolled out in a prescriptive way. To be effective, all have to be tailor-made. The business of securing funds for the arts is more than a simple trade. A process enabling alliances to be struck between those with financial resources and those with few, it lays a path to the future beyond the parties directly involved. It is a barometer of power relations in society and thus a measure of its civility.

FOUR

REDISCOVERING CIVIL SOCIETY AMID THE MARKET AND THE STATE

Never doubt that a small group of thoughtful committed citizens can change the world. Indeed, it is the only thing that ever has.

(Margaret Mead, www.mead2001.org/faq)[1]

When I began work at LIFT in London it was at the height of Margaret Thatcher's Conservative government, and market values were in the ascendancy. Deregulation of state monopolies and growth of the financial services sector appeared unstoppable. Colossal bonuses were awarded to successful financial traders. Champagne and money flowed in city bars and civility seemed in short supply. A government intent on improving Britain's overall productivity encouraged this aggressive pace of business. For the first time since it was established after the Second World War, public funding for the arts had to justify its existence in competition with more apparently worthy demands on the public purse such as education, housing, crime prevention and health. Every area of activity seemed to come second to the market and be subject to analysis in accounting terms. If we were to make advances in this climate we needed greater understanding of where the Festival fitted in the interplay between public and private sources of support and how best to articulate our position to these sources.

This chapter will describe how practice and crisis revealed the formal and informal funding context in which LIFT evolved; how the political climate influenced support from both public and private sources; and how we learned that the civic, commercial and arts worlds are intimately intertwined.

The arts in Britain – a tapestry of support

Britain's cultural institutions are underpinned by a combination of funds from local and regional government, from businesses and foundations, and from voluntary participation and ticket sales. At the centre of arts funding in the UK is Arts Council England (ACE). Scotland and Wales have their own councils. The Arts Council of Great Britain, as it was formerly known, was established after the Second World War by Royal Charter (1946) 'for the purpose of developing a greater knowledge, understanding and practice of the fine arts . . .' and to increase 'the accessibility of the arts to the public' (ACGB 1967). As part of its Royal Charter, ACE's activities were to be at arm's length from government and political interests. In the decades since incorporation, ACE has undergone repeated reorganization in response to changing emphases on, for example, London's arts at the expense of the regions and vice versa, and shifts in priority between 'popular' art and art for art's sake. Its current structure has a presence in each region with offices responsible for disbursing funds locally. ACE receives funding from government via the Department for Culture, Media and Sport (DCMS). Government funding of the arts via ACE currently stands at £335 million in 2003/4, rising to £410 million in 2005/6. In 1986, when I began work at LIFT, it was £105 million.

Public funding of the arts began after the Second World War. Forty years later in the 1980s, a wave of new funding initiatives emerged from ACE in an effort to make arts organizations more efficient. All were informed by private sector business models; many were based on American funding schemes. One such, Incentive Funding, was launched in 1987 to reduce a 'welfare state mentality' as Richard Luce, UK Minister for the Arts, put it. The aim was to encourage arts organizations to become more 'financially enterprising', to 'improve their commercial management skills' (Wu 2002: 56) and to become more successful at generating funds from other sources, including the private sector.

LIFT was encouraged to apply to the scheme and underwent detailed scrutiny by an accountant who, vowing as he came through the door that he was not there to pass comment on LIFT's artistic programme, then proceeded to do so. His comment as the excruciating meeting ended was that the only way to generate more income would be to programme more commercial productions but that he did 'admire the enthusiasm of you ladies'. He clearly found it incomprehensible that the only reason LIFT was viable at all was the organization's willingness to take artistic risks backed up by already considerable management and entrepreneurial acumen. After attending numerous subsequent meetings, it emerged LIFT was not eligible for Incentive Funding as it was better suited to organizations that had catering facilities and premises that could be hired out. It was clear that LIFT fitted neither the accountant's nor the government's model. The Incentive Funding débâcle was followed in 1991 by an ACE appraisal. This process took LIFT apart piece by piece before longer-term funding was granted.

The only route to diversifying LIFT's funding remained commercial sponsorship. In its most ancient form, to sponsor someone means 'to stand surety for someone or to support or favour him or her strongly'.[2] More recently, it has come to signify a business relationship between a provider of funds, resources or services and an individual, event or organization that offers in return some rights of association that may be used for commercial advantage.

Association for Business Sponsorship of the Arts (ABSA)[3]

To encourage sponsorship of the arts among businesses, a business membership organization, ABSA, was set up in 1976. During the 1980s the organization grew to extend the market ethos of arts sponsorship promoted by the Thatcher government. It was also a lobbying organization to increase opportunities for and effectiveness of corporate promotion via the arts. It was much influenced by US models of business sponsorship that emphasized fundraising and sponsorship more aggressively than was the norm in the UK at that time. ABSA's work was dedicated to raising the profile of sponsorship through press lobbying, a series of awards, receptions and ministerial acknowledgement for new or exceptional sponsors of the arts. My first encounter with ABSA came early on in LIFT's investigation into how the organization should go about the search for sponsorship. Fenton and I sought advice from the organization's Director, Colin Tweedy, who, although supportive of LIFT's efforts, acknowledged that our productions were not an obvious choice for sponsors.

In 1984, ABSA's role had been strengthened through the introduction of the Business Sponsorship Incentive Scheme (BSIS). ABSA administered this on behalf of the government. This was a different incentive scheme from the one initiated by ACE described earlier but all were tied to the Conservative government's free market policies.

LIFT succeeded in securing a BSIS award to bring artists from Nigeria to London in 1987. Applying for this incentive award was not a straightforward process. The award was aimed at encouraging businesses to sponsor the arts by matching new sponsors' money pound for pound. This additional money was destined for the arts organizations, and in return they had to produce more benefits to the business through additional performances, education projects or other artistic outcome.

These benefits were difficult to perceive by businesses in the early stages of negotiaton and hence rarely provided any real incentive for the business to sponsor the arts. These awards were always an afterthought for the business but, needless to say, we filled in the forms as though they had been the determining factor in the business's decision to sponsor. At times, we felt encouraged to describe the business's reasons for sponsoring with more commercial motivation than had originally been the case. This had paradoxical effects. It meant that any public good instincts on the part of the sponsor were made invisible, forcing their motivations to fit a commercial ethos. The business–arts relationships fostered by ABSA at that time rarely made any reference to the civic context in which all parties existed. This exaggerated emphasis on the commercial came to be counterproductive.

In Margaret Thatcher's heyday, suspicion of the arts was reinforced by an overlay of class resentment and anti-intellectualism. The dominant tone was one of utilitarianism, philistinism and spiritual desertification. The arts were seen to be the domain of a self-indulgent social elite with which the government did not identify. In some cases, this was justified, with moribund arts organizations taking their annual handout from ACE for granted, while remaining artistically static and limited in the spectrum of audience they attracted. The contemporary arts were seen as an irritant, questioning Conservative ideals or somehow making a fool of the public.

As work on LIFT unfolded, patterns of support on which the arts depended began to reveal themselves. Many of these patterns still exist. They bring with them advantages and disadvantages but all colour the way in which the arts are resourced in Britain.

There are many people who support and engage in the arts through practice, participation and funding from all walks of life. The most visible of these is a fluid group of people who are seen and see themselves as the guardians of public arts activities. They are often referred to as 'The Great and the Good', whose support is often based on an aristocratic tradition of dedication to things literary and aesthetic. Some members of this group are aristocrats; some are powerful through riches and status acquired in other ways such as the law, business, academia or public service. Over the years of LIFT's existence, this latter group has expanded and the role and visibility of hereditary aristocrats has diminished. 'The Great and the Good' populate the boards of arts institutions and charitable bodies of all kinds, not just the arts. Their position is a point of reference for social aspiration and contribution to the public good among the newly rich.

Much establishment art is resourced through the leverage of class and the invisible 'favour books' of mutual obligation operating among 'The Great and Good' and those who aspire to be among their number. The Royal Family is at the nexus of this social hierarchy, and although it has to be said that the Royal Family are not renowned for regarding the contemporary arts as a priority, the

Prince of Wales gives broad support via his role as patron of a number of arts organizations.

Britain's system of honours, knighthoods and peerages acts to strengthen activities in the public realm, including the arts. The system has a mixed reputation. At its worst, a knighthood can be more or less bought via financial contributions to the political party of the day. At another level and more positively, it is a system to encourage people in power to work for the common good. At times it is only too obvious which individuals are intent on gaining a knighthood and doubtless many go about the task in quite a determined and cynical way. In spite of this, what the system does offer is an additional route to leveraging resources and influence from people in positions of power towards less well-resourced areas of society and those activities, such as the arts, seen to be for the public good. Fundraisers for the arts needed to be aware of these social and power dynamics in order to enlist project champions to elicit support from others. They also needed to be aware of the unspoken cultural rules about what can be asked of people and what cannot. These conventions can only be apprehended through advice and practice, although there is a growing literature on elite giving in the UK and US.[4]

To speak of the arts establishment in this way, generalizations are easy. Of course every single person has different motives, levels of interest and social awareness. Attitudes and generosity are only ever revealed through attempts to engage individuals. First of all, there are a few wealthy individuals who get involved in the arts simply because they think it is a good thing and they are personally inspired to do so through background or education. These are philanthropists who regard giving to the arts as part of their duty. The most honourable philanthropists look for no promotional or other return and consider that they learn from a connection with the arts. They do not make a song and dance about getting involved, often wishing their support to be anonymous and private.

These individuals usually give in recognition that the focus of their support is saying something new; that their help can really make a difference; that they will see friends regularly in an interesting setting; or that they will have an authentic connection with a world beyond their day-to-day life, or with a younger generation of people they would otherwise never meet or be able to encourage or learn from. It gives them a sense of connectedness and community from the privileged end of the economic and social spectrum. They give because they understand that financial power brings with it responsibility, and in order to learn they have to take a risk and make connections with people who do not necessarily care about the status they may enjoy elsewhere. In order to know who they are beyond their social status, the privileged need channels of social communication opened up by the arts as much as the arts need them.

At its worst, philanthropy can be a front for the worst kind of self-promotion, exploitation and hypocrisy and just a way to get near to the lead actress or actor or a sense of vitality that the phil-anthropist may crave. At its worst, the pyramids of social aspiration driving support for the arts and charitable giving can operate against wider arts involvement, merely serving to prop up the status quo and the impression that the arts are just for 'posh' people.

This means that arts organizations that are seeking to break down these social barriers have to consider carefully not only their artistic programme but also the culture via which money is secured for this. If your artistic programme is doing one thing, but the social rela-tions being fostered behind the scenes are all emphasizing glitzy receptions and social aspiration, then at some point you will be perceived as inauthentic. LIFT does not get it right every time, no one does, but we have always maintained an awareness of these potential pitfalls and structured our fundraising efforts accordingly.

UK arts funding and internationalism

The mid- to late 1980s was an era of thumping the patriotic drum with emphasis on 'British' notions of art and traditional art forms. The government department responsible for the arts was called the Department for National Heritage. The name itself gave its affairs a historical tilt. Ideas of keeping channels of communication open beyond Britain's shores or promoting culturally diverse views of Britain were seen as anything but a priority. As Britain's horizons seemed to be closing in we, and others, became still more motivated to keep them open. There was no provision within the national arts funding system for bringing international arts to Britain. Responsibility for this lay with a small organization called Visiting Arts (VA), set up in 1978 and still relatively new when LIFT began. VA was directly funded by central government through the Foreign and Commonwealth Office, housed in the British Council. Cultural expenditure emphasized countries with which Britain had strategic diplomatic interests or fences to mend. The budget for exporting British culture was well known among international arts presenters as being much larger than that for importing culture from abroad.[5] This imbalance meant that LIFT often felt like the guest at everyone else's parties, rarely able to pay for hospitality in return thereby risking abuse of the goodwill of artists and international festival peers.

Of course, individual members of government did not privately share this xenophobic view, nor did enlightened policy-makers. Nevertheless, this was the atmosphere that they and we were trying to alter. LIFT was at the centre of contemporary arts practice that was seeking to question established views of Britain. It was inevitable that this was an uncomfortable place to be. Interestingly, in contrast to the policy landscape, those business sponsors with international interests whom we managed to attract were much more alert to the value of keeping open channels of communication between Britain and the rest of the world. These connections helped us overcome the dominant political ambience of the day.

Nevertheless, in this climate the search for sponsors of the international involved high degrees of lateral thinking. In 1986, Neal had made a research trip to Nigeria to make contact with artists who were forging ways of reflecting contemporary cultural reality in the country. As is often the case, artists working outside officially recognized organizations were making the most interesting work. Dancer, choreographer and director, Peter Adegboyega Badejo, was one such artist. His progression was hampered by institutional stasis and the politics of academia in Nigeria. He was keen to make a new dance drama examining the problems confronting farmers in Nigeria and to reveal how political, colonial, religious and civilian regimes repeatedly seek to hijack the people's traditional cultural forms for their own glorification. These cultural forms have evolved over millennia to express, celebrate and re-affirm the history of each particular culture, their collective experiences and their beliefs as a community.

With echoes of our own struggle to keep cultural communication alive, we were constantly on the hunt for new sources of support. Knowing of our wish to fund the visit of Badejo and his company, Tim Stockil of ABSA sent a clipping from the *FT* about Cussons International, a British company doing well in Nigeria through sales of Elephant Power detergent. A sponsorship proposal was drafted and sent to Cussons International in Manchester, followed up with a phone call and visit to meet the Chairman, John Zochonis. We asked Cussons to sponsor Badejo's company, Kufena. They agreed to do so, making their payment in Nigerian naira so that the unfavourable exchange rate between naira and pounds sterling did not come into effect. Badejo received the sponsorship in Nigeria to resource a period of rehearsal to a value of £5,000 (equal to 25,000 naira). This enabled Badejo to fund Kufena's creation of *New Earth* and bring the production to LIFT '87. Unusually, we were able to apply for a Business Sponsorship Incentive Scheme[6] award to match the foreign currency in the UK and thus secure additional resources for the company's visit to London. The sponsorship was administered in Nigeria via the British Council. This sponsorship enabled us to swell resources for international cultural connections at a time when public funds had little flexibility.

In the early 1990s, the wind began to change. ACE perceived that the UK arts scene did not exist in a vacuum and began to embrace an international perspective. This acknowledged that LIFT and other UK presenters of international work needed to be able to make programming decisions on artistic merit alone, rather than simply inviting arts companies from countries diplomatically interesting for Britain at the time. This change of direction was vital if Britain was to maintain artistic inspiration from beyond its shores.

The national trend of conservatism made for a very particular time in London's regional government too. London's government is made up of 32 local boroughs brought together in a London-wide civic authority, the Greater London Assembly (GLA). In the 1980s, it was called the Greater London Council (GLC). The GLC had wide-ranging regional responsibilities including those of arts, education and international relations. The imposing building housing the GLC sat just over the Thames from the Houses of Parliament. Under the socialist and idiosyncratic leadership of Ken Livingstone, the GLC became a thorn in the side of the Conservative government. It was the GLC that had first recognized LIFT with public funding (together with VA) and had widely acknowledged the asset represented by the cultural diversity of London's peoples. Support for local festivals and recognition of the importance of London's cultural diversity was seen as subversion indeed, adding to the wider perceptions of inefficiency and annoyance held by central government. So in 1986, the Conservative government simply abolished the GLC in the name of efficiency and as part of the wide-ranging regional and local government reforms sweeping the country. Ken Livingstone was to secure sweet revenge when he was elected Mayor of London in 2000, to the consternation of the New Labour government for whom he had become an irritant in equal measure.

This shifting political landscape at both national and London regional levels was to affect work at LIFT dramatically. It meant that, without a civic authority to acknowledge the benefit of LIFT to the capital, there was no obvious civic partner to which we could harness private sector support. Practically speaking, this meant that there was no one who could offer the appropriate level of civic recognition to any sponsor we might secure for a major international event, or be a third partner in the complex funding partnerships required to ensure such events were possible. This became clear after trying to secure private sector support for Peter Brook's *Mahabharata*. Whatever effort we put into generating support from businesses, without a regional civic authority to embrace the interest such a production could bring to the city itself, the venture was doomed to fail. We found a suitable venue in Docklands: Warehouse O. This was an area designated for urban regeneration in London's East End. The London Docklands Development Corporation was responsible for leading this regeneration effort and they were prepared to back the theatre venture financially to a certain percentage. A commercial sponsor was interested in backing the venture, but the combined resources proved inadequate without additional investment from civic funds. In most other cities included in the world tour of *Mahabharata*, the city was a major financial partner in renovating or adapting a venue for the production. These included Barcelona, Adelaide, Frankfurt, New York, Perth and Avignon. Several of the venues remained as a new arts venue for the city. London lost out in this regard and the production went to Glasgow in 1988. Designated to be European City of Culture two years later in 1990, a range of partners was galvanized to fund conversion of the Tramway performance space, still a major showcase for international contemporary artists. London's struggle continues to provide a permanent venue of the scale and style we sought then.

The Thatcher revolution forced examination as to how and why public expenditure was distributed to particular fields and the interplay between different sources of funding both public and private. Great expectations were held that funding for cultural activity would come from the private sector. There was little understanding however, in either policy-making or arts circles, about how this would be done long term and how an appropriate balance would be struck between public and private funds. The experience of juggling these relationships in London forced new ways of thinking about LIFT's role in achieving that balance.

Balancing funds from private and public sources

The advantages and disadvantages of private and public funding are ever changing. Among the responsibilities of fundraisers is that of staying alert to when this balance tips out of kilter. During the 1980s and early 1990s it became the barely questioned view that arts organizations should build closer and closer relations with business.

Never without strings, the cumulative effect of this proximity had wide-reaching effects. In an impressive and comprehensive survey of corporate art interventions in the 1980s, art historian Chin-Tao Wu lays bare the impact of corporate interventions in

Britain and the US (Wu 2002). She exposes the dubious proximity of relations between those who are powerful in the business world and those who are trustees of publicly funded cultural institutions. We were part of that picture.

While honouring Wu's critique of this dangerous proximity, what is to be done? My view is that public money is fraught with dangers too. It can be used directly or indirectly to censor troublesome or politically sensitive work. An unquestioned reliance on permanent state funding of theatre and opera companies frequently militated against vibrant programmes at such institutions in Britain and in the former Soviet Union for example. At a 2005 arts sector conference in London it was pointed out that most of the organizations funded by ACE in 1945 are still on the list indicating at least a degree of institutional stasis (Knell 2004).

With the best of intentions, public funding can sometimes end up having more subtle deleterious effects. Public funding aimed at building equity between cultures for example can often end up doing the opposite. Artists who see themselves simply as practising their art realized the only route to funding is found in emphasizing ethnic or race origins. Contrary to intentions, such funding has served to marginalize and infantilize artists through the reductive notions that can result from ethnic definition. Paradoxically, it succeeds in separating artists from the main flow of contemporary practice, encouraging assumptions about artists and audiences that narrow opportunities for engagement across cultures. Particularly devastating when these effects combine with assumptions of programmers, Shobana Jeyasingh, choreographer, describes the impact:

> There are still venue managers who believe the most appropriate audience for a British artist of Asian origin is the 'Asian community', as if that were a homogenous entity. And the fixed triumvirate of race, culture, and art still generates the inevitable starting point of much critical comment that deals with the work of such artists – comment that is at times closer to anthropology than artistic evaluation.

> (Jeyasingh 2002)

Politically correct policies (and funds) can produce heavy burdens of representation for artists. Outstanding art is the most positive starting point for funding rather than policy aims. When responsible for seeking arts funding, all these potential dilemmas must be borne in mind.s

While alert to the ill effects of private sector funds, having access to these can, on occasions, counter the constraints of public funding. Scarcity of public funding and the need for public accountability mean that decisions to fund new initiatives are inevitably sluggish. Public accountability and risk do not necessarily go together.

For example, LIFT had difficulty in securing public funding when it began working with young people. In the climate of the early 1990s, the arguments for international arts in education had yet to be fully taken on board by funders. The only arts funding relating to international visits focused on bringing prestigious national companies to Britain. It did not extend to education projects. Any funds had to be etched from the main budgets of arts organizations in competition with other demands. British Telecom (BT)'s sponsorship of LIFT's Education Programme in 1993 enabled us to launch a fully-fledged programme. Although the sponsorship itself proved to be short-term, public funding was secured for this area of LIFT's activities only in subsequent years. Public funding is often confined within geographic boundaries. We experienced more parallels with international business in the way that artists worked, constrained neither by national borders nor administrative boundaries.

In the diplomatic field, when Britain had severed cultural relations with Argentina following the Falklands War in 1982, LIFT was told unofficially that no public funds should be seen to be supporting the visit to LIFT '89 of artist, Eduardo Pavlovsky, from Argentina. Luckily, by this time, we had secured sponsorship from the Baring Foundation. This protected us from government pressure and ensured we were able to invite Pavlovsky to perform in the Festival that year.

When speaking about the LIFT experience of sponsorship to arts managers in India, South Africa, the USA, Latvia, Poland, Slovenia and Turkey, it has been necessary to confront the paradoxes of the curious tapestry of support that has evolved to support arts practice in the UK. Britain is lucky in many respects that there is a tradition of support for the arts – even if that support is fragile and paradoxical. At its best, this means that a traditional cultural reluctance to talk directly about money has established social norms whereby overt commercial messages do not appear as a backdrop to plays on the national stages. Brand names are kept off the stage. At worst, arts support in Britain just reinforces a self-referential and self-congratulatory social hierarchy hampering arts organizations from critiquing the status quo. Nevertheless, for all the drawbacks, contact with other countries reveals the relative ease of building allies for the arts in the UK. In economies at a stage more akin to wild-west capitalism, supporters for the arts are harder to find, and commercial sponsors have little compunction about demanding that corporate logos be put centre stage or only give their money after the event, and then reluctantly.

The interplay between state and private funding remains complicated to say the least. The eternal hopes that private sector funding will be sustainable have not been borne out. It remains notoriously fragile. The volatile changes in the business world mean that people stay in their jobs for a very short time. The nature of arts sponsorship is such that each individual, whatever the professional reasons for choosing to sponsor something, has personal reasons for doing so. As a result, sponsorships rarely survive if the person who originally decided on it moves post. In the early years of sponsorship, this personal dimension of sponsorship was dubbed 'the Chairman's whim' or 'the Chairman's wife's whim'. In other words, support was entirely dependent on the personal enthusiasms of powerful individuals. For all efforts to extend sponsorship decisions more widely across the company and to embed sponsorship culture into regular corporate practices, in reality little progress has been made in this regard. Sponsorship decisions still rely on personal enthusiasm at whatever staff level they are taken. For all efforts to professionalize the process, the decision to sponsor still transcends the professional imperatives of individuals to touch on the personal.

Although highly critical of the damaging and divisive effect that an unswerving dedication to the market has had on the public realm in Britain, I have reluctantly to admit that it has had some good effects. Maybe these were unintended side effects, but they have nevertheless forced people in the arts to have a more direct responsibility and connection with their audiences, supporters and the civic realm with which private support is intimately intertwined.

Public funding gives arts organizations a degree of continuity and allows them to develop relationships with other sectors over time. Hence, a combination of public and private funds has provided a way to ride both horses and achieve a degree of stability and independence. Therefore the funding landscape that has emerged in Britain, between public and private sectors and trusts and foundations, makes for an exceptionally strong base for a dynamic cultural life. What is more, and very significantly, I believe that the proximity that has grown up between arts and business over the last two decades has paradoxically placed the arts in a better position from which to critique the very market values that forced this closer relationship with business in the first place.

Nevertheless, no balance can be achieved without better understanding of the dynamics of an even bigger picture – that of civil society and the role played by the arts alongside other sectors.

Civil society emerges from a civic vacuum – LIFTING London

When abolition of London's regional authority began to affect the quality of life in the city the public realm began to deteriorate fast. This brought home to many people in the arts, business and other walks of life that market forces alone could not address strategic issues of common concern. There was little necessity for LIFT to articulate its civic role and responsibility prior to this. Every day, every person working, living or visiting central London was confronted with failures in the city's management. For example, changes in central government policy relating to social security benefit combined with absence of a London-wide policy on homelessness had devastating impacts on individual lives and resulted in great numbers of people sleeping rough. This was the most visible impact of abolition of the GLC. The streets deteriorated too. Potholes and broken pavements became a hazard to cyclists and pedestrians. The absence of a city authority and its effect on cultural life became obvious to us in several ways, particularly in LIFT's informal role as ambassador for London abroad and in celebrating the city's cultural diversity at home. In this climate, we had to face the fact that a political context unsympathetic to the arts in the city was unlikely to change overnight. It seemed a small organization such as ours had little power to improve the situation.

One day this feeling of powerlessness became tiresome and I thought of trying the crossing-the-street game. In my mind, I walked away and looked back at an imagined wall with many other small fry angrily complaining as they banged their heads against it, endlessly berating the civic vacuum and a lack of funds as insuperable obstacles to change. The thought that it might be possible to take action brought with it a change of spirit.

Having moved to a new place in my mind, I began to look around for signs of hope and took steps to engage with other organizations attempting to improve matters. I found there were other people speculating about new ways of doing things – or doing them differently already. The experience of a civic vacuum made people realize that they had to invent their own civic networks. They had to think beyond their own immediate need for money, taking action outside the normal structures if they were to achieve their goals.

Two key organizations helped us see how we might do things differently. The first was Common Purpose. The second was Vision for London. Both had been started by visionary women who believed in the power of connecting people to each other and to the city of which they were a part in ways that transcended formal organizations or party politics. Both had profound influence on the way that LIFT came to regard its role in the city and on the way that we designed subsequent communications across the sectors.

Common Purpose, founded by Julia Middleton, is an organization bringing together leaders from different sectors to address particular civic issues in year-long education programmes.[7] In 1989, Middleton realized that if Britain's cities were to survive profound

future economic, social and cultural changes, then leadership qualities in a greater number of informed individuals needed to be
improved. She sensed that an ability to interact in civil society, in
that space beyond formal job roles or party politics, was critical. An
ability to take leadership without formal authority was essential.
Common Purpose was her response.

LIFT was introduced to Common Purpose via American arts
researcher and facilitator, Jean Horstman, who was advising the
organization about how the arts might play a part in its programmes.

In the late 1980s, I embarked on Common Purpose North
London, the area where LIFT was based. Each of the programme
days combined talks and visits to relevant organizations affected
by public policy in the area concerned. On the criminal justice day,
for example, my group spent the day in London's women's jail,
Holloway. We met inmates, ate the same food, and learned about
opportunities for education and training in the prison regime.
During the rest of the day, we learned about different aspects of the
criminal justice system and how they interrelated, for example
sentencing tariffs; the resettlement of offenders; and police efforts
to counter the drug trade in the King's Cross area.

This combination of activities provided opportunities for formal
and informal communication between participants and those
organizations visited. I gained new insight into pivotal London-wide
issues: without a civic authority for London, many organizations
were bemoaning the lack of a strategic overview of planning
and land use issues. It was hard for Londoners, in competition
with other British cities, to make claims to central government and
to promote the city abroad. The experience highlighted that one
sector's challenge is frequently another's opportunity and expanded
my ideas of the role of the arts in other areas of life.

The second organization that came to be a great inspiration
was Vision for London (VfL). Started by Esther Caplin, VfL was
invented to fill the gap in civic discourse about planning and architecture issues that existed after the abolition of the GLC. VfL held
meetings on a range of topics in different venues. This peripatetic
programme, like LIFT and Common Purpose, had the virtue of
taking people to parts of the city they would otherwise not know

and encouraged different sets of people to converse, share practice and exchange information.

At LIFT, we began to perceive our role in a civic sense beyond the theatre world. We realized the art we staged was a way of bringing people together across all sorts of levels of London life. Rather than see ourselves as a small organization simply putting on shows and constantly frustrated by civic inadequacies, we audaciously began to see ourselves as a larger catalyst with a wide embrace and a special role to play, based on celebration rather than complaint. This was the germ of an idea that turned into our own civil society experiment – a programme of events and a conference called LIFTING London. We organized this with guidance from Common Purpose and VfL.

How do you raise morale in a city as enormous as London? At LIFT, we felt that, unless we addressed ourselves to this question, we would drown in frustration. Amid a decline in the urban fabric, economic fortunes and the civic pride of London, we felt a need to focus on the city's assets rather than its problems as a way of generating hope.

First, during the LIFT '91 Festival, we brought London itself into sharper focus than previously by drawing five events together in a city-wide series of public performances entitled LIFTING London. These included *Flying Costumes, Floating Tombs* referred to earlier; the Angell Town Festival, a local festival in Brixton of which more to come; *The Man Who Lit Up the World*, a carnival celebration of the life of African-American inventor Lewis Latimer; Lord Dynamite, about Alfred Nobel, inventor of dynamite; and *Los Angeles Poverty Department Inspects London*, portraying the reality of living on London's streets, a project devised and performed by homeless Londoners.

These performances helped refine the form and content of a conference that followed in March 1992. At the conference, we did not set out to tell LIFT's story; instead we set the stage for others to tell theirs. The goal of LIFTING London was to challenge accepted ways of doing things, to make the link between policy and practice, and to counter a more usual view of the arts as constantly moaning about money. We hunted for stories of local initiatives that, because they had tackled seemingly intractable challenges in unusual ways, had succeeded in overcoming these to inspire people at local, regional, national and even international levels. A focus on the positive rather than the negative gave delegates courage in their own fields, and inspired policy-makers about the importance of supporting those efforts that at the outset might appear small scale.

It is true we knew that we ourselves would face a challenge in getting the conference off the ground, funding it and getting people to attend a civic event run by an arts organization. But at least we would be taking action and in that effort building connections for the future and gaining clues as to new ways of doing things. In the process we would gain greater understanding of our role in the city and be building links to people working in very different fields from our own. We needed influential people to back the idea. Ian Hargreaves, the Managing Editor of the UK's financial newspaper *FT*, was interested in urban and social issues and he agreed to put the company's name to our initiative. With this endorsement, it was then easier to go to public funders and secure financial support to develop the idea. Gradually the bricks fell into place and we secured Cabot Hall, a prestigious conference venue at Canary Wharf and national symbol of the ascendancy of business, to host the event. A LIFT ex-colleague, Helen Marriage, was by this time leading the arts programme at Canary Wharf and secured permission for us to use the hall.

It was important that the voice of the people running projects was heard, whether they were 16 or 60, whether they had spoken at a conference before or not. Finding the right balance of people to tell the stories was akin to casting a play. Those with a policy or strategic overview of the relevant fields were invited to give their view as to why more of these success stories were not happening. This was a way of getting project people together with policy-makers, but in a different relationship than that normally experienced, more frequently one of supplicancy alone or with adversarial qualities provoking a feeling of 'us' and 'them'. Esther Caplin of VfL fine-tuned the programme, speakers and documentation. Our aim was to create an atmosphere of hope, encouraging a sense that we were all in the same boat, all trying to make a difference but that the difference was frequently made in unconventional ways and often from the margins. We chose stories from housing, education, arts and business, all from people with whom we were already in touch or might wish to work:

- Angell Town: Dora Boatemah told the story of the tenant-led refurbishment of a run-down estate.
- Islington: Andrew Morris and students described new approaches to post-16 education.
- From Stratford East to Broadway: Philip Hedley told the story of *Five Guys Named Moe*.
- Korda: Carolyn Hayman described a venture capital company with a difference.[8]

Angell Town: the tenant-led refurbishment of a run-down estate

Dora Boatemah was the tenant who led refurbishment of the Angell Town Estate in Brixton, south London. LIFT met Boatemah when invited to organize a local Festival celebrating completion of the first phase of re-building[9]. This was one of the LIFTING London events in LIFT '91. Residents had been faced with terrible practical difficulties every day in an earlier era. Vandalized garages provided easy shelter for drug-dealers and arsonists. The majority of residents spent their time defending their homes from burglary, squashing cockroaches and agitating for a transfer to new accommodation. The nearest shop was a quarter of a mile away. There were no communal facilities on Angell Town. Anyone admitting to an Angell Town address was unlikely to secure a job. One day, Boatemah decided to do something about it; she was fed up with living for a future transfer that would never come.

The amazing thing that Boatemah did was concentrate on the need for communal facilities before tackling the inadequacies of individual accommodation. She had a vision of the neighbourhood and set out to bring it about. The local authority's plan for physical refurbishment of Angell Town did not have this emphasis – there was no provision even for consulting the tenants. It was also a hard-won struggle to convince other tenants, many of whom needed patience indeed to wait for provision of communal facilities such as a launderette and crèche before the discomforts of their own accommodation were addressed. Boatemah's most ambitious idea was to incorporate a recording studio very early on in the building programme. She believed that the young people living there needed creative activities. If she could generate hope with the young people, then this would spread to parents and neighbours. Her ideas and advocacy captured everyone's imagination and resources began to flow in, from successful musicians with a commitment to that part of London, from radio DJs and from the builders contracted to refurbish the estate. Through Boatemah's vision a whole neighbourhood was turned around. Furthermore, her actions contributed to national legislation that no estate could be refurbished without tenant consultation.

The lessons this story held were that, in order to turn something round, something has to turn round in you. You have to look not beyond yourself for someone to make the first move, but to make that first move yourself. In Boatemah's case it was to make a commitment to the place where she lived, rather than wishing she lived somewhere else. Then it was to create a vision of what the place could be like and enthuse other people, capturing their imaginations so that they could move beyond their own direct self-interest. Then it was 'fight, fight, fight'. Boatemah's other lasting legacy was to believe in young people and their abilities and to fight for resources for them at an early stage in the regeneration process. Her local vision helped change national policy.

Islington: new approaches to post-16 education

The social, cultural and economic reasons for many young people failing at school are only too easy to catalogue. More difficult is trying to address them. In north London a series of initiatives had been developed that had a significant impact on individual lives. Three students told their story in public for the first time. Andrew Morris, an educationalist with specific expertise in post-16 curriculum development, interviewed on stage Roshen Bhurtha, Jynee Tsang and Kim Vinall, all students known to him personally.

Roshen Bhurtha told us of what he had gained from being mentored by Bernard Wiltshire, a barrister from a cultural minority background like Roshen. Wiltshire introduced him to a world he would not normally see. Bhurtha commented:

> I got a sense of the atmosphere and an inside view of the workings of the court. I saw that there are two sides to the job – the glamorous side and the boring side. The boring side didn't put me off.
>
> (LIFT 1992)

Bhurtha subsequently gained the courage to embark on studies for an extra A-Level and to apply to university.

Jynee Tsang came from a family with no experience of higher education and did less well in her A-Levels than expected. With the help of student counselling, Tsang was able to clarify what she wanted:

> The student counsellor helped me to think clearly and understand what I wanted to do. I was going to her two or three times a week when I was feeling really low.
>
> (LIFT 1992)

This support and her own determination enabled Tsang to achieve a place at university to study maths and science.

When Kim Vinall became a mother she was faced with a choice of staying on income support or returning to a dead-end job. Instead, she opted to embark on an Access course at the local college. Once a certain number of credits were gained, a place at university was guaranteed. Vinall reflected that the anti-education values with which she was surrounded in her youth were difficult to overcome:

> An Access course is like an access to life. It opened my mind completely. It was hard because for the first time the values I've had all my life got smashed down. I had to start examining everything. Education does that.
>
> (LIFT 1992)

Morris and colleagues looked at how these initiatives might inform national strategy. Initially, the schemes arose without overall co-ordination, devised by enterprising local educationalists in response to local need. They were aimed at promoting access to post-16 education, progression from it and flexibility in the curriculum structure. So successful were they that an alliance of institutions and funders set up a project to pull them together into a coherent system for post-16 education and training at a national level. Local experiment informed national policy.[10]

From Stratford to Broadway: *Five Guys Named Moe*

'If you design a show to be a transatlantic hit – don't be surprised if it sinks mid-ocean.' So commented Philip Hedley, Director of east London's renowned Theatre Royal, Stratford East. In 1985, performer and musician Clarke Peters devised a 40-minute divertissement based on the music of Louis Jordan, a hero from his childhood growing up in Harlem. Initially this was to amuse colleagues in the Green Room of the National Theatre where he was working at the time. Soon, Peters persuaded the Theatre to stage three late-night performances. Philip Hedley was in the audience and invited Peters to develop a full-length show, believing it would be perfect for his local audience in Stratford.

In 1989, the show was presented at Theatre Royal to critical and audience acclaim. West End Producer, Cameron Mackintosh, saw the show and agreed that they had to transfer it to a commercial run in central London. Key elements of the Stratford presentation were vital to maintaining the informal atmosphere of the show – being able to bring drinks into the auditorium and making sure that the audience was mixed. The mixed audience was made possible by a cheap ticket policy. These dimensions were maintained when the show moved to London's West End in 1991. Soon afterwards, a transfer to Broadway was negotiated with plans made for tours to cities beyond New York, to Europe, Australia and the Far East.

The phenomenal success of *Five Guys Named Moe* came in part because it was never designed to be a hit. Rather, it demonstrates that if you set out to serve your local audience, be responsive to truly expressing experience at a local level, you are more likely to have a success on your hands. The Theatre Royal has a 118-year history of working with the community on its doorstep. Joan Littlewood, the theatre's Director in the 1950s and 1960s, described this process as a continuous loop between the audience and the stage and back again. In this way, local experience acts as laboratory for expressing and refining human expression. If it works sublimely at home, it is more likely to travel.

This philosophy was confidently borne out in the evolution of *Five Guys Named Moe*. Its evolution also illustrates the delicate interactions and interdependencies of the theatre ecology in London. The successes of the commercial world are dependent on risks taken in the subsidized sector. A continuum of opportunities, scale and personal connections mean that an idea has the time and place to incubate and be tested with different audiences and at different scales before reaching its full potential. London's international reputation for theatre does not rest on the successes of the West End and the mainstream houses alone. It emerges from delicately interwoven relationships from local to mainstream level, an ever-changing arts ecology of creators, supporters and audiences reaching across London, elsewhere in the UK and internationally as well.

Korda: A venture capital company with a difference

Taking a different view of risk and incubation was the work of Korda and Company. Just like the stories in education and the theatre, this venture capital company realized that new business ideas do not arise ready-made out of nothing. They need nurturing. Alex Korda founded the company in 1982, after working in large companies. He said:

> I was looking for a way to commit crazy mistakes for myself rather than fighting internal politics. My intention was to develop a platform on which to build technologically-based businesses without any capital.

(LIFT 1992)

Together with his business partner, Carolyn Hayman, whose experience spanned government and consultancy, he amassed contacts among a wide range of scientists, technological experts and people with access to capital.

Korda's first company collapsed. The four subsequent companies thrived. Nevertheless, by 1988, Korda and Company decided they needed to raise additional capital. This was secured from 6 sources, following 130 approaches. The Korda seed capital fund of £5m was launched in 1989. Korda differs from mainstream investors because of its intimate involvement in the evolution of the companies they finance. The company aims to find a project with sound technology, ambitious scale, and people with some understanding of the challenge they are undertaking. The company does not look for perfect business plans. They assess the individuals rather than the technology. Korda will help the project to develop and to identify new capital, aiming to withdraw its support in time.

Challenges of supporting innovative business practice proved to be the same as supporting innovative practice in the arts. Just as ensuring London's economic vitality rests on the support and incubation of new business ideas, the vitality of London's cultural life is made up of an ecology of activities in which the most local level is inextricably linked to the flagship institutions and personal relationships at local, regional and international levels. In the arts world, it is at small scale that people's talent and ideas are incubated and tested first before they are ready to be displayed on the main stages, the same with business. It is not without coincidence that those with the least resources have the greatest ability to set the stage for others. They have the strongest motivation for leaps of imagination to overcome the obstacles that face them. They have nothing to lose by experimenting with different approaches, satisfying their own creative curiosity and questioning the status quo. It is often because people are connecting at a level not determined by money alone, but by their own motivation to do something against the odds, that an initiative takes on an energy inspiring to others working at a different scale. Initiatives at the edge prefigure the mainstream and are the initial locus of innovation.

LIFT's civic role

Just as when Fenton and Neal set out to discover how to put on an international Festival, LIFT now realized that it had to discover how to make a Festival for London and examine in greater depth its civic role. In spite of a lack of civic leadership, we realized that we had connections with a very wide range of people from policy-makers to local project leaders without whom the policy-makers could not do their job. Simply by setting out to extend an invitation, to offer hospitality rather than being a supplicant and shouting about our own assets, we had changed our view of ourselves. In so doing, we changed others' perceptions of LIFT and began to build a constituency of support that has been a foundation for building partnerships over subsequent decades.

LIFTING London provoked questions about the balance of relationships between market, state and civil society. This helped us to get a better feel for where we should fit in an era when these roles were changing. Sir Ralf Dahrendorf, a distinguished commentator in this field, was asked to summarize our meeting. At best, he insisted, government can provide only a loose framework for activity – the rest lies with civil society. This concept of civil society was being lost and was in great need of reinvention in a world of increasingly rapid devolution of responsibility from central government to local arenas and from public to privately run services.

This dimension of life has since been described as:

> the arena of uncoerced collective action around shared interests, purposes and values. In theory, its institutional forms are distinct from those of the state, family and market, though in practice, the boundaries between state, civil society, family and market are often complex, blurred and negotiated. Civil society commonly embraces a diversity of spaces, actors and institutional forms, varying in their degree of formality, autonomy and power. Civil societies are often populated by organizations such as registered charities, development non-governmental organizations, community groups, women's organizations, faith-based organizations, professional associations, trades unions, self-help groups, social movements, business associations, coalitions and advocacy groups.
>
> (LSE's Centre for Civil Society 2004)

Dahrendorf reminded us that civil society is made up of a plurality of autonomous associations practising civic responsibility and it is this that sustains life in a free society[11]. Indeed, he asserted: 'This is what ultimately makes life worth living.' Associations of civil society depend on the joint efforts of non-governmental and governmental agencies; 'partnership' is not always the most appropriate description of the relationship between agencies. He explained a degree of tension was to be expected between the initiatives that grew out of an immediate sense of need and those with formal responsibility in the field. Dahrendorf pointed out that it was a common mistake to think that legislation can solve everything. He reminded participants in LIFTING London that the energy and commitment of people acting in one place are often more effective. 'But,' he said, 'lighting one little candle requires a whole lot of people who are prepared to do it.'

Just two years earlier, images of thousands and thousands of ordinary people assembling in Prague had inspired others all around the world that change is possible. The playwright, Vaclav Havel, had helped to found Civic Forum in Czechoslovakia and was made his country's President in 1989. Civic associations had overturned a system that had ceased to serve human needs. Those images inspired us in attempts to bring about change in London.

Samuel Pepys, lover of London par excellence, would perhaps have agreed with us when he wrote: 'Strange to see how a good dinner and feasting reconciles everybody' (Pepys 1980 [1665]). When there are difficult questions to address, festivity can play its part. Through calling a meeting in an atmosphere of constructive critique, opening up conversations between sectors, between people running projects and policy-makers responsible for a strategic overview, LIFTING London brought people out of their individual boxes to celebrate achievements to be found in the city. A civic conversation across sectors, cultures and ages generated a sense of hope among those in search of it, even a sense of neighbourliness. It connected LIFT to its own civic responsibility and set a tone of communication in response to perceived need. This step came to influence the way we programmed the Festival and how we viewed the audiences and constituencies that the programme brought together. It also taught us about the limits of the market and that commercial sponsorship and civic life are intimately intertwined. By taking the risk of taking action, it contributed greatly to our own strategic thinking. For the time being, LIFTING London made our lives easier until the next crisis hit. The Czech example of the power of civil society would come to inform a response to more subtle and all-pervading threats posed by the inequities of globalization that would build to a crescendo in the late 1990s.

But for now, attention at LIFT began to focus more and more on how the Festival could engage young people in the theatre and, through performance, encourage their engagement in civil society.

FIVE

ENTER YOUNG
THEATRE-MAKERS

Culture is not something extra, like say a sixth finger on a human hand. Culture has been rightly said to be to society what a flower is to a plant. What is important about a flower is not just its beauty. A flower is the carrier of the seeds for new plants, the bearer of that future of that species of plant.

(Wa Thiong'o 1993: 56–7)

Fenton and Neal believed that for the Festival to flourish in the long term, ways needed to be found of engaging future audiences, participants and artists.

Confident that the Festival provided an outstanding resource for engaging the imaginations of young people, the question was how to do this consistently and well over time. Ample evidence existed as to how theatre could engage artists and audiences on a one-off basis. How to effect continuity of genuine engagement across generations and cultures in wider groups was more challenging. This chapter tells how LIFT set about doing this through the Festival's education programmes, and professional and youth international exchanges.

LIFTING London had reminded us of the value of interaction beyond everyone's formal roles when faced with a civic crisis in the late 1980s. As LIFT's relationship with commercial sponsors became more challenging and their commercial demands more clamorous, these questions of engagement beyond institutional walls became more urgent. What we did not realize was that engaging with a younger generation would inform how LIFT engaged with businesses.

In the early 1990s, strange to say, we barely recognized that globalization of the economy was the trend to which the arts world was responding. LIFT was continually working to present performance in the most authentic context possible. This quest led LIFT to make a shift in its understanding of internationalism. Rather than an international approach being simply a two-way street between home and abroad, LIFT began to see the dynamics of international exchange like a multi-way street with a need to connect the Festival more solidly both at home and abroad. This sense challenged the status quo. Clues for direction came from other Festivals grappling with the same issues. Theatre Director, Peter Sellars, for example, had recognized that to present an international arts festival in Los Angeles it was no longer tenable simply to present classical opera in the grand arts centres.

> The 1990 Los Angeles Festival offers art of social continuity and challenge, the work of artists who are defining and redefining the concept of community in their lifetimes.
>
> The ultimate task is the realignment of the cultural distribution system in America to create a world in which Americans – Americans of colour, first generation, second generation, third generation, natives – begin to see images of their own lives and the lives of others which are personal, accurate and sufficiently deep; a world where political discourse is not dominated by 30-second television spots about the flag, but where notions of patriotism are grounded in a knowledge and love of what our land actually is and who really lives here; a world in which there is room for private feelings, difference, controversy, sophistication and trust.
>
> (Sellars 1990)

If LIFT was to reflect the reality of London and its peoples, this could be achieved neither in the space of one festival alone, nor through one generation of traditional theatre attendees. LIFT began to imagine how international artists might be directly connected to young people by embarking together on creative adventures.

Following an initial pilot phase in 1991,[1] a fully-fledged Education Programme was launched in 1993 under the aegis of Education Director, Tony Fegan. As a former drama teacher in a large London comprehensive school, Fegan knew the role challenging performance could play in the lives and learning of young people and their families. When he and his students worked with artists from South Africa in LIFT '91, Fegan saw the exceptional additional potential brought by an international dimension. These experiences laid the foundations of the LIFT Education Programme.

The LIFT Education Programme

Participation happens at several levels. At the simplest, LIFT offers young people and their teachers access to LIFT performances through discounted tickets and background information. Education packs provide information about selected shows, their country of origin, and their cultural and historical context. Teachers are encouraged to use these as a starting point for introducing different cultural perspectives to subjects across the curriculum. A period of study culminates in a visit to the LIFT production and workshops either before or after the performances. Much effort goes into making direct contact with teachers in advance of the Festival for planning theatre visits and associated lesson content.

At a more ambitious level, LIFT's international artists provide a catalyst for teachers and UK-based artists and young people to work together over a longer period. The performances by young people are not kept in some special box but are billed in the programme alongside the other LIFT shows for presentation to the public on a par with other LIFT productions. Shows of varying scale are made and performed in the young people's own neighbourhoods, or in mainstream arts institutions or public parks. Public performance is vital to ensure the rigour, excitement and authenticity of creative cultural exchange for everyone involved.

Performing for a public is always challenging, the experience is of such intensity that those directly and even indirectly involved have an opportunity to awaken new skills, even to bury grievances to create new stories of success. Previously disaffected students can change their own and others' perception of them. Such educational and social values of participation in theatre-making are a resource that LIFT offers to young people in both schools and out-of-school youth arts settings. On occasions, schools and groups of elderly people have been encouraged to work together.

The normal Festival rhythm was biennial and each LIFT season from 1991–5 included work with young people. But a more intensive period of experimentation called OUT of LIFT happened during 1996, traditionally a non-Festival year. The question guiding this season was: how can theatre be created with, by and for young people? The centrepiece was *Factory of Dreams*, a large-scale public event in Brockwell Park, south London, created by 120 13-year-olds working with a team of artists, led by French pyrotechnician, Christophe Berthonneau. This project was seminal in the evolution of LIFT's work with, by and for young people. It demonstrated how creative exploration releases the dreams of young people to illuminate the public realm, thus enabling the young people to play a part in civic life.

A sense that such social and creative celebration was desirable emerged from a time of increasing political and social polarization in the late 1980s and early 1990s. The interests of the individual were emphasized above *all* others, and Thatcher's dismissive comment that 'There is no such thing as society' rang in our ears.[2] As moves towards the first ever National Curriculum were made in Britain, LIFT was concerned that the space for creativity in schools was being eroded through a prescriptive approach to how and what could be taught with an emphasis on the 'harder' subjects. As budget cuts hit home, schools could offer fewer part-time opportunities for practising artists, thus further eroding both the place of the arts in school life and sources of livelihood for artists.

An invitation was extended to Berthonneau to work with students in a London school. Berthonneau and Groupe F have devised and realized many large-scale civic, sporting and national celebrations across the world. The company was responsible for pyrotechnic illumination of the Eiffel Tower in Paris for Millennium

Eve, and more recently the opening and closing ceremonies of the 2004 Athens Olympics. LIFT first invited Berthonneau to stage his work in London in 1995 with *Birds of Fire* on the River Thames. The company returned to LIFT with *Un Peu Plus de Lumière* (Battersea Park, 1997), *Garden of Light* (Victoria Park, 2001) and *Joueurs de Lumières* (Victoria Park, 2004).

Berthonneau welcomed LIFT's proposition, seeing the project as an opportunity to test his creative abilities in an arena away from the spotlight of civic celebrations. The frantic pressures of an international schedule gave little time for reflection whereby creative energies could be refreshed or deep connections made with the cities in which Berthonneau and his company worked. Without reflection, imagination quickly loses its wings. The increasingly commercial values dominating life in Britain were coming at that time to erode community life in France as well. This coincidence of circumstances, hopes and aspirations gave rise to *Factory of Dreams*.

LIFT invited a group of London artists from different cultural backgrounds and different art practices to devise the project with Berthonneau during an initial week-long period. The team included Dominic Campbell, carnival designer, pyrotechnician and open-air animateur; Sofie Layton, mask and puppet-maker and creator of large-scale sculptural forms; Gavin O'Shea, composer and music technologist; Andrew Siddall, pyrotechnician, physical theatre performer and producer of open-air events; and Ali Zaidi, visual artist, sculptor, film and carnival designer.

A proposal for pupils to take part was put to Tony LaMothe, Head Teacher of Stockwell Park School, south London. LaMothe immediately welcomed the plan, seeing that such a challenging venture had the potential to bring pupils, staff and parents together, to raise pupils' aspirations and to change both internal and external perceptions of the school through public performance. The UK-based artists took up residency and worked with teachers across the curriculum in preparation for Berthonneau's second working visit.

One hundred and twenty pupils aged 12 to 13 were selected to work on the project from the school's Year 9, a group not occupied with examinations and with flexibility in their timetable. It turned out that the hardest part of the project was asking the pupils what their dreams were. They were so rarely asked this question, particularly in a school context, that they found it difficult to answer.

Encouraged by the artists, pupils began to generate ideas. Their visions took the shape of, for example, excelling in football, having their own homes, becoming an architect, or safeguarding the future of the planet. Once images were formed into artefacts in clay or on paper a visit was made to the local park to help the young people (and the artists) imagine how the scale of the eventual production would communicate to and involve an audience. With the artists' guidance, the pupils' images were magnified and, in the process, they learned about the properties of materials needed to sustain this change of scale. Music was written and recorded by the young people. Further ideas about fire and light were explored in subjects across the curriculum. Different traditions of celebration were explored through the over 40 cultural backgrounds of the young people in the school. The young people began to perceive that they could contribute to society beyond their family or school.

Eight months later, over two nights, around 8,000 people travelled to south London at dusk from all across the city to see *Factory of Dreams*.

> The city is recharged by cultural injection; good art is about people coming together and several thousand of them created a transient, but moving sense of social communion in the pleasant acreage of Brockwell Park . . . teenagers at Stockwell Park School participated in a ritualistic procession of giant lanterns and carnival puppets . . . a papier-maché queen was transfigured in a fireworks display that climaxed in one almighty orgasmic whoosh that left us limp with pleasure.
>
> (Michael Coveney, *The Observer* 1996)

Teachers and students reflected on the project. Headteacher Tony LaMothe commented:

> Because of the way LIFT Education projects work, creativity is always an outcome but along the way there is the opportunity for young people to develop listening skills, an appreciation for individual

talent, teamwork, planning, organizational and communication skills and to experience major success in their young lives.

(LIFT 1997)

Akbar Hosein, Head of Design and Technology, commented:

Initially there was chaos. Then the things which were complex at first, like moving work between departments, became simple in the end, because we learnt to rely on the pupils and each other and approach problems on a more friendly, honest basis.

(LIFT 1997)

Paul Brown, the School's Workshop Technician, observed:

Since Factory of Dreams, certain pupils will no longer disrupt the class if they do not understand what is going on. Instead they will later go to other pupils and ask them.

(LIFT 1997)

Nikki Jones, an educationalist, who had attended the final performances recognized:

Having worked for so long in London schools, I knew just what an incredible feat of energy dealing with the logistics and fears, prejudices and egos, the performance would have demanded, the real joy for me was the achievements of the pupils, who are so often not allowed to show their true talent.

(LIFT 1997)

This shared activity in the public sphere brought a new dimension to the young people's learning and to the experience of teachers, parents and public alike. We were embraced by something that was bigger than all of us.

LIFT education and international cultural exchange

A second LIFT education initiative illustrates how the LIFT principles of participation, equity and public creation have been augmented by international cultural exchange for young people and arts educators. Phakama, meaning 'lift up, take control' in Xhosa, was initiated by LIFT with Sibikwa Community Theatre, Johannesburg, in 1996. LIFT had a long association with South Africa through presenting theatre productions in the Festival. Following the end of apartheid, LIFT was interested in collaborating with an emerging generation of artists and in helping to initiate a venture that could build creative skills among young people in both South Africa and London.

Project Phakama resulted from a number of arts educators who observed that remarkable educational results emerged from participation by young people in out-of-school activities focused on the ideas and experience of young people themselves. Increased emphasis on literacy and numeracy skills in schools eroded the possibilities of group learning and shared critique that the arts educators observed in these out-of-school arts settings. Such informal youth arts activities are often invisible or barely tolerated by mainstream institutions in their local areas. Part of their draw is that they provide risk, real (not realistic) learning, and a different ambience from the status quo. Young Phakama leaders saw the venture as a route to forging a voice and creative responsibility in their communities, and even a route to economic survival.

Phakama as of 2004 is connected to youth arts groups across South Africa and other countries in the SADC region.[3] It is also working in India and Brazil and continues in London.

Phukama's way of building qualities of intercultural creative projects came to inform LIFT's communication with businesses. Description follows of a Phakama session:

Project Phakama – learning creative leadership

In 2000, I took part in a Phakama residency in Mma-batho, Northern Province, South Africa. Approximately 80 young people from the local area, from Gauteng, Western and Eastern Cape, and Northern Province came together with around 15 tutors and trainee tutors from South Africa, Mauritius, Mozambique, Namibia, Lesotho and London. Some of the young South Africans had visited London the previous year to join with Phakama youth there.

The format of a residency is now well established. Individual groups research and create pieces of theatre and performance in their own regions. Representatives selected by their peers join tutors and young people from other regions in the international session. Over a nine-day period a new work is created from individual pieces, performed to the public in response to a specific location in each city, often outside a conventional theatre. Thus art and life are merged, a link forged between the act of creation and daily life helping to maintain a creative approach to other aspects of existence. Rather than imagination being kept in the box called 'art', each performance takes inspiration from the spirit of the place and reflects it back to makers and audiences alike.

The Mmabatho residency's theme was the lives of women. Members of the regional groups, aged on average between 11 and 25, interviewed their mothers, aunts, grandmothers and sisters. The performances, many of which were researched and performed by young men, raised urgent questions: the common experience of violence and traditional gender roles.

Phakama's guiding principle is inclusivity, drawing on the imaginations and skills of the group. The rhythm of creation at times has an inward focus and at others looks to the outside world. Phakama's form and process enables regional groups to become one and each individual participant to feel a part of the whole. The first few days concentrate on building a shared creative responsibility with an emphasis on name games; agreeing ground rules for living and working together; sharing and critiquing work from the regional groups; and visiting places of local significance. The group tangibly begins to gel when the performance location is encountered for the first time; participants immediately respond by imagining scenes in situ, placing the scenes of others and devising new scenes in response to the material around them. The performance place inspires both curiosity and generosity. Mealtimes give groups opportunities to mix, debate, connect and converse, often animatedly. All participants now have a common project to talk about. As work progresses, more shared experience is generated on which to base conversations. It becomes easier to talk and ask questions, enabling younger and older participants to organize around an emerging reality.

Sharing skills and responsibilities is another guiding principle made explicit during a session called Give and Gain. Everyone fills in two strips of differently coloured paper. On one, participants write what they wish to gain from Phakama and, on the other, what they wish to give. On the wall is placed the shape of the sun. It is divided into sections representing all the skills and responsibilities that go into making theatre: production; direction; dance; acting; song; movement; finance; publicity; marketing; box office; front of house management and audience safety; lighting; stage management; and, finally, in the case of Mmabatho, liaison with the traffic police. It may be that during any particular session individuals choose to emphasize what they wish to gain in skills or expertise. One may be brilliant at acting, but wish to learn more about production and finance. In this way, each individual can be part of a group in which someone more experienced has decided to share his or her skills. The other benefit of the skills' wheel is to see at a glance the part one has chosen to play in the making of the whole. My role at the session was to advise on fundraising and I wished to gain skills in movement.

Multiple layering of responsibility flows through all projects – leadership and skills are distributed. This dimension bears luminous lessons for developing leadership qualities toward civic and cultural engagement. Three levels of leadership are at play: young participants, trainee tutors and tutors. Although the tutors appear to be in charge, their main task is to guide and step back. When they step back, the next generation of emerging leaders takes responsibility. Among the young participants, natural leaders emerge and organize games, and guide others in the negotiation of ground rules or living arrangements. The trainee tutors emerge from the group of young participants. Through connecting to a real project, about all too real issues explored with great energy and creative risk, leaders emerge with new skills and abilities put to the test.

South Africa's future, just as Britain's, depends on 'setting the stage for a shared future' – Phakama's subtitle. In the performances created, each group works with cultural and individual skill levels and differences to reach a negotiated solution, celebrating differing viewpoints and creating something new out of the tensions.

The final performances of the Mmabatho residency took place in two houses located on either side of the main four-lane highway into the city. Audience members were led through the rooms to witness stories abstracted and shaped from original research. From a tree in one garden hung strands of poetry created in the six different languages spoken by the group. The audience explored the poetry tree with the aid of torches. The traffic police arrived to close the highway while the audience crossed the road between the two houses. The police came prepared for regular duty, but soon joined in dancing and singing with the car-drivers, passers-by, audience and performers, changing, for one moment, the life and routine of the city.

Extensive research into the qualities of learning and perform-ance that emerge from out-of-school youth-based arts activities such as these has shown how such settings offer an atmosphere of risk and revelation. Big questions of society come to front stage, and age barriers crumble when young people lay claim to civic engagement, social responsibility and cultural continuity for their own communities (Heath and Smyth 1999).

LIFT's Education Programme tests principles of shared learning[4]

Education Director Tony Fegan's vision of LIFT as a learning resource had been partly inspired by a project with arts educa-tionalist Anna Ledgard the year prior to his joining LIFT. At that time, Fegan was Head of Performing Arts in Queen's Park Community School and Ledgard was Education Officer at the Puppet Centre, a national arts advisory body. Both were united in a desire to build a corpus of knowledge, values, professional prac-tice and ideas to underpin collaboration between artists, teachers, children and communities.

The visit to LIFT '91 of Handspring Puppet Company and the Market Theatre Laboratory of Johannesburg offered UK artists, teachers, young people and audiences first-hand engagement with artists from a country at a turning point in its history.

Motivations for engaging in a shared project were multiple. Handspring was keen to work with Faulty Optic, a leading company of innovative artists they had long admired. The Market Theatre Laboratory performers (visiting London for the first time) were interested in running drama workshops with young people. The Tricycle Theatre was looking to strengthen its education programme. The school saw an opportunity to widen the curriculum with a cross-cultural, arts-based project.

Collaboration on this scale required a clear structure for planning and reflection to decide on priorities and build relationships. In Ledgard's words, 'it proved a hornet's nest of conflicting assumptions' in which mutual respect between artists and teachers was fragile and differences surfaced in approach to learners.

The production they produced with the students was based on the life of Stompie Moeketsi, the child murdered by Winnie Mandela's bodyguard.[5] Called *The Life of Themba*, this technically accomplished piece involving shadow and Bunraku puppetry, rap and storytelling was performed on the main stage of the Tricycle Theatre prior to performances of *Starbrites*, the production presented as part of LIFT by Handspring Puppet Company.

The difficulties of working across boundaries

Students had left with a sense of achievement, the school and teachers were satisfied, but the artists remained frustrated, feeling they had gained little in the exchange of creative ideas. A shared commitment to the rigours of performance had avoided failure but improved working principles were needed if such projects were to succeed. Much of LIFT's work over the next decade concentrated on finding a methodology enabling artists and schools to work together in a way that did not compromise their respective principles, priorities or cultural perspectives. These principles came to inform how we shaped our learning programmes for business and public sector worlds.

Principles of shared learning

1 All projects are participant-centred, in the words of Fegan:

> allowing for as many entry points as possible, each participant brings their own skills, life experience, curiosity, passion – and also a readiness to put themselves at risk by saying something unexpected, or simply being, in their own way, different.
>
> (Ledgard 2006)

2 Action and reflection lie at the heart of collaborative creative learning. Reflection is impossible to detach from the creative process. When opportunities for reflection are in short supply, simply allocating time for individual and collective reflection proves of immense value to participants.

3 Collaborative art forms are central. When embarking on shared experiment, relying on well-honed expertise in one particular area does not allow for surprise. Shared risk and uncertainty make for shared serendipity and discovery.

4 Particular histories and cultures experienced through LIFT performances are the starting points, developed further through the particular cultures and histories of participants. The cross-cultural and cross-sectoral nature of learning projects actively bring together international and UK artists, from a range of experience, cultural backgrounds and abilities, including adult helpers and parents where possible.

5 Specific places and locations are fundamental to collective creation. This not only challenges the status quo of conventional theatre practice but also allows for new meaning and confident new connections to be forged with particular places.

LIFT's learning cycle

Each event is followed by sessions of internal (and sometimes external) assessment, planning and projecting forward from individual shows. This iterative internal reflection is a big part of LIFT and an attempt never to rest on one's laurels, always asking: How

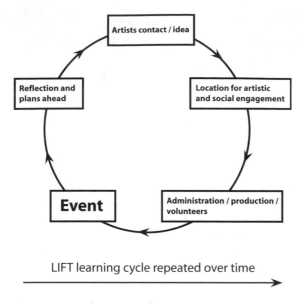

LIFT learning cycle repeated over time

Figure 5.1 LIFT learning cycle

did this work? What are the principles that lead us to go forward or backward from here? As with Christophe Berthonneau's fireworks, each show is a rehearsal for the next.

The international youth dimension of LIFT sparked creative activity in the public sphere in compelling ways. Testimony from teachers, students, parents, and civic and community leaders bore witness to this.

LIFT's Education Programme made vivid the quality of learning to be gained from youth arts activities in the public sphere. Could we move the businesses from which we secured support beyond their instincts to splash branding or enhance corporate reputations, going into each situation with a fixed idea of what was to be extracted? Could we assert somehow to business the value of the public realm as a place for imagining, learning, rehearsing and adaptation? These underlying strategic questions became a constant refrain urgent to address if we were to survive the next crisis.

PART TWO

Strategic Conversations

Burrow awhile and build, broad on the roots of things.
(Browning 1864: 301)

SIX

BLEACHED BONES AND STARTING AGAIN

Human life begins on the far side of despair.[1]

(Sartre 1943: 311)

In 1994, crisis did indeed hit. Two things happened in one month that produced a radical development in business relations at LIFT. The first involved a momentous event in Britain's banking history. News broke that one of Britain's oldest merchant banks and one of our longest-term supporters, Barings Bank, had crashed. The news was shocking. Closer to home, concern struck as to how Barings' change in fortune might affect LIFT. We had an application for funds waiting for a decision by the Baring Foundation. Ironically, because the Foundation's support was of the philanthropic kind, we had been encouraged to apply for sponsorship of a production that was of little interest to other, more commercially motivated sources of support. We were able to leave our application to the latest moment so confident were we of the Bank's commitment to us. We would just confirm our application when we had all the information required. On returning to the office a few days after news of the Bank's collapse, we made enquiries and discovered that the Foundation was in turmoil and all decisions had been frozen. For us it spelled near disaster. We had left the application so late that with no funds from Baring's there was a glaring hole in our budget for the forthcoming Festival. There was little hope that the money would be found from elsewhere.

Nicholas Baring, whose individual support we had enjoyed since 1986, was a member of the Council of the Baring Foundation.[2] He had attended many of the productions we had staged. Beyond his sponsorship support, Baring was never too grand, remote or rushed to act as a sounding board when we were faced with situations in need of counsel and connections.[3] He was someone we had grown to trust. Soon after the crisis, we received a call. We learned that ING, the Dutch company now in charge of Barings, had agreed to honour existing commitments of the Foundation. In LIFT's case, as nothing was signed, the position was unclear. Enquiries were being made to establish whether another Foundation would take over responsibility for LIFT. In due course, we were referred to the Esmée Fairbairn Foundation, who agreed to support LIFT for the subsequent three years. The crash of Barings Bank threatened to destabilize LIFT too, but in the end, this reverse turned out well for us. Amid the profound shocks detonating around him, Baring had not forgotten organizations dependent on the Foundation's support.

The second event never reached the newspapers. For LIFT, however, it was equally historic. BT, the sponsor of the first year of LIFT's Education Programme, decided not to sponsor the second. The company had taken a risk in sponsoring the first season and the sponsorship represented the largest LIFT had ever secured. We were aware that the results were uncertain and that real benefits for the sponsor would emerge after a second Festival. In all our discussions with BT the benefits of a long-term partnership were emphasized. LIFT knew that a one-off sponsorship would be less likely to build visibility than one that lasted over a longer period. A second year's sponsorship was not dismissed in these discussions and we naturally hoped that it could be negotiated in due course.

There were some great achievements in that first year. In spite of our best efforts, however, we did not succeed in securing reams of press coverage for the sponsorship in the national papers. This was one of the outcomes sought by both the sponsor and us. In common with other community efforts, we found it difficult to persuade the press that front-page material was to be made from articles about young people finding a voice, or as one teacher described a project, 'tackling racism in the head'. The sponsors were disappointed and even accused us of not giving them value for their money.

We made mistakes. On reflection, the scale of the project in its first experimental year was perhaps badly communicated. This is not to say that any information given was deliberately misleading, rather that in describing projects in the future for which there is no common experience as a basis for discussion, it is extremely difficult to ensure that a sponsor's expectations are realistic. Perhaps, in spite of our very best efforts, our organization was not set up to deliver the hard marketing return that was expected by the company. At the time we had only the beginnings of an in-house marketing department to make the most of the promotional opportunities that LIFT's activities might offer. To make matters worse, one of the projects supported by BT had not been the creative success we would have liked.

On the sponsors' part there were confusions too. They perhaps perceived our organization as more slick and sophisticated than it was – or indeed than we would want it to be. Our sponsorship came through the regional office of BT and there appeared to be tensions between this office and the national sponsorship office, making for confusions and delays in decisions. For all the rhetoric of benefits and accountability, little clarity emerged about how the project was to be evaluated. A gap between the rhetoric of good corporate citizenship and the 'hard' marketing benefits sought by the sponsors developed as a consequence. As a result my colleagues and I spent hours in discussion with the sponsor, often at cross-purposes. Over time, it became glaringly obvious that there was a fundamental paradox in marketing-based sponsorship that went to the heart of some of the most acute challenges faced by our society – issues of engagement across cultures and fostering the potential of young people. A relationship based on advertising of necessity focused on discussions about the size of the company's logo on LIFT's publicity material, the amount of press coverage secured and so on. There was no opportunity via which the company could learn through engagement with the young people or the arts it was supporting. It became obvious that marketing measures of success were at odds not only with society's needs but also with the long-term interests of the adaptability of business itself.

These two events, the crash of Baring's Bank and BT's withdrawal from what we hoped would be commitment to long-term sponsorship of LIFT's Education Programme, plunged me into despair. After ten years' raising money for the arts in the context of the time, my working approach, and even integrity, leapt into question. I sensed a deep concern about the application of commercial sponsorship to youth arts activities. The weight of this realization made it difficult to lift the telephone one more time to raise funds in the language of marketing. A radical new approach was needed.

Of course, for many in the arts in the UK, the idea of getting sponsorship from businesses had always been an anathema. This was an attitude fostered by 50 years of subsidy, a predominant culture of art for art's sake and the socialist instincts of many arts-makers. Many companies were seen as evil personified, and having anything to do with them was seen as selling your soul and supping with the devil. How could I be naive enough to think it could be otherwise? What was my position on this? Was it possible to find a way of connecting the two worlds that made sense from the business perspective and yet was consistent with arts principles of social justice, and political and aesthetic critique? And anyway, the nature of a business was as varied as the idea of an arts organization. An entrenched position on the inevitability of core differences between business and arts allowed for no differentiation between businesses, or even for a business to change its behaviour. And if public sector services were being privatized, where did this leave the idea of public service? What was public, and what was private and how did the arts relate to both, or either?

An isolationist approach on the part of the arts did not appeal. We had learned from LIFTING London that all sectors are interdependent. What is more, socialism and capitalism seemed to be merging worldwide. If capitalism is the system we are stuck with, how do we try to do something about the culture of capitalism in which we live? Do we just stay out of the conversation or try to offer critique in other ways?

To continue securing funds for the arts from the business world, we had to have answers to these new questions. The dual crisis of Baring's collapse and BT's sponsorship decision forced a return to first principles and examination of my own role and values. I had always been an interpreter/translator between cultures of one kind or another. Convinced that the theatre and celebration in my own life actually helped survival, I wished to discover the role of theatre for others as a space to think and feel and even survive. Maybe it would be possible to find a new way of doing my job. A different way of speaking was needed; one that would allow a completely different conversation to happen through a mode of engagement that was not *directly* commercial, but instead was firmly based in the civic sphere and on principles of shared learning.

The route to a new language

My mind buzzed with questions in the effort to discover anew the role of the arts with no directly commercial application. What was the interest to business of young people exploring their potential and abilities? What was the value of encountering worlds other than your own? What was the role of celebration for our times? What was the role of the artist who questions accepted ways of doing things? What was the value of cultural activities in the public sphere? What was the value of the public sphere? These were very different questions from the ones we were used to asking, namely: Which productions are the most commercial and easiest to sell to sponsors? How big should their logo be on the printed material? How many tickets do they get to shows? How much is the sponsorship worth? Who sits next to whom at dinner? And so on. This new direction embraced the whole Festival, controversial shows included. If we were to generate new forms of relationship and generate revenue to do so, then we needed to explore these questions in much greater depth. It was soon clear that to start a new conversation we needed a new language that went back to basic beliefs about theatre itself.

Talking to artists alone would not help illuminate such issues. We were all talking about the same things. Since my particular focus had been the business community, I needed business people to talk to but different business people from those in arts and community affairs departments who, whatever the stated community policy of their company, could not escape marketing measures of success. They could not have broader conversations; there was no logic within their day-to-day jobs that would allow it.

It emerged that there was indeed a hunger for people in business to embark on different kinds of conversation beyond the boundaries of their own organization. For the most part, they were not those responsible for making connections with the arts, with rare exceptions. Years earlier, when LIFT's engagement with businesses was solely defined by a marketing approach, Catherine Graham-Harrison of Citibank had made me stop and think when she asked if we could enable her colleagues to learn more about the theatre. I was to discover that those people in businesses interested in different conversations beyond the walls of their company rarely had the arts in their view. They were largely in charge of strategy or long-term planning, management or leadership development in departments well away from formal connections with the arts.

My route to this discovery was circuitous and began with the Royal Society for Arts, Manufactures and Commerce (RSA), which had embarked on a project exploring Britain's future competitiveness. Initiated by some of the UK's leading corporations and business thinkers, *Tomorrow's Company* established the attitudinal changes required to maintain Britain's position in a global economy.

As a Fellow of the Society, in 1994 I attended sessions of *Tomorrow's Company* and recall a discussion about how the report should be disseminated. Would its fate be just like a million others, relegated to a shelf, never to be read? The thought occurred that something more persuasive might be valuable, a project that brought to life the challenges faced by people in business. Perhaps what was needed was a play, a soap opera or a television series? Everyone laughed at my suggestion. There was one exception, a young Belgian, Alain Wouters, who worked in the planning department of Shell. At last, someone had emerged with whom to float ideas in earnest.

Wouters explained that there was a desire to engage with people from other disciplines, including the arts, in the search for solutions to new pressures on companies such as Shell. The broad picture I gained was one in which globalization of the economy was producing growing economic uncertainty for established businesses. The removal of geographic barriers went hand in hand with escalating technological capability and flows of information. There was a gradual recognition that the skills and attitudes increasingly sought in the business world looked more and more like the everyday practice of the arts world, one in which uncertainty and openness were embraced. Heightened levels of competition meant that businesses had to think more creatively simply to remain in business. As a result, the relationship between the two worlds was changing. There were inklings that businesses might indeed have something to learn from the arts, not only through the art or performance itself, but also in how arts organizations were structured and managed.

More or less at the same time, another line of enquiry was under way. It came to our notice that the musician Brian Eno belonged to an organization called Global Business Network (GBN). The idea that a musician was a member of a business network was mysterious enough to provide an excuse to write to him. A letter was sent introducing LIFT and explaining our aim to develop a different kind of relationship with people in business from the one we had bungled to a degree with BT. Brian Eno was generous with his encouragement and sent with his reply a book by Cambridge academic, Charles Hampden-Turner. Gradually, as I read *The Seven Cultures of Capitalism*, I became more and more excited. Through the fog, some distant shapes began to form.

The book reveals that the values, habits and cultural styles more usually associated with the arts and social development are the key to economic success. Culture is defined in its broadest sense: as worldview and basis of values with different approaches to time, ideas of the hero, and the relationship of the individual to the collective. Could it be that by illuminating culture through all the performances we staged that we may be giving people insight into the culture of others and thus their own? And that this might be of interest to business? This revelation was the start of something different. A letter went to Hampden-Turner in the hope of gaining better understanding of some of the concepts he was exploring. He too was generous with his advice and ideas and was convinced that theatre could offer much to the field of business learning, particularly in navigating across cultures.

The development of new ideas is not linear. It is more a meandering journey in a maze of corridors, some with blank walls and others with magically opening doors. During my journey, faces sometimes remained blank, and some people learned to move away when they saw me coming, thinking my line of enquiry too off the mark or my tone too earnest and oblique. New concepts and new vocabulary came slowly. Sometimes the person with whom I found myself in conversation was also struggling with new ideas and looking for new allies and ways of explaining the world. Whenever that happened, although few coherent words had been exchanged, a kind of resonance sprang up, giving me confidence to stay in touch and continue a dialogue with that person, opening a door to new ways of understanding barely expressible thoughts.

A breakthrough happened one evening when Eno invited me along to a meeting of GBN in London. A young American woman was speaking at the meeting about a project she had been facilitating in Scotland. Something about the subject matter sounded new and refreshing. Here was someone at a business meeting emphasizing the importance of learning from different perspectives and that the future of business was founded on strong connections across sectors.

That evening was my introduction to two people who came to influence LIFT's future direction: Barbara Heinzen and Arie de Geus. These two plus Gerard Fairtlough, a colleague I met subsequently, specialized in scenario planning. Scenario planning is a discipline that describes how the present might evolve over a given period of time. It enables organizations or societies to think about and take action in the environment in which they exist. Scenarios are imaginative stories of the future based on strong research into inescapable forces combined with instinctive insight into uncertainties from a diversity of people. Through this process, organizations, individuals and societies can learn to adapt to changes in the world around and reduce the number of unknown threats. It was taken for granted in this arena that culture was an extremely important dimension but there was a paucity of tangible evidence.

Keen to know more about Heinzen's perspective we arranged to meet. I learned Heinzen had come to London to do her PhD on the role of multinationals in international development and, after finishing her thesis in the mid-1980s, had been eager to find work. She had offered to do a speculative assignment for Shell in the hope that they might subsequently hire her. The question she was set by the Planning Department was to identify the next newly industrializing countries based on their cultural characteristics. Wincing slightly at the echoes this question held of old cultural stereotypes, she realized it did identify a real corporate need. Having an idea about how a country might develop and when it would need more energy would enable Shell to make more confident long-term investment decisions.

Heinzen's research revealed the relationship between a country's social indicators and its economic development as seen in Figure 6.1.

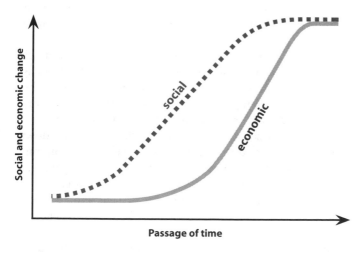

Figure 6.1 The double-S curve

Source: Heinzen (1984)

Social indicators included life expectancy; literacy; school enrolment; access to a water supply; men in agriculture; and percentage of salaried and wage earners. Economic indicators were gross domestic product (GDP); agricultural production per male worker; per capita steel consumption; per capita energy consumption, etc.[4] With access to a data base built up over 30 years of these statistical indicators, Heinzen was able to create charts comparing social and economic indicators. She found that an improvement in social indicators preceded the rate of economic development. Contrary to received wisdom, it was clearly demonstrated that social foundations precede economic growth and when combined created a double-S curve.

This information turned on its head the political idea of the 1980s and early 1990s with which we were struggling at LIFT. Economic growth was seen as the first step in social survival. Community responsibilities, including investment in health and education, were thought of as the luxury of wealth, pushed out like a widget at the end of the manufacturing process. Heinzen argued however that social foundations were the pre-condition for economic development. Evidence that this was so was exciting indeed and it was with mounting curiosity that I absorbed all the information Heinzen could offer.

She went on to show the double-S curve divided into four different stages as shown in Figure 6.2. The first represented the stage when social foundations were being laid down, the second when economies were becoming creative and taking off, the third when there is massive growth in consumption and, finally, the fourth occurred when both social and economic change slowed down. Slow at first, the rate speeds up over time, and levels off as economies reach maturity, i.e. their social indicators are more or less at a maximum and economic growth has levelled out. This last stage was when the economy was pausing to breathe or resting on previous achievements. In the mid-1980s, this point had been reached by mature Western economies with their saturated markets.

In a third diagram boldly entitled *Past, Present and Future of the World on One Page*, Heinzen argued further that we are reaching the limits of one kind of world system and that the dominance of

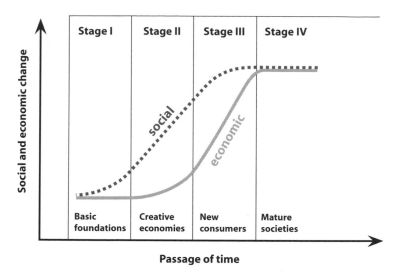

Figure 6.2 Late twentieth-century changes
Source: Heinzen (1984)

the mature Western industrial economies can no longer be taken
for granted (Figure 6.3). The natural resource base is finite and
dynamic, and will be under increasing stress as population and
material consumption both increase. This stress will force us to
invent new social, political and economic systems. These, in turn
will be shaped by values and culture, i.e. how people relate to
each other and to the natural world that sustains them. Within a
pluralistic cultural world, we are at the start of attempts to build an
ecological economy that necessitates negotiation between cultures.
Heinzen cautioned:

> Our ability to respond to these pressures will be conditioned by
> the ideas and beliefs we hold. Cultural values, intellectual fashions,
> policies, political rivalries and basic emotional assumptions about
> the nature of man, society and the natural world will all shape our
> responses and ambitions.
>
> (Heinzen forthcoming)

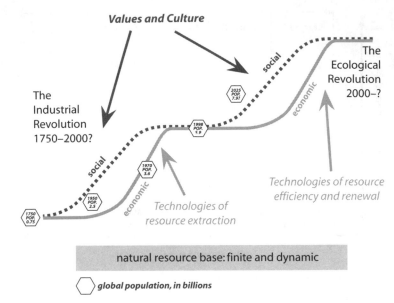

Figure 6.3 Past, present and future of the world on one page

Source: Heinzen (1984)

Here at last were compelling arguments as to why cultural issues were coming to the fore for the business world and of course for all of us. Heinzen's diagrams offered a clear signpost as to why we at LIFT needed to rediscover the place of theatre in the making of culture in a wider sense. Theatre quite obviously has a role to play in exploring 'basic emotional assumptions about the nature of man, society and the natural world'. Heinzen's ideas indicated a route to making a direct connection between the arts and ways of bringing other perspectives to corporate thinking. If Heinzen is right, our ability to think about more than the bottom line could get us all out of trouble.

More evidence came to light showing that culture is the key to change. Systems thinker, Donella Meadows, indicates the places in which it is possible to intervene in a human system (Figure 6.4). The

Figure 6.4 Places to intervene in a human system

Source: Meadows (1997) © B.J. Heinzen 1991

least effective are numbers: subsidies, taxes and standards; some-where in the middle are rules: incentives and punishments; rising in effectiveness are the power of self-organization, the goals of the system, and, finally, at the most effective, the mindset or paradigm.

Again this indicates how it is culture, in the sense of the para-digms and mindsets we use to interpret the world, that is funda-mental to changing attitudes and actions. Unless we acknowledge what paradigms we live by, how can we change them? To become conscious of the profoundly held beliefs by which we operate means being challenged in one's assumptions. One way of making those assumptions visible is through cultural exploration and engage-ment with others. Meaning in the world is constructed through culture, which is constantly changing and being made and remade. Through witnessing other people's culture, we are able to sense our own. For mindset or paradigm to shift, negotiation and shared experience is needed. Culture cannot be made in the abstract. If business were to re-imagine its role, then part of that re-imagining might take place in the context of LIFT. This possibility went way beyond the existing idea of business–arts relations.

Called for in these ideas was fundamental questioning of the system in which products are manufactured and sold. Such questioning would not justify the arts for their contribution to the national economy simply as a vehicle for advertising or one of the 'creative industries'. Instead, the arts could be a way of unearthing and renewing 'our basic emotional assumptions about the nature of man, society and the natural world'. In this sense, LIFT could restore the theatre to its role of critique and recreation.

The evening I met Heinzen, I also met Dutchman Arie de Geus. When quizzed on whether he thought business had something to learn from the arts, he did not brush aside my enquiry. Later I was to learn that he had looked seriously into how the arts could give early signals of structural change in society. Importantly too, in his role as Head of Group Planning at Royal Dutch Shell, de Geus had asked: what if longevity and long-term survival is taken as a measure of corporate success rather than the demands of quarterly results? This question provided the basis of research into the factors that enable companies to last for more than 200 years.

Four common factors enable long-lived companies to adapt and survive. These include responsiveness to the needs of the environment (in a broad sense) in which they exist; a strong sense of identity through generational flow and a sense of stewardship; a tolerance of experiments; and, finally, financial independence.

Very few companies last more than a paltry 13 years. De Geus points to the reason:

> Corporations fail because the prevailing thinking and language of management are too narrowly based on the prevailing thinking and language of economics ... companies die because their managers focus on the economic activity of producing goods and services, and they forget that their organization's true nature is that of a community of humans. The legal establishment, business educators and the financial community all join them in this mistake.
>
> (de Geus 1997: 9)

I was reminded of a comment made by film producer, David Puttnam, that brought home the destructive impact of minute financial control that excludes all other styles of thinking and communication: 'How have we allowed the language of the accountant to dominate? If you only think about the bottom line, don't be surprised if you sink to it' (in conversation 1994). Puttnam had made his name in the creative and volatile business of film production so perhaps he would say that anyway. However, de Geus's critique of the numbers obsession from someone working in a large corporation was completely new to our ears. With business efficiency as the mantra of the day, the stories coming out of Shell were very useful for us to be able to tell as we made the arguments for different forms of learning and civic alliance.

The profitability of a company was found to be a *symptom* of corporate health, not a predictor or determinant of it. This ethos ran counter to the business orthodoxy of the 1980s and early 1990s and showed values and sensitivity to the external environment as key to long-term survival of an organization.

A culture of measurement had seeped into every part of life as though measurement was somehow an infallible determinant of certainty and stability, be it in business, the arts or education. This kind of obsessive measurement holds within it an implicit defensive quality – a way of justifying ourselves to others. Measurement can only refer to the things that we know about. It cannot bring related but unconnected things together in a context when the things to be measured are unknown. In the fields of education and organizational achievement, most measures of success relate to individual achievements. In the face of growing evidence that learning takes place most effectively when engaged in what is called situated learning, as part of a community of practice, measures of individual success are inadequate. In this light, existing measures can be deemed to skew the education process away from the most effective routes to learning. Of course ways of keeping on track are required, but to take these as the only measures of success is counterproductive.

When asked to give a view as to whether business would have something to learn from the arts, de Geus pointed to three other key ideas: how the arts point to the future, how the brain perceives the future and how organizations learn.

The first was that de Geus was intrigued by how the arts among other factors were often seen to prefigure social change. It was not clear however how useful information could be drawn from the range of artistic expression to be witnessed in any era. De Geus relates how the French government had actually taken this idea seriously and, at the time of President Brezhnev, had sent researchers to Moscow to discover whether real change was about to happen in Soviet society. This was done through looking at the theatre. One of the researchers recounted to de Geus that it was very important to look at the fringes of art, especially if artistic expression is strongly controlled. 'You must look in whatever little space of freedom there is for art to express itself.' One should not only look at the art itself, but also at the audience. If the audience is purely an art establishment audience, then this is of no interest. The more representative of different sections of the population, the more interesting an indicator of change the theatre represents.

De Geus introduced us to the findings of neurobiologist, David Ingvar, and cognitive psychologists, Francisco Varela and Humberto Maturana. Ingvar revealed how every moment of our lives is occupied with making hypothetical pictures of the future, or time paths, in response to new information and choices that might face us (Ingvar 1985: 127–36). The brain does this by doing two things: it imagines an outside world in the future with certain possible conditions and then it immediately decides what action to take or what needs to be done under those conditions. The human brain does not try to predict one single future. It imagines a wide range of possible futures, and for each one of those futures it makes time paths, saying, if this happens, then I will do that. The brain not only creates these time paths, it stores them. So one is constantly making a 'memory' of possible futures.

Maturana and Varela remind us that knowledge is socially constructed: 'the world that everyone sees is not *the* world but *a* world which we bring forth with others. It compels us to see that the world will be different only if we live differently' (Maturana and

Varela 1987: 245). The collective dimension of knowledge construction tuned with the essentially collective nature of making, watching and participating in theatre.

De Geus pointed us to the work and ideas of Peter Senge (Senge 1990), who describes the ways that organizations can learn and adapt to changes in the world around them. The learning organization openly acknowledged that companies were made up of human beings with the usual range of human frailties and it was they who had to learn if the organization was to do so. Senge's book challenged images of contemporary leadership as a result. In contrast to the idea of the leader as a lone hero steering the ship in a particular direction, pushing and pulling the levers at just the right moment, the idea of the learning organization implied that the most appropriate contemporary leaders were more akin to coaches and enablers, encouraging learning across all the organization's employees.

Although rare examples existed of a willingness to learn and imagine the road ahead in unconventional ways, machine and engineering metaphors in management theory were far more common. The language of management rang with terms such as company re-engineering; total quality management; just-in-time delivery systems and so on. The idea of organizational learning contrasted refreshingly with all this language of control. To admit that an organization needs to learn is to admit that it doesn't know everything and cannot control everything. The world cannot be made according to a single view. This tuned with the picture of organizational and personal upheaval witnessed in the large organizations with which we were familiar, but ran counter to the exaggerated images of unbridled power and control that many large companies had taken on in the public imagination.

In order to learn, de Geus asserts, any business must ask: What is a business for? Is it just a machine for making money and returning value to shareholders? Is it an organization for creating goods and services for use in wider society? What does it choose for its own measures of success? Returning value to shareholders was the common view, but this inhibited the ability of business to think long term let alone learn to adapt.

Other evidence emerged that questions of civic connection were intimately connected to processes of wealth creation. In his study of the comparative economic and civic success of different regions in Italy, political economist Robert Putnam established that successful regions did not become civic simply because they were wealthy:

> The historical record strongly suggests precisely the opposite: they have become rich because they were civic. . . . Social and political networks are organised horizontally, not hierarchically. . . . Citizens in these regions are engaged by public issues, not by patronage.
>
> (Putnam 1993)

These qualities of engagement are the foundation for building social capital – the asset that above all others determines a region's economic and civic destiny. Communal social capital is created when engagement is built across socio-economic divides and around transcendent interests such as, believe it or not, choral societies, literary circles or theatre.

I had set out to seek answers as to why business in particular might need theatre. I had discovered on the road why it was that we all might need theatre to survive faced as we are with the challenge of moving from an industrial to an ecological economy. The business models adapted by the arts sector were not unaffected by this discovery.

Identifying champions for LIFT's business project

These ideas gave confident foundations on which to build our quest for a new form of relationship with business that was not primarily about fundraising but about questions of broader public collaboration and negotiation. Well-known champions were needed if we were to make something practical happen.

Economist Will Hutton had written frequently about the need for a profound shift in culture if Britain was to maintain its competitiveness while fostering a viable social fabric. He was invited to become a LIFT Director and help shape our business project, whatever this would turn out to be. We needed the endorsement of other well-known individuals or organizations if we were to engage participants less confident of the timeliness of our experiment. Charles Handy's book *The Empty Raincoat* was among the first reaching a popular audience that indicated the business world was in difficulty: i.e. that many people in corporate life were looking for a renewed sense of purpose and meaning. It seemed that, even for people working in business, money alone did not provide sufficient motivation for getting up in the morning.

Handy was asked for a meeting. Some weeks later, my colleague Lucy Neal and I crunched across the gravel to his front door and rang the bell. We were ushered into a large room with a roaring fire and two big sofas. Handy was silent as a basilisk as our ideas tumbled onto the expanse of carpet between us. He said not a word and I wondered if we were just wasting his time. But then he agreed that he would help us in any way he could. In due course, he and his wife Elizabeth hosted a series of lunches for us to meet various key business people. Over the next few months we met a number of their friends and colleagues, all people trying to steer their various organizations through choppy waters. Many were politely interested in our attempt to change the dialogue between business and the arts. When it came to embracing such an idea more wholeheartedly, they admitted that it was not a priority to engage the contemporary arts as a way of seeing the world more clearly. It was clear that we did not have an immediate and obvious market, but we needed to hone our product nonetheless in these early days. The lunches helped us to rehearse our case, test our forms of expression and gain confidence. The Handys knew that informal occasions such as these bring people together across levels of power far more speedily than embarking on a round of formal meetings. Some of these conversations bore fruit immediately; some laid the foundations of alliances forged some seven years later.

We also knew that a media partner would be valuable in lending weight to our venture. The *FT* had supported our civic conference, LIFTING London, two years earlier and once again we extended a request for endorsement. David Bell, Chairman, was happy to back our business experiment and assigned his colleague,

Andy Anderson, the then Managing Editor, to help us think the project through. A young journalist, Krishna Guha, was assigned to document the venture.

In late 1994, we had enlisted a good line-up of people to help us devise a project for LIFT to launch on the unsuspecting world. There was the music and global business perspective of Eno; the financial establishment and management perspective of Anderson of the *FT*; the business strategy experience of de Geus; the business and social philosophy perspective of Handy; the economics and media experience of Hutton; the market strategy experience of Paul Askew, one of LIFT's long-standing advisers; Heinzen's experience in economic development and ecology; and, finally, another member of GBN and close colleague of de Geus and Heinzen, Gerard Fairtlough, who had recently retired as Chief Executive of biotechnology company, Celltech, and had practised and written about creative management (Fairtlough 1994). Also involved was Ian Wigston, at that time Director of Innovation at investment bank BZW.

We held a brainstorming meeting starting with a deliberately simple and open question: 'Has business something to learn from the arts?' This was precise enough to explore what possible practical roles there might be for LIFT to play in answering this question, yet open enough for all involved to take a view. The range of expertise, age and perspective of those present ensured that we were evolving something satisfactory for both an eventual business constituency but also fitting with LIFT's values and organizational capacity.

Why would the people we had brought together wish to be there? Needless to say, each and every one of them would have individual reasons we could never know. At a time of great change people need to get together in order to know what they think. It is from one another that they get a fuller sense of what is going on. People also enjoy being needed, helping to get something off the ground and testing their expertise in a new context. The LIFT project could help clarify for them that their general themes were in tune with a local reality. At a time of great turmoil, they sensed perhaps that new ideas very often come from the edge and that it was important to maintain channels of communication between the centre and the periphery. They also doubtless had a sense that maintaining a vibrant cultural life in Britain depends on individuals addressing how that can happen.

It went without saying that the backdrop to our discussion was globalization, the escalating power of technology, resulting hyper-competition and a growing sense of Britain's social fragmentation. In addition to this base, there were fresh issues facing businesses. In markets where there were fewer hiding places for bad corporate behaviour; people in business were being forced to address ethical, cultural and environmental issues as never before. How were managers to balance the many ambiguities with which they were faced? As the state's responsibilities shrank and those of business grew, there were even people asking 'What is business for now?'

We were reminded by Eno not to over-revere artists. Too many were stuck in their own boxes too and would benefit from sharing conversations with completely different people in order to know better what their role was in this changing world. The LIFT project could be a learning venture for artists as well.

Having established that there was a value in learning across these boundaries, we were faced with the challenge of how such a venture could be organized. LIFT faced several obstacles in devising a new way of connecting with businesses. Connections with the theatre were still not likely to be a business priority, so we would have to design a programme so that decisions to take part would be easy.

In the back of my mind, I had always held the plea of Citibank, to help us connect their employees behind the scenes to the artists in the Festival. One approach might have been to design a creative programme for one specific corporation but this felt somehow not quite right for LIFT, more conscious now of our civic role. Whatever we came up with, it had to have at its heart a way to connect people to the artists we were presenting but also a way of reconnecting people to the public sphere.

We had wide-ranging discussions around the form of the venture. It was Handy who crystallized how it could be done. The idea was simple:

Let's invite people to attend events in the Festival and then we'll talk about their experience. Artists should be part of the discussion then people can hear what they had in mind when they were putting the show together. Ask how they got it off the ground and worked together.

(LIFT 1994)

This was the start of the LIFT Business Arts Forum – an opportunity for business people to reflect on the world around them via LIFT events and through conversation with artists. There was a secondary objective to generate revenue to the Festival. We were confident that, if the primary ideas were right, then the secondary objectives would be fulfilled. Once we'd come up with this central idea, other suggestions came thick and fast. Will Hutton described a conference he had helped to guide where business people were encouraged to address environmental issues.[5] Participants were put together in small-scale syndicate groups, enabling people to move beyond mere courtesies or the soapbox tendencies of large gatherings to have a depth of dialogue that was rarely possible in conventional conferences. We would do the same and put people in small, mixed groups so that they could engage in discussion across disciplines.

Finally, we tackled the question of recruitment. How were we to find people to take part? We all knew that the challenge for business people would be to find the time to engage with such a programme outside their work environment. Our challenge would be to formalize a way for people to engage with the Festival and for them to legitimize their participation with colleagues and family members.

Our advisers clarified that the programme would be best aimed at those individuals who were already in a position of leadership or moving into one. For emerging leaders, it was a way to develop a view from the other side of the street and to see where their work and their company or working perspective fitted in a wider cultural, social and political context. It was a programme for people in positions of operational responsibility, not first and foremost for those in the conventional roles of community or public relations.

If letters inviting people to take part in LIFT's business project arrived on LIFT letterhead, they would probably end up in the

waste-paper bin or back in the arts and community affairs departments – the very departments we were trying to circumvent. It
would be better if these letters could be written on someone else's
letterhead. Bell agreed that invitations should be issued on *FT* letterhead and a list of relevant names was suggested to us.

How would the finances work? Just as people pay to do a course
at a business school, we would charge a fee for participants and get
venue and catering costs sponsored wherever we could. The surplus
above costs would go towards LIFT's core costs of presenting theatre
to the public. This would change the nature of business funds
generated by the Festival. Unlike the marketing sponsorship LIFT
continued to seek, these funds were not tied to the marketing
demands of sponsors and thus could be reinvested where we chose.

Our initial meeting drew to a close having reinforced our conviction that we were embarking on something with promise. We had
many practical suggestions and further contacts. Now we had to
shape the project into something we could launch on the world
without over-extending LIFT through diversion of energy and
resources into areas too far removed from our core activities.

SEVEN

GIVING BIRTH TO THE LIFT BUSINESS ARTS FORUM

Each venture,
Is a new beginning, a raid on the inarticulate
With shabby equipment always deteriorating
In the general mess of imprecision of feeling.

(Eliot 1940: 203)

That initial meeting established plans for the first year of LIFT's Business Arts Forum. There was a session to introduce participants to why they might find it valuable to learn from a contemporary theatre festival. Then we invited people to attend at least four LIFT '95 events in June and July. Everyone was put in 'syndicates' with private sector people, artists and a facilitator to translate between the worlds. Participants were encouraged to attend events together and take partners, colleagues, family or friends to events as well – thereby making a link between people's inside and outside work personas. At the end of the Festival, we held a session to talk about what participants had seen. They were asked what they would do differently in their work as a result of their experience. Participants' fees funded Forum activities.

Planning and preparation took place alongside my regular sponsorship-seeking responsibilities at LIFT. The Forum was just one tiny part of LIFT's overall activities. The priority of the organization remained the presentation of shows to the public and the facilitation of learning programmes for young people. The Forum was our own action research experiment as to how we might develop a more fruitful and appropriate relationship with business in a globalizing economy. It was intimate and small scale.

This schedule of meetings and events developed as illustrated for 2001 in Figure 7.1. An initial, day-long meeting was followed by a second prior to attendance at four evening performances over the period of the Festival. A final afternoon and full-day session brought participants together to reflect on the performances and speculate about how they might do their work differently as a result of the shared experience.

Various reasons lay behind the design of the first Forum. We proposed taking people to several events so that they had a range of experiences. They saw productions of different form and content from a range of cultures attended by different audiences and set in different locations in London. Journeys to events took them through parts of London they never knew existed. The experience disrupted routine. It led participants to walk in other worlds, thus enabling them to see their own differently.

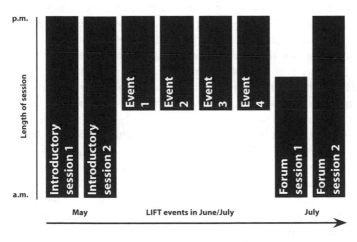

Figure 7.1 LIFT Business Arts Forum Timing Plan 2001

Our challenge in recruiting people to the Forum was to identify who participants might be and then to reach them. As mentioned before, letters written on LIFT letterhead were unlikely to have an impact. Anything with arts or theatre in the title would be seen as too 'soft' an environment in which anything useful could be learned by the 'hard' world of business. We needed the invitation to be extended by people who would be naturally respected in the business world. It was agreed that letters of invitation should go out on *FT* letterhead signed personally by Bell, with Handy as the co-signatory.

Box 7.1 *FT* letter of invitation to take part in the Forum

27th March 1995

Dear Chairman of X Company

Since 1981, the LIFT Festival has staged eight seasons bringing 3,000 artists to London from over 60 countries. These artists are not only immensely popular in their own countries, but also working at the frontiers of cultural expression wherever they are. The Festival is a resource of international innovation and insight that business people should not ignore. We are inviting a selected group of 25 companies to participate in a Business/Arts Forum running through the Festival this June and July. This is an outstanding opportunity to bring new ways of learning into your company in an exciting and enjoyable way.

In a business environment facing structural transformations, there is much to be learnt from the innovative arts. Artists are also the antennae of society and illuminate changes which will have profound implications for us all. For these reasons, we firmly believe that there are ways in which businesses can learn from the Arts, just as the Arts have been learning from business over the last ten years.

The pressures on you are doubtless too great for you to participate personally. We propose that you nominate an individual you consider will be of Board calibre during the next ten years. This person would be invited to attend four productions in the Festival followed by participation in a day-long seminar on 7th July working with both artists and people from other businesses.

We hope that your company will wish to participate and encourage you to respond at the earliest opportunity on the LIFT form enclosed.

Yours etc.,

David Bell   Charles Handy
Chairman   LIFT Patron and Forum Adviser
Financial Times

For all the personal attention given to the *FT* letters, they drew disappointingly few responses. Each and every letter was followed up with a telephone call to discover the response or to see if the letters had been passed on elsewhere in the organization. Their destination in the company, or whether they received a response at all, was a barometer of each company's responsiveness to the outside world. While these letters were being sent, other routes to recruitment were being pursued – via membership of GBN; via people who had been long-term supporters; or through friends and any other contacts we could call upon.

In the first year we recruited people with senior roles in a range of functions such as strategy, finance, research and retailing, from a range of companies including British Airways, De Beers, Hewlett Packard, PepsiCo, Marks and Spencer and RTZ. Most were recruited through word of mouth, a couple were referred to LIFT by their chairmen or eventual recipients of the *FT* letter.

In the '95 Forum, we simply set out to test whether there were insights to be gained from the Festival by people in business. *FT* journalist, Guha, had studied the links between art and structural change in society as part of his degree. He was thus well placed to document people's reactions to the Forum and to capture their impressions following the Festival (LIFT 1995).

The introductory session was held at the *FT* conference centre and lasted about four hours. Proceedings began with a welcome from Bell, followed by a talk from Handy explaining from his perspective as a teacher of managers why it was that the LIFT Forum offered such a rich opportunity. He had a firm belief that all the management primers in the world were not worth as much as the lessons to be found in works of great literature and the theatre. He recounted that he had recently undertaken a straw poll of the first intake of students to London Business School who were now all captains of industry. He asked them what they most remembered from their time there. Was it those accountancy classes? Was it the lessons in international strategy? It turned out to be none of the formal offerings. For those students the most memorable and valuable experience had been going to the theatre. What is more, it had been going to the theatre in Prague. This was a curious result and needed more explanation.

Handy went on to describe that during that particular year he had taken a group to Czechoslovakia to experience at first hand the centralized command economy of the Communist bloc. There happened to be a gap in the formal series of talks and visits to factories and local dignitaries. Handy improvised and arranged for his students to visit the theatre. He remembers it may well have been the theatre of Vaclav Havel, writer and director, who would become leader of the Czech Republic some 20 years later.

What the students remembered from that time was attending a performance of Sophocles' *Antigone*. What's more, the production was in Czech. Antigone's dilemma was how to choose between right and right, whether to bury her brother or obey the law. The experience of the play spoke down the centuries and communicated beyond language the nature of human dilemmas.

Handy reflected that the position of a leader is a lonely one. Few formal guides exist when faced with moral choices. Essentially, Handy said, leadership is about love and death, loneliness and responsibilities. Leaders face countless questions. How do you end things graciously? How do you decide where your responsibilities begin and end? How do you keep your counsel and choose between good and good or bad and bad? These lessons are not found in management textbooks. Guidance is more often found elsewhere, among the eternal truths of the human heart – more frequently the subject of literature, art and theatre. These reflections of Handy's ex-students were made when they had reached the top of the tree. They had spent a long time looking upward to the tips of those branches on the way up. Now at the top, they realized the most valuable insights came from looking down and around to a world where they were not the centre of attention and power and they could find places quiet enough to listen.

Handy reassured our first-year intake of Forum participants that what the LIFT Forum offered was an opportunity to walk in other worlds in the company of other people who cared not at all who these participants were in their own particular tree. This introduction reassured the participants who wondered what they were doing there. For some, the idea of contemporary theatre was alien. Prejudices about a snobbish and exclusive arts world ran deep. Handy's status in the business world was such that, by being in the room and validating the Forum through his own experience, he was reassuring others that, even if they had no idea what they were getting themselves into, there was something worthwhile to be experienced here. He and others had visibly moved their feet in our direction, to stand by us.

During the second part of the evening, participants were allocated to small groups introducing themselves to one another and to their facilitator. By way of introduction they also sketched out what they hoped to get out of their journey over the next few weeks. People wanted to get fresh ideas to stimulate more creative approaches to their work, even to test themselves in a different environment, to get a better sense of ideas coming from the edge and elsewhere in the world, from outside their 'comfort zone'.

Fenton and Neal introduced the programme, including that year: *Birds of Fire*, Groupe F; *Noiject* by Japanese dancer and choreographer, Saburo Teshigawara; *Zumbi* by Black Theatre Co-op; *Jozi Jozi* and *The Suit* from the Market Theatre, Johannesburg; *Murx den Europäer! – Ein patriotischer Abend* from the Volksbuhne Theatre, Berlin; *Cirque Plume* from France; Bobby Baker's *Take a Peek* from the UK; Deborah Warner's *St Pancras Project*; *The Madwoman of our City* from The Company, India; the National Theatre of Craiova's *Phaedra* from Romania; *The Tale of Teeka* from Les Deux Mondes, Canada; and *Seka Barong of Singapadu* from Bali.[1]

Then it was time to make the practical arrangements. It was imperative that we secured people's ticket bookings at the earliest opportunity as some of the shows were already selling fast to the public. We charged £750 for each business participant in the first year. This sum included two tickets each to four shows. We had primed participants to bring their diaries with them in order to co-ordinate their theatre visits with other members of the group. We also needed to impress upon participants that, if they said they were going to a show, this represented a financial transaction between LIFT and the box offices of the individual Festival venues. We asked them to ensure that, however late in the day, they let us know if they could not make a performance. We did not want to leave empty seats and disappointed people in a queue outside the theatre when this could be avoided.

We held the final day of the Forum on the last Friday of the Festival. The quality of physical space needed was very important. We became aware that a conventional conference centre, too mani-cured and functional, was not what we were looking for. Neither should we use a theatre space – in the dark with raked seating. It was clear that, to encourage an atmosphere of shared learning, we needed to find a space that did not communicate in any way that any of the participants were experts, delivering wisdom from a podium to a passive audience. We needed a physical space that would encourage greater equity between participants and a sense of everyone sitting at the same level leaning forward to listen hard to one another. There had to be scope for including an element of the session that did not emphasize rational analysis but exploration of a more performative, non-verbal kind. The physical space changes the performance.

We also needed a space to fulfil more practical aspects such as a sufficient number of rooms for the smaller discussion groups and somewhere for lunch. Needless to say, we also needed it to cost very little. Eventually, we found a space. It was an old building of the Central School of Art and Design. A central big room with a golden-coloured wooden floor had a domed skylight. Several smaller rooms led off this with natural daylight in all of them. There was a dining space nearby with a caterer on hand. The building had a certain history to it with a great amount of Victorian detailing dating from the Arts and Crafts movement. All these details gave a sense of history and respect for learning to the setting for that final day that made it somehow separate from the pressures of daily life.

The overarching questions we had posed to people at the outset were: 'What did you learn from LIFT events, their creation and management? What would you do differently in your work as a result?'

The first part of the final day was spent teasing out what people's experience of the shows had been. We were encouraging people to express their reactions honestly. We were not asking people to use literary critical language, or talk in a scholarly way about the artistic influences or traditions that had led to the creation of this or that piece. Those discussions of LIFT shows could be found elsewhere. Nor were we asking people to make a judgement about whether this was a 'good' show or not. We were asking people to make visible to others their impressions, what their experiences were of attending the show. The shared experience itself was undeniable, thus people's different reactions had to be respected and, via this shared experience, people could see just how differently the world was perceived by others.

To accustom people to a different form of discussion and to break the ice, we had opened the session with some exercises that were quite familiar to theatre practitioners at the start of rehearsals. Anyone looking on would have seen the room full of people making strange noises to indicate mood, wandering around the space with their eyes closed, or listening hard to master a complicated rhythm.

When it came to the more rational analysis, the facilitators of the three groups were Heinzen, Fairtlough and de Geus. To aid their discussions, they had asked us to get hold of a tool that was frequently used to help in facilitation of group planning processes.

It was a white board with hexagon-shaped magnetic cards. This elegantly simple tool was new to me. I watched as participants noted down impressions at random from the Festival and then, later on, silently clustered those impressions into common themes. It was a brilliant device for assessing what interconnected changes in culture or the world might be understood from everyone's pooled comments.

We set participants a task on the Forum day – to interpret their experience and attempt to communicate it to other participants and an invited audience. This challenge focused people's minds and called on their joint creative skills. This was as demanding a task for the artists and arts administrators taking part as it was for the business participants.

We had asked someone to chair the last session of the day. Somewhere we had learned that British Airways had on its payroll a Corporate Jester. To learn that someone actually had 'Corporate Jester' on their business card was surprising, containing as it did echoes of Shakespearean fools speaking truth to power. But Paul Birch, the Jester in question, was clear that this function was vital if an organization was to maintain its equilibrium and not be blinded with its own rhetoric. Paul was used to facilitating people to think creatively across departmental boundaries and was a good chair for the final session of the Forum.

One of the ideas that was raised during the brainstorming session with advisers all those months before was that, as well as 'push' in a venture, you need 'pull'. This means that, as well as validation from the outset, you need witnesses to the end result towards which people would be working. This was also a way to extend the influence of the discussion beyond just the group involved. (The inspiration for this was the Prince of Wales' Business Leaders' Forum on the environment where, at the conclusion of the meeting, participants presented their findings to the Prince of Wales.)

The audience for our findings came to be called, somewhat tongue-in-cheek, the Imperial Council – a group of people who would be invited to come and pass judgement on our deliberations. We would encourage participants to ask whoever they would like to be a member of this. In the event, only a few participants asked people to come along. Paul Askew asked his nine-year-old son Thomas. Barbara Heinzen asked a publishing friend, Carolyn Dawnay. LIFT invited Board members, Will Hutton and Bob Palmer, and artists, Keith Khan and Ali Zaidi.

The room was quiet and each Forum group entered one by one. Each came up with a completely different form of presentation, none of them a straightforward verbal explanation. There were impressions of chaos interspersed with moments of joy and puzzlement. The performances demonstrated how something meaningful could be created out of thin air simply by engaging in intense conversation in a serious and focused context.

The Forum process was without question a valuable one for people involved, but it was somewhat mysterious to outsiders. In fact, the idea of the Council turned out not to be such a good one. People arriving had not seen many or any of the LIFT shows. They were not part of the group and hence felt estranged from the process. Participation was the key to insight. It did not work second hand in this case. We did not repeat this experiment in later years and just accepted that it was difficult to spread the conversation beyond the people directly involved in the experience throughout.

The aim of that first session was to see if there were lessons to be learned from LIFT by people in business. We established that there were.

Handy observed:

The theatre speaks to your heart and spirit as much as to your brain. Business ought to organise itself more like the theatre. Find ways of engaging the heart as well as the minds of its actors and audiences – create an experience for employees and customers that leaves them standing up and clapping.

Seeing the LIFT show, *The Suit*, showed Askew that:

when you get into an institutionalised form of neurosis in response to a crisis you get into a horrible trap. Business can get into neurosis equally well – it may be a sudden crisis or a crisis that happens very gradually, but this is counterproductive.

Others commented:

An artist has a vision of how he or she wishes to reflect and shape the world; it matters not at all where the material comes from. There are no rules about departmental boundaries or definitions.

No LIFT '95 production featured a star at the centre – a move away from single heroes to team and ensemble presentation seems to be a common theme. If everybody wants to be a hero, how do you establish trust and shared values?

All troupes fostered an atmosphere of respect for each individual on account of their skill.

And from one of the business participants there was a clear realization that:

We must hear a minority view even if we don't like it.
(All quotations from LIFT 1995)

Advisers were delighted that the Forum had provided a space for diverging views to be voiced and experimentation to take place. It had provided a place of genuine engagement and ways to test and adjust one's assumptions.

It was not only business people who got something out of the Forum. Artists gained insights too. Through extending whom they spoke to beyond colleagues or their usual audiences they felt a greater sense of connection to a world beyond their own. Difficult at times, there had been an honesty and directness of engagement, seldom encountered elsewhere with audiences or public funders. Artist Bobby Baker and Beverley Randall of Black Theatre Co-op found being under the spotlight a painfully testing experience. On a positive note, both recognized in retrospect that the Forum had been valuable. Baker commented that her participation encouraged her to renew her view of what artists were for in society. Randall's participation proved pivotal in changing fellow participants' understanding of black experience in Britain during discussion of *Zumbi*. This show linked the story of Brazil's runaway slave leader with contemporary struggles of black communities in Britain.

LIFT gained from the Forum as well. We had opened up a new way of looking at the role of theatre and had made new allies. At the most basic level, we had generated a full-page article about a theatre festival on the management page of the *FT* rather than the arts page. But looking to the promotional benefits alone was just echoing the promotional ambitions of the corporate relationships we were trying to reconfigure. We had to look for something more. The Forum that year made only a modest income over its costs. This was because it had not recruited as large a number of participants as we had hoped. The most important thing that we gained was intangible, but worth a great deal. It renewed our self-esteem in our dealings with business and our public funders. It reminded us that theatre was not just entertainment, a badge of status or a vehicle for advertising. We were not just a drain on the public purse. We had a valuable role to play in encouraging people to look anew at their world, particularly by engaging in wider public discourse a sector of growing power. Our experiment to forge a new relationship with businesses had worked.

At a personal level, the experience had felt like floating somewhere between worlds, hovering and listening, to capture the form of things as we brought everything together to turn it into practical action. Talking to Neal and Fenton about this feeling, they remarked that they had felt the same when they had started the Festival, as though they were 'being pushed from behind'. Vaclav Havel describes how he became 'an instrument of the time' and was 'pulled forward by Being' (Havel 1992: 17). It sounds self-important to name such things. In an attempt to be accurate about this experience, however, it has to be recorded. The sensation was so strong and novel. Simply put, by setting out to ask a question, it seems others had found a place to ask questions of their own.

In the process of putting the Forum together, we found that the spectres of gender relations and stage in life raised their heads. In the orchestration of the roles of all involved, the fine and invisible texturing of place, space, food, timing, form and content was made possible through the delicate interplay of younger and older women and younger and older men. These reflections bore significance as our understanding evolved of the Forum's role as spark for civic discourse and shared learning.

Havel's *Summer Meditations* were a steady guide throughout the period of questioning. Echoing the saying 'the road to Hell is paved with good intentions' Havel emphasizes culture and civility and the need, not to think one will build Utopia, but that survival depends on a never-ending willingness to engage in conversation and self-education.

> There is no simple set of instructions on how to proceed. . . . It is a way of going about things, and it demands the courage to breathe moral and spiritual motivation into everything, to seek the human dimension in all things. Science, technology, expertise, and so-called professionalism are not enough. Something more is necessary. For the sake of simplicity, it might be called spirit. Or feeling. Or conscience.
>
> (Havel 1992: xvi–xvii)

Such principles and values, if they are to be incorporated into the everyday life of organizations, need formalizing in practical ways with implications for organizational structure and routine. Now is the moment to reveal how LIFT evolved as an organization to juggle its artistic aims and values, roles and responsibilities and readied itself to facilitate artistic activity, widening civic and human connections.

EIGHT

TAKING STEPS
INTO THE WORLD OF
ORGANIZATIONS

A frog in a well only sees his piece of the sky.

(Chinese proverb)[1]

The value of sharing conversations across working practices was demonstrated in the first Business Arts Forum. Everyone had gained insight in some way. We sensed that inviting younger participants into the Forum would bring new perspectives to all. Linking young people with people from other generations and unfamiliar worlds brings many questions. Examination of our own organizational ethos and structure was required if such conversations were to happen on a long-term basis. Furthermore, if this route was to be taken, more information about the internal workings of large organizations was needed and a greater sense as to why young participants and people in business might benefit from such links. Research in the UK and US gave direction. But, first of all, what was LIFT like behind the scenes? What organization was orchestrating these connections in wider society?

LIFT behind the scenes: how is the programme put together?

LIFT's *raison d'être* is to present the best of contemporary theatre from around the world. It is an open question as to what the 'best' contemporary theatre is and 'contemporary' as a concept emerges from a singularly Western view of modernity. Judgements are inevitably subjective and ultimately those of the Festival Directors. Programming decisions are made through an accumulation of factors and views.

On average, around 17 to 22 productions were presented in each Festival season from 1981–2001. In the search for artists and productions, the Festival Directors undertake research visits to parts of the world about which they wish to know more or build long-term cultural relations. Points of contact come through a variety of informal and formal routes: artists' networks, other festivals, the cultural departments of embassies, or via the British Council or other countries' cultural organizations. Productions are chosen because they reveal in a new way what theatre can be.

Such breadth of programming ensures that the Festival fulfils its mission and reaches the audience numbers merited by its artistic vision and public funding. Many other factors come into play when deciding on the programme. Several companies will have their own touring schedules under way, so may or may not be able to visit London. When inviting companies from distant countries – China, Australia or Vietnam for example, effort is put into finding other potential national and international tour partners with whom to share costs.

Each production has its own budget that balances across the Festival as a whole. Several events in each Festival are free to the public. The more popular shows that are ticketed are able to generate higher box-office income and larger audience numbers than the more experimental ones. Depending on each show's ability to generate ticket income, sponsorship or funding from their own government's cultural resources, they will receive a greater or lesser amount from LIFT's public subsidy pool. The majority of these public funds are generated per production or per project, so, in fact, the flexibility of LIFT to invest funds exactly where it likes is limited.

As the Festival developed, simply bringing shows from abroad proved an insufficient response to the complexities of international cultural programming. Consideration of the circumstances in which such work was produced was required. As the Festival grew and international festivals worldwide multiplied, LIFT recognized the need to invest in the artists furnishing the programme and hence took on a commissioning role. In the commissioning process the Education Programme often served as a laboratory, building relationships with artists and testing ideas in their early stages.

Commissions proceed step by step over long periods, sometimes spanning two Festivals. UK Theatre Director Deborah Warner, for example, was inspired to work on an idea outside the constraints of mainstream theatre. At the outset she had no clear idea of the specific building in which she wished to create a performance. LIFT researched many possibilities, from an abandoned mental asylum to a 1930s cinema, now a bingo hall.[2] Warner's imagination was finally caught by Euston Tower, an unprepossessing office block towering above a busy crossroads in one direction with lush views over Regent's Park in the other. Permission to use the empty building resulted from painstaking research as to who had power to decide on its use for a theatre production. This took time, so meanwhile a production team was put in place, the funds raised, and permission to use the building finally secured. *The Tower Project* was two years in development. Following the run in London, it was remounted in Perth and New York where it became *The Angel Project.*

Artistic inspiration, financial and production considerations, venue availability and specifications, unshakeable determination and *extremely* hard work: these are the building blocks on which the programme is built. Information feeding these choices comes not only from judgements of the Festival Directors but also from views of other colleagues in charge of production, finance, education, communications and fundraising.

Working principles

Balance has to be struck between the roles needed to deliver the artistic vision in an ideal world and the funds available in the real one. Ways of managing significant risk and multiple layers of uncertainty have been built at LIFT. What the organization says it will deliver to the outside world has to be consistent with the organization's internal capacity. Each person working on the Festival is taking the risk that each project will happen although funds are rarely confirmed at an early stage. This collective act of faith demands high levels of trust. This is the job of the Festival leaders, to ensure that at every stage no colleague is exposed to risks of which they are not aware, thus endangering the layers of trust built with people in the city and internationally on which future reputation and working relationships depend. If less money is found than was indicated in the first place, then modifications to the project are negotiated at each critical stage.

Work on the first Festival in 1981 began at least a year earlier with Neal and Fenton working together with a group of friends. Guiding principles were laid down from the start, namely that nobody was an expert or professional. Everyone took responsibility for his or her own area. It was assumed that everyone would discover how to do things by doing them. The motivation was a wish to do it. Although nobody was paid, accountability to others was taken as a given. Fenton and Neal relate that everyone was required to deliver a report on their work without which the job was not completed.

More formalized roles and responsibilities evolved as the organization grew. Twenty-five years or so later in 2004, LIFT had a core staff of 9 people rising to as many as 70 during LIFT performance seasons. Beyond the core team, everyone else worked on a part-time, freelance or voluntary basis, sometimes having a long-term co-thinking role working on specific projects as LIFT Associates. A list of all 900 people who have ever worked on the Festival can be found in Fenton and Neal's book (Wend Fenton and Neal 2005).

If organizations are to survive, they must evolve to stay in tune with changing needs and resources, both internal and external. A picture follows of how LIFT developed from 1981 to 2004. This snapshot of the organization provides a glimpse of the organizational context in which an intergenerational flow was built into the Festival's life, enabling the Business Arts Forum in its turn to make links between generations.

Mission and values

Roles and responsibilities in any organization derive from a clear sense of purpose and values. Collective articulation of these extends ownership to all involved, acts as an aid to decision-making and helps supporters and partners know more about the organization's aims, values and ways of working. LIFT's artistic mission was first formally articulated around 1999 following discussion between staff and Board members:

> An opportunity for artists from around the world and the people of London to celebrate and explore together what makes the world tick.

Four qualities were expressed as to how the mission was to be achieved:

Quality
To present a programme of theatre and performance from around the world that demonstrates excellence and inspires new ways of seeing.

Adventure
To invest in the new and the unexpected by commissioning artists and creating the right contexts for their work.

Celebration
To offer enjoyable opportunities for celebration, affirming the commonality of human experience and the power of the creative arts.

Connections
To explore key relationships between artists and people, making connections across the city, and between London and the rest of the world.

Four values were articulated as informing the work of LIFT. These were:

Respect
Honesty
Hospitality
Generosity

(All from LIFT 2005)

Organizational roles, responsibilities and legal status

At the heart of the organization were and continue to be the artists LIFT commissions individually or as members of a company. The ongoing life of the organization depends on: voluntary Board members; formal and informal advisers from a wide range of sectors – especially when embarking on a new area of activity; full-time paid staff; part-time paid staff; freelance contractors and LIFT Associates; Festival volunteers; and student placements.

LIFT's legal status is a limited company with charitable status governed by a Board of Directors. Board members number about 12 with a range of backgrounds, in the arts, law, human rights, management, business and the civil service. The Board's main role is to provide a strategic overview, approve the Festival budget and to ensure financial probity. Meetings are held three or four times a year. The Chairman is both organizational guide and figurehead whose skills have changed depending on what was required for each chapter in the organization. For example, in order to prepare the search for sponsorship in 1986, a Chairman with a high public profile was needed. As mentioned earlier, an influential figure in the cultural and political world, Lord (Grey) Gowrie, was invited to fulfil this role followed in 1990 by Tim Waterstone, a business entrepreneur who had revolutionized bookselling in Britain. Waterstone's experience of managing organizational change helped lead the Festival through a period of consolidation in the early 1990s when greater accountability was required of LIFT by public funders.

As Waterstone's period with LIFT came to an end, a political change was in the air. LIFT was gaining confidence in advancing cultural discourse both within Britain and abroad. To help strengthen this role, defence lawyer and human rights advocate Helena Kennedy was recruited as Chair, followed by Amelia Fawcett, a business-woman with a long record of community involvement. Fawcett was called upon to guide LIFT through another period of radical change – that of a change in artistic leadership and form of the Festival.

In the early 1980s, LIFT was set up as a biennial festival simply to present shows to audiences. Initially everyone worked unpaid on a part-time basis. A small number were paid by the second Festival but still worked on other things between Festivals for the first decade. Only in 1991 when funding was assured from London Boroughs Grants Scheme and ACE was LIFT able to shift into another gear. This stability enabled more to be made of the potential offered by each performance through initiation of the Education Programme and investment in longer-term relationships with artists, audiences, young people, schools and teachers.

The organization is still led by the vision of the artists it presents and still sells tickets to shows. Each new show brings with it the possibility of building different audiences or challenging existing audiences and artists to engage in new ways. Hence the greatest shift has been from an organization that puts on shows, to one that still puts on shows, but regards these shows as an opportunity to spark greater discourse, insight and connection among the artists and audiences with whom it engages through workshops, seminars, commissions and research. This is possible through the relationships of trust the Festival has developed with different constituencies and an expansion in the number of LIFT staff responsible for building those relationships. The LIFT Education Programme, incorporating the Student Placement Scheme, Volunteer Programme, Teacher Forum, Business Arts Forum and Project Phakama, has increased the opportunities for ever-widening circles to engage with LIFT.

This section offers a snapshot of the evolution of roles and responsibilities.

Core team (as at 2004) working full time

- The Festival Directors were responsible for everything in the first Festival. By the second some of these responsibilities were devolved to an administrator. Broadly the same since then, the Festival Directors' responsibilities include researching and making decisions about the artistic programme, fundraising advocacy, guiding LIFT's strategic direction and maintaining an overview of fundraising, finance, staffing, internal and external contracts and communications.

- The Education Director was appointed in 1992 to lead LIFT's projects with school students, teachers and youth arts groups in the informal education sector. As access to the artistic programme widened and deepened, this role came to be called LIFT Learning Director. A learning traineeship post was instituted in 2001.

- During the early Festivals a staff member co-ordinated the budget, administered contractual issues and sometimes took on artistic responsibilities working alongside the Festival Directors. This job ensured that all the artistic ideas were budgeted and that projected income and expenditure balanced across each production and the Festival as a whole. This role and its name changed between 1981 and 2005. In 1987, the role of General Manager became more formalized but was still undertaken on a limited contractual basis. In 1991, when LIFT's organizational consolidation was under way, a full-time appointment was made. As the Festival increased its commissioning role, this post took on more and more producing responsibilities. In 1997 its name changed to Administrative Producer to reflect this greater responsibility. The role included management of staff, Board liaison, producing, fundraising from private and public sectors and managing an organizational strategy review. A freelance, part-time bookkeeper and accountant worked with the Producer.

- A Development Director was appointed for the first time in 1986 to set up LIFT's sponsorship campaign. After 1995, when the Business Arts Forum was begun, the role of seeking business sponsorship became the responsibility of the Adminis-

trative Producer and a Development Associate working closely
with the Festival Directors. In 2002, fundraising from the
private sector and trusts and foundations became the responsibility of the Head of Communications working with the
Fundraising Manager.

• A department of Communications and Development was
instituted in 2002 including three staff: Head of Communications and Development, responsible for private sector relations,
all print, media and communications strategy; Director of
Marketing, responsible for marketing and box office; and a
Fundraising Manager, responsible for applications to trusts and
foundations and for all receptions.

• The Marketing Director 's responsibilities cover LIFT communications, marketing strategy and copy for the LIFT programme; graphic design, print and web services; media space
and fly-posting services; photographers; and box-office liaison
and contracts with venues on ticket prices and numbers.
Marketing was managed on a freelance basis until 1993, when
it became clear that year-round continuity was needed and an
in-house Marketing Director was appointed.

• The full-time Office Administrator ensures that the office runs
smoothly: answering telephone calls, liaising with cleaners and
photocopy, telephone and computer engineers, welcoming
visitors, and dealing with job applications, interview appoint-
ments, staff meetings, etc.

• A Programme Manager was appointed full-time prior to the
LIFT '01 Festival to assist liaison with the theatre companies,
artists and curators and to take on individual projects.

Freelance, part-time staff working on long-term projects

• Artists are the lifeblood of the organization, taking on many
roles and responsibilities: performing; directing; designing;
leading education projects and other projects such as launch
celebrations; documentation; staff training; facilitation of
meetings; and evaluation.

- LIFT has always had a press consultant on contract. At the beginning of each Festival cycle, scope and priorities of the press campaign are set. These range from promoting individual shows, to raising the profile of LIFT as a whole, to managing announcements of major strategic change.
- The Business Arts Forum Director's role began as a research experiment in 1994. The role was contracted on a freelance basis as funding was confirmed for each cycle of the Forum. In 2005 the Director became a LIFT Associate advising on an occasional basis as the Forum evolved further.
- The Teacher Forum Director, a part-time LIFT Associate, initiated a learning programme to renew teachers' creativity in 1999. The LIFT Learning Associate addresses strategic educational and arts issues, which LIFT Learning practice is well positioned to co-ordinate. The Associate's part-time, freelance contract is based on the financial viability of each stage of the project.
- The Student Placement Scheme was introduced in 1999. This is to provide longer-term learning opportunities for UK and international students of arts administration, production, marketing or education. Placements take on significant responsibility and their experience forms part of their college assessment. A work experience scheme exists for school students.
- The part-time Learning Co-ordinator manages all placement interviews communications and appraisals, assists on the Business Arts Forum and liaises on other learning programmes.
- Project Phakama was first managed by the Education Director and then became an independent initiative with its own co-ordinator and freelance facilitators, housed at LIFT. Part of LIFT Learning, Phakama's young leaders are commissioned on occasion to lead aspects of other LIFT programmes.

Festival staff

- The Production Manager ensures that each show can be staged in accordance with the vision of the artists and that public performance licences are secured from the relevant London borough. This involves work ahead of time to ensure that each show fits with the theatre spaces available; the required number

of seats are possible; and sets and props can be shipped or made
if necessary. The task of staging 17 to 22 Festival productions
across London demands balancing a consistent LIFT approach
with the vastly different working practices and levels of support
in each venue.

The Production Manager works with one production assis-
tant, several volunteers and other production managers on the
more complex shows. All work on a freelance basis to equip,
install, licence and de-rig each show.

- The Artists' Manager takes care of all the international travel
  arrangements, visa requirements, accommodation and local
  transport needs of visiting artists. This role is taken up three
  or four months before each Festival.

- Group Hosts provide the bridge between the receiving venues
  and the LIFT organization. Each host speaks the language of a
  LIFT theatre company, and provides the interface between
  artists, theatres and other venues and the LIFT organization.
  Group Hosts take care of day-to-day pastoral needs, payment
  of per diems, airport transfers and local transport.

- Volunteers made up the majority of staff for the first Festival
  in 1981. Volunteers continue to fulfil a variety of roles from
  helping the production team, to selling programmes, to stew-
  arding at open-air events and helping at receptions. Now
  recruited by advertisement and from a variety of colleges and
  informal routes, LIFT's volunteer scheme has evolved into a
  more formal study and work experience programme.

- The Club manager is appointed on a freelance basis during each
  LIFT season with responsibility for production and programming of the Club.

- Every season incorporates a discussion programme to tease
  out issues of interest from each production and bring people
  together around those questions. A Discussion or Talks Co-
  ordinator has filled this role, again on a freelance basis.

In continuous evolution, a snapshot of LIFT's organizational
structure in 2004 is reflected in Figure 8.1.

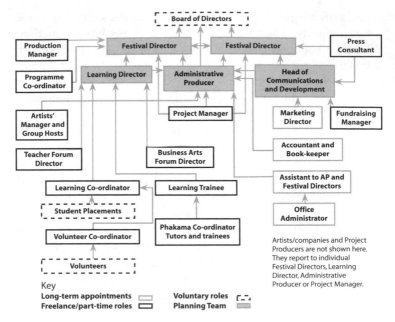

Figure 8.1 LIFT organization chart 2004

Meetings, meetings, meetings and lunch

When risk lies at the heart of an organization, culture and form of communications become vital to address. Responsibility for overall direction and communication is the work of the Planning Team, made up of Festival Directors, Administrative Producer, Head of Communications and Learning Director. This group meets every Tuesday to set strategy and discuss operational issues, alternating between the two areas each week. No external meetings are scheduled on Tuesdays. This cycle incorporates a fortnightly staff meeting combined with a lunch, cooked in turn by each staff member. Food is very important at LIFT. These lunches enable formal and informal interaction among the entire team, building collective ownership of risk and solidarity in the face of that risk. Each new influx of student placements takes part in a group induction session scheduled to coincide with one of these lunches. This aids extension of LIFT ownership to newcomers through formal and informal interaction with old-timers and an introduction to organizational roles and responsibilities, mission and values. These rituals and intergenerational connections provide moments of certainty amid multiple layers of uncertainty.

Walking in other worlds

Back to the Forum and conviction was dawning that inviting young people to take part in the Forum would benefit both young people and adults. Such a move would be consistent with LIFT's civic aims and artistic ethos. If, however, such shared learning between adults and young people was to be built, it needed a three-way fit: the aesthetic and public role of LIFT; the values of education for young people; and alignment with the interests of business and large public sector organizations.

Specifics needed to be established if intergenerational learning connections were to be made. LIFT had its own hunches and experience, but it was time to take a look in greater detail at the world of large organizations and conduct formal research into how these partnerships might be shaped and argued. There were well-publicized cases of businesses supporting youth arts activities, but cases of companies learning from young people were less well known. Still less well known in the UK were companies learning from the arts and young people at the same time. The search for precedents involved two research periods, one in the UK and one in the US. This section sets out the findings that most influenced future developments.

Several steps figured in the effort to step deeper into the world of organizations in 1996. First of all, I had to ensure that the study was worth undertaking not only from LIFT's point of view but also from my own, as this would take time and resources. The starting point for the interview process was a belief that adults had much to learn both from international theatre and from young people who were just starting out on their adult life. This was twinned with a desire to widen connections and learning experience for young people in London.

Cases of 'cool hunting' were well known, whereby fashion house researchers hung out among young people, usually young urban black people, to pick up on how jeans and other clothing were being customized. These trends were then exploited for mass production. This was not the kind of learning and observation that we had in mind. The relationship pictured was one where learning and engagement was truly two-way. As we had established through the principles guiding the Education Programme, that would only result from a degree of vulnerability and risk on the part of all involved. Adults would be encouraged to engage with the young people to address questions of common concern stimulated by the theatre. The young people would be risking conversation with unfamiliar people in unfamiliar settings. Both adults and the young would learn about different ways of doing things, different modes of discussion, and be able to step into places often closed to them. Embarking on the interview process, it was not necessary to have a precise picture of what the ideal relationship might look like, but it was essential to have the idea of a general shape and principles.

Looking outwards and inwards

I was not attempting to become an expert, but to get a feel for and think laterally about the world I was about to enter. From experience of sponsorship and the Business Arts Forum, the world of large organizations was not unfamiliar, but a much more subtle grasp of human development issues was required to overcome the common assumptions about the arts I was likely to encounter. The first step was a look at the management shelves of large bookshops. A look at the titles, chapter headings and indices of the books revealed common business parlance and daily challenges, frequently using specialized language. I looked for the human questions concealed in that language that might connect with what our world had to offer. These gave sufficient pointers to spark a conversation and persuade people that my curiosity about their working life was genuine. The aim was to encourage people to talk, not to have a full understanding of their world. Indeed it emerged that unfamiliarity helped. Talking to someone outside their field gave people an opportunity to voice concerns and ideas in a way that sometimes proved to be new and refreshing.

A further inward look was needed. Did the human questions the research might reveal have overlaps with our activities and organization? Did my vision of how my area of work could evolve fit with this wider picture? Was our organization set up to deliver such a relationship? How might it need to change? Did we wish to do this? What might we gain from a new departure? What might we lose? In consultation with colleagues it was decided that sufficient scope existed to embark on the study.

Resourcing the research

Work on the research needed funding. By now political changes in London had affected arts education policy and practice in the capital. Following discussion with London Arts Board (LAB), the regional arts funding organization, it was agreed that a study primarily aimed at providing a foundation for shared learning at LIFT would also hold interest for LAB, at that time speculating about how it could make its limited resources go further in building local cross-sector arts partnerships for the benefit of young people.[3] The track record of the Business Arts Forum and connections provided through our team of advisers convinced LAB to fund the research as their strategic aims had much in common with those of LIFT. Funding for the study was approved.

Making contact with interviewees

Once the grounds for research were established, contact was made with interviewees. Just as in our earlier cross-sector ventures, LIFTING London and the Business Arts Forum, a project champion was needed. Arie de Geus made an introduction to the London Business School and members of their Leading Edge Research Consortium, a group of businesses sharing practice on how business strategy is developed through people.[4] Interviews were set up with members of this group, human resource managers or directors in a range of companies and public sector organizations. Others were added to a final list, including Appleyards Peugeot Dealers, BP, BT, Glaxo Wellcome, Hewlett Packard, Marks and Spencer, Midland Bank, Ogilvy and Mather, Royal Insurance, Tesco, SBC Warburg, and a large management consultancy that wished to remain anonymous.

As lines were redrawn between the sectors, it was clear that links beyond organizational walls were needed in the public sector too. Organizations interviewed included the London Borough of Redbridge and the National Health Service.

People needed a guarantee of legitimacy or reassurance that my questions were well researched before agreeing to be interviewed. Referral by someone they recognized and respected was invaluable. Once the report was completed a copy was sent to interviewees asking for comments as to accuracy and seeking permission to publish. Permission to publish the findings was given by inter-viewees at the time (1996). The findings offer a glimpse of organizational life in the mid-1990s; many of the same pressures revealed by the research related here still exist, others have become more insistent.[5]

Interview questions included:

- What external pressures are affecting your business?
- How are your management development processes changing in response?
- Have you called on the arts and/or community engagement to provide professional development for your staff?
- Have you made any formal connections between your arts and community affairs departments and your staff development programmes?
- Do any of these programmes make connections with young people?

Research findings

Inside the ordered office buildings lay a surprise. Acute levels of uncertainty were encountered and in both private and public sector organizations; I witnessed people trying to work out a way ahead.

Drug company, Glaxo Wellcome, with deregulation of the National Health Service, could no longer rely on an unquestioned demand for drugs from a single huge client and faced real competition for the first time. This exposed difficulties previously obscured in an era of unhampered growth. The Human Resources Director observed that managers had difficulty in dealing with the situations of ambiguity experienced in periods of change. Tension resulted from a culture dominated by a scientific approach. Making sense of situations did not always suit conventional forms of communication such as written reports on paper but needed more generative styles of conversation and multiple modes of interaction. New ways of learning, and a coherence of company values and behaviour across departments and managerial levels were needed. All senior managers and Board members had undergone appraisal. One-to-one coaching was undertaken and changes only seen after months.

In turn, introduction of budget holding and the internal market were profoundly affecting management culture in the National Health Service. Faced with finite resources, spending priorities had to be set and publicly accountable ways found to do so, affecting people's working relationships and approach. There was a need to rebuild confidence and renew a sense of purpose. Creative forms of interaction were considered useful in countering a climate of uncertainty.

Supermarket chain, Tesco, faced reductions in the number of out-of-town large store developments permitted. With geographic expansion ruled out, diversification and continuous innovation provided the only ways of maintaining a competitive edge. The Head of Human Resources described the need for cross-functional working and self-organizing teams in the search for innovation. Tremendously challenging and highly emotional, the demands new ways of working made on staff raised the need for issues to be tackled at a deep-rooted level.

BT had been opened to worldwide competition through deregulation. New technology and increased competition forced transition from a public utility company to one in which communications and multimedia converged. This demanded completely different management and leadership skills, attitudes to markets, brands and customers, with wide-ranging implications for internal organization, communication and concepts of service. Some 125,000 people took voluntary redundancy. The majority were engineering staff and middle managers. Comprehensive appraisal and training schemes for all remaining staff were introduced.

Royal Insurance was struggling to improve internal communication in response to new technology and increased pace of competition. The Group Management Development Manager described how everyone was operating in his or her own silo, often refusing to accept that there were others two floors below doing the same job but in a different silo.

In the face of these now familiar but almost overwhelming changes, there was less and less place for 'permission-seeking, linear thinkers or those with an authoritarian, hierarchical and status-bound approach. Everywhere, the issue of personal responsibility, lifetime learning and adaptability gained ground' (Rowntree 1996). Organizations were obliged to become 'flatter', more flexible and creative, requiring different leadership qualities. Individuals could no longer rely on a 'job for life'. Responsibility for career management and personal development increasingly fell to the individual. When the hierarchy was less clear, people had to be ready to work alongside people on an equal basis, and assess what they wanted to do, sometimes making a horizontal move or developing their skills for redeployment elsewhere. Career paths took a zigzag and individuals were compelled to ask more frequently, what do I really want to do and how do I learn to do it?

Hewlett Packard (HP) was more familiar with fast-paced change. The ratio of computing power to price continued to increase at a dramatic rate, forcing creative approaches to collaboration with other organizations. Relatively small investment was now needed to enter the market, increasing competition for larger players such as HP. Light-footed management was required to keep pace. By the mid-1990s the product cycle had reduced to 18 months and sometimes even 9. Many products were in effect being tested on the market. Now companies were in a relationship of close co-evolution with the learning pace of customers.

Accelerating speed of communications also meant that there was no longer a hiding place for bad company practice. Increased scrutiny put greater demands of accountability on organizations that had before been less open to public gaze.

BP had acknowledged these dynamics. For example, faced with growing public scrutiny of the company's social and environmental record, among other measures, BP had afforded greater importance to government and public affairs matters. A new department was created, made up of those dealing with external affairs, those responsible for health and safety and those responsible for regional operations worldwide.

With national boundaries diminishing in importance, under-standing of cultural differences was becoming vital. Investment in the emerging markets of Eastern Europe and Asia needed well-nuanced approaches in the advertising industry. Ogilvy and Mather's Head of Management Development remarked, 'To think that a market will remain uneducated and unsophisticated for more than two and a half seconds is crass.'

Cultural awareness was not only called for in an international context. Where a range of internal functions had been contracted out of organizations, new forms of relationship and interdependency between large and small organizations had emerged. These changes required an awareness of organizational cultures of many kinds and the unconscious ways in which 'things are done round here'. It could no longer be assumed that everyone behaved with the same set of assumptions and would just pick up on unspoken modes of behaviour across different scales of operation, depart-mental, national or even gender boundaries.

It was clear from all the interviews that the only response to continual change was a willingness on the part of both individuals and organizations to learn new ways of doing things. Staff facing redundancy inevitably faced retraining. Remaining staff embarked on programmes varying from specialized leadership schemes to company-wide ventures to learn just about anything.

The qualities and skills needed to deal with change and foster innovation could be developed by building relationships beyond institutional walls and by gaining greater cultural sensitivity and openness.

Did connections with the arts or communities figure as a route to adaptation?

None of the companies interviewed in the UK had made a connection between the learning and management development needs of their staff and the activities of their community affairs departments. There were a few, very few, examples of the arts being incorporated into these companies' attempts to effect change and encourage innovation. Where these existed, they were one-off examples, emerging from the personal interest of a visionary Senior Manager or Director. Where secondment schemes and voluntary work in communities or with young people existed, they rarely involved an arts dimension nor were they regarded as a mainstream route to professional development. Where knowledge of such links existed, the arts and connections to communities were viewed as a dimension of the company's charitable activities.

BT, echoing other organizations, saw its role in relation to arts and community affairs as 'being a good member of society and dedicating a percentage of profits to charities' (Rowntree 1996). Connections with communities came after the profits were made, not before.

Nevertheless, a programme combining training and marketing at BT brought groups of clerks, administrators and managers together in a series of town centres to interview the public about attitudes to BT. Relieved of the day-to-day pressures of the workplace, staff had a way of testing their view of BT's role in wider society. The programme also improved communication with colleagues of different status within the BT hierarchy. Untapped potential was revealed among staff. Not much was said about the programme's effectiveness at increasing sales. This seemed to be less important than the impact of the programme on individual morale. The BT interviewee commented: 'there was warmth, a catalytic effect. It was a fantastically positive experience. I'd carry on doing it for ever and a day' (Rowntree 1996).

Members of staff at Appleyard, a Peugeot dealership in Chesterfield Derbyshire, were encouraged to pursue a dream and to view work as an integral part of life. The key had been to foster openness and trust in which people could admit their failings rather than assuming they had to be right about everything. This changed atmosphere was found to be far more helpful to the company. Sceptics who thought that it would encourage people to go off and do something else were proved wrong with evidence of increased staff loyalty, reduced absenteeism and improved staff communication.

Managers at HP had taken part in Operation Raleigh, a youth expedition scheme, but, while recognizing the benefits of youth and community connections as a route to management development, had not yet considered the arts as a resource in this way.

Investment bankers, SBC Warburg, recognized that staff benefited from participation in youth mentoring schemes. Mentoring was actively encouraged at a senior level in the company. Around 30 individuals from SBC Warburg were mentors to a group of young people at a school in south London. In the words of one of the mentors paired with a 15-year-old student:

> I have learned an enormous amount from my mentee, about how he sees the world. We are now very good friends. My communication skills at work have improved considerably. I'm so much better at listening than I was. He's helped me to understand other people – and my own children will be teenagers in due course!
>
> (Rowntree 1996)

At retailers Marks and Spencer (M&S) a rare example was found of the arts contributing to staff development. The Managing Director was concerned about poor communication across departmental boundaries and job status. Convinced the solution lay in greater contact with leaders in arts and science, he initiated the M&S Arts and Science Club. Among the first guest speakers were the internationally renowned contemporary artists Christo and Jeanne-Claude. Their description of wrapping the Reichstag building in newly unified Berlin was compelling enough for members from different M&S departments to organize their own trip to Germany. Efforts by some members of staff to focus the Club more directly on commercial issues were energetically countered. This non-work ambience helped people to leave their job descriptions at the door. Attendance was voluntary, but certainly made more compelling as the Managing Director was himself a Club regular. It was unusual to share informal time with someone of such seniority in the organization.

UK arts company Opera Circus (whose commercial division is called Lively Arts) organized an event with partners of a large management consultancy to encourage communication across the group, and stimulate creativity among the team. Partners in the consultancy and their spouses worked together in Portugal over several days to create a performance of their own with guidance from the artists. The project was welcomed by some as the source of 'a sense of joy not experienced for many years'.

This initial foray into the world of organizations in the UK had given a sense of the day-to-day realities of organizational life. It had offered strong evidence that there was a role for the arts and community connections in the personal development of managers. Nevertheless it revealed few alliances of the civic kind that I sought across the boundaries of arts, businesses, young people and communities.

Stories from the US

I was eager to discover other examples, gathering shapes to weave back to LIFT. In periods of change, stories from other sectors and other countries provide inspiration for different ways of doing things. Stories from home are fine, but stories from abroad are often better for the purposes of advocacy. This is especially true when they come from a country assumed to be setting the pace in innovation and wealth creation. With the expansion of new technologies and the Internet boom, the US was on a roll. Britain's 'special relationship' with the US was very much in the ascendant in 1997 and there was a sense that America was shaping the future. A Winston Churchill Travel Fellowship funded me to extend my research to the US. Contacts were made through our existing network of Forum advisers.

Paired Youth Adult Scheme, New York
Outward Bound Center

I learned that Colgate Palmolive, a large corporation, and New York Outward Bound Center (NYOBC), a non-profit organization, had set up the Paired Youth Adult Scheme. The NYOBC ran physical adventure courses for young people in state schools and for employees in companies. The programmes helped to build physical and mental achievement, trust and teamwork. Approximately ten Colgate staff members volunteered to spend a weekend with an equivalent number of young people.

A manager at Colgate related how she had embarked on a five-hour canoe trip on the Hudson. Behind her a young man struggled with equal determination. Later, when they were comparing notes, she admitted that she had nearly given up but felt she had to keep going because she was the adult. He admitted he had to keep going because to give up would be cowardly. He felt if he could complete a trip like that, he could see his schooling through. The Colgate manager subsequently helped with his ambitions. Colgate participants acknowledged the personal benefits of taking part. Participation is voluntary. Indeed, there was a reluctance to consider the programme as being a formal part of management and personal development. It was felt this would diminish its quality of authentic human encounter and shared adventure.

This caveat stayed with me. Just as I was attempting to make the arguments for gaining professional development through connections with young people and communities, it was a warning that this professionalizing approach might undermine the very thing it was attempting to achieve. Voluntarism on both sides is vital in ethical facilitation of intergenerational connections.

United Parcel Service's Community
Intern Programme

United Parcel Service (UPS) has, for 30 years, run internships for managers in neighbourhood hostels or community projects. This is a company that operates largely on the street. Managers need to respect cultures other than their own; to overcome fear of HIV and Aids, drugs and alcohol; and to become more compassionate. In order to stay in tune with its changing constituency, managers need to change their attitudes too. The Programme Manager stressed that the number one challenge in business is communication and understanding. This programme, he says, 'gets ten out of ten for encouraging people how better to understand people'.

As for the hostel, how do they benefit? The co-ordinator of the UPS Programme at Henry Street Settlement in New York says the UPS interns bring hope to residents. This hope springs from the interns, who are seen as being successful in life, letting down their guard and listening. Real openness and communication has developed before they leave. Internship fees contribute to Settlement income. In some instances, UPS staff have sponsored the education of young people or helped the organization long term. The Programme needs detailed co-ordination and only works with a dedicated staff member.

Santa Fé Community Youth Mural Project[6]

In 1992, the townspeople of Santa Fé, New Mexico, were enraged by an escalation of graffiti on buildings around the city and called for custodial sentences for perpetrators. The Head of Education at the New Mexico Museums' Service, Sue Sturtevant, persuaded the city council to allow her time to devise an alternative. A City Arts Commission was set up with advice from local artists running the city's art warehouse project for teenagers. The Santa Fé Community Youth Mural Project was approved by Mayor Debbie Jaramillo.

Professional artists were invited to submit proposals for murals on the city's public buildings, a condition being they worked with groups of young people and consult with the neighbourhood in which the mural was to be located. The young people were identified through an informal referral system via the police, community organizations, schools and word of mouth. The young people were paid for their work and they received official acknowledgement on completion of the Project. Artists acted as artist mentors to the young people, directing research, design and technical execution.

As part of the research process, the memories of older residents were gathered. This channel of communication provided an opportunity for prejudices about young people to be overcome and for a sense of achievement to be developed on the part of all involved. Around 60 murals of outstanding quality have been completed in the city. A 78 per cent reduction in graffiti was recorded.

Santa Fé provided a further vivid example of how the arts and young people could contribute to changing attitudes in the workplace and wider society at the same time. This time it involved adults, young people and artists working with the city's Solid Waste Department. The recently arrived Managing Director of the Department, Cindy Padilla-Cessarich, knew she needed to raise morale among her staff. She had an idea that the mural project might be able to help her accomplish her aims.

Artists were invited to submit proposals for working with young people to paint four new white garbage trucks. Nancy Sutor and Chris Cardinale were chosen and embarked on research with a group of around 20 young people looking into the waste processes of their city, from house to house collection, to landfill sites in the mountains. They considered the manufacturing cycle, and reflected on the excesses of consumer society and issues of sustainability. They also interviewed the garbage collectors.

The murals brought recognition to the frequently thankless job of garbage collection and raised awareness of how much and what was thrown away. One truck carried portraits of some of the collectors and drivers (this was the most popular in the Department). Another depicted manufacturing processes and mountains of waste emerging out of houses. A third was decorated with graffiti-style flames and heroic swirls with 'EXCESS' emblazoned over the truck. The fourth had huge, iridescent bluebottle flies all over it.

A remarkable project, it fulfilled the aims of managing change within the Solid Waste Department, providing artists with new challenges and giving the young people a solid grounding in the disciplines of artistic life. It also raised public awareness and civic discourse about sustainability and has since inspired the painting of the interior of the public buses.

Learning beyond institutional walls

Just what was it about the arts and cross-boundary learning that was vital to contemporary organizations and broader society? Shirley Brice Heath, Professor of English, Education, Linguistics and Anthropology at Stanford University, had conducted research over a ten-year period that provided the clue. Heath and her team had looked into the question: 'What characterizes learning environments that draw reluctant learners and young people from unstable and sometime dangerous communities into superlative demanding performance?'

Heath's research revealed that conventional US schools are failing these young people and that many found their way to out-of-school organizations such as Boys and Girls Clubs, athletic clubs and, most significantly, arts clubs. Heath's research established that the most dramatic educational results emerge from young people's involvement in youth-based arts organizations in out-of-school settings. Instinct and interest leads these young people beyond existing institutions to places where they can set the trajectory and content of their own learning.

When compared with a control group from across the US, described as 'the national sample', the statistics are startling. Young people participating in community-based arts organizations are

> twice as likely to win an award for academic achievement, eight times more likely to win a community service award, and four times more likely to participate in a maths or science fair. They are also 25% more likely to report feeling satisfied with themselves and 31% more likely to say they plan to continue education past high school. Moreover, these young people are more than twice as likely as those in the national sample to see themselves working to correct economic inequities.
>
> (Heath and Smyth 1999)

The part played by out-of-school, youth-based arts organizations in these young peoples' lives is pivotal. Young people are creating their own institutions to replace those that are either absent or not responding to their sense of meaning and security, providing a safe haven thus helping young people's survival. The arts settings provide continuity of communal connections and faith in possibilities. They sometimes even provide a route to economic activity, helping young people make their own workplaces. Rather than being teachers, the role of adult artists and mentors in these organizations is as enabler and listener. They set the standards, rigorous standards, able to stand up in the public realm. They do not rule out ways of doing things but encourage a rigour of approach and excellence in performance and execution. They call for the best in people and help set the values of the group. What is more, the research shows that engagement with out-of-school arts activities actually increases the school attendance of these young people and shapes their roles as citizens. These findings provided the foundation for considering why we all need a public and civic sphere from which to learn, particularly at times of great upheaval.

Artists have a particular role to play in this context. They can see where others only peer into the fog and hark to voices at the margins. Expressed another way by the writer, James Baldwin: 'This is the only real concern of the artist, to re-create out of the disorder of life that order which is art' (Baldwin 1970: 75).

Beyond institutional walls

The research conducted in 1996 and 1997 showed that engagement beyond the walls of any one organization or discipline helped respond to crises and change. Leadership qualities sought in the business world were effectively developed through engagement with communities and young people. Colgate's Paired Youth Adult Scheme had encouraged learning across generations and BT's staff had gained tangible motivation from engaging with communities. In some instances, the arts had proved to be a catalyst for the development of attitudes of openness and learning across boundaries of organization, culture and generation. The contemporary arts had helped people cross boundaries between departments and job status at M&S. The Santa Fé Mural project stood out, building learning across organizational and generational boundaries to contribute to public education, civic awareness, artistic creation and young people's learning and transition. It was this example that I held in my mind as I imagined the shape of what might be pursued in London.

The research process had provided a foray into a world beyond the theatre, to examine more closely the pressures on business and public sector organizations. It made clear that, when faced with great change, people in all organizations, and of whatever age, benefit from connecting to and learning from beyond institutional walls. This learning cannot happen in the abstract. For it to work effectively it needs tangible and authentic shared projects. Engagement that transcended job, economic and age status via creative projects over time made for particular qualities of learning. This led to a question about what the arts teach.

What is it that the arts teach?

Elliot Eisner, Professor of Education at Stanford, has long been an advocate of the special qualities that the arts teach, namely:

- that problems can have multiple solutions and that multiple perspectives can be brought to bear on any one question.
- that circumstance and opportunity change what is created.
- that neither words nor numbers are the only ways of knowing.
- that small differences can have large effects.
- to understand and make judgements about qualitative relationships.
- to work through and with the limits of materials.
- to articulate what is difficult to express.
- to seek experience that is available from no other source.
- to see that arts' position in the school points to what adults believe is important.

(Eisner 2000)

What attitudinal changes are sought in large organizations?

Interviews revealed that the qualities and skills needed to survive change and foster innovation in organizational settings bore remarkable similarity to these qualities of learning through the arts. Required was:

- vision and an ability to take responsibility;
- an ability to draw on a full range of skills and potential;
- an ability to overcome deep-rooted emotional and behavioural obstacles, such as fear and prejudice;
- an awareness of different cultures and value systems;
- managing diversity, fostering skills and potential in others;
- an ability to grasp and articulate complex, interconnected relationships;
- an ability to regard chaos and ambiguity as positive and creative;
- openness and trust;
- the creation of learning individuals within learning organizations;
- a continuous search for excellence.

Approaches needed in the two fields, arts-based youth development and business innovation, were too similar to ignore.

A picture began to emerge of how the Festival could spark the intensive and intimate connections necessary to personal and civic alteration. From our engagement with others' roles in society, we became more confident of the Festival's role in facilitating creative engagement in the public realm. We needed to look in more depth at the space we were drawn to frame and the implications this perspective held for the Forum, for those involved and for the overall vision and structure of LIFT itself.

PART THREE

Imagining a Cultural Commons

I never used to respect strangers . . . that changed when I started working a little bit more and having fun.
(B. Rodrigues, student participant in
LIFT's *Factory of Dreams* project)

PART THREE

Ethnographic Cultural
Comparisons

NINE

COLLECTIVE LEARNING

The poet's eye, in a fine frenzy rolling,
Doth glance from heaven to earth, from earth to heaven;
And as imagination bodies forth
The form of things unknown, the poet's pen
Turns them to shapes, and gives to airy nothing
A local habitation and a name.
(Shakespeare, *Midsummer Night's Dream*, 5.1.12–17)

The main impulse for the Business Arts Forum came from a sense that sponsors of youth arts activities were primarily motivated by the need to build brand recognition and image. This approach did not, we thought, pay sufficient attention to broadening possibilities of learning and adaptation across the board.

As understanding grew of the so-called creative industries, they were widely hailed for their contribution to the national economy. Less attention was paid to how creative activities that eventually become commercial begin first in the civic realm, in youth arts activities and shared interest associations. It was this non-commercial form of creative activity that was the focus of our attention. We were now convinced that shared creative learning had its part to play in bringing people together across generations, sectors and cultures to focus on shared projects or issues of shared concern.

US economist Jeremy Rifkin claims that, when the commercial sphere begins to engulf the cultural sphere, the social foundations on which commerce itself is built risk destruction. Commerce inevitably takes things out, extracts things from a common well of ideas, passions and experiment where culture is made, where values are intrinsic (of and for themselves) rather than co-created for any monetary value. Rifkin chides cultural institutions caught in a 'kind of neo-colonial limbo between the government and market sectors' dependent on paymasters in these realms, receiving grants for the delivery of policy or 'in return for some marketing or promotional benefit' (Rifkin 2000: 255). Rifkin throws down a challenge, claiming that: 'Bringing culture and commerce back into a balanced ecology, then, is likely to be one of the most important political tasks of the coming age' (Rifkin 2000: 252).

The precise role of LIFT in restoring such balance in its own activities needed repeated experiment.

Ideas into practice are described in this and the following chapter. Description of LIFT's steps in bringing adults and young people together leads on to description of other, similar programmes that it sparked under the auspices of GBN, the Oxford Research Group and London Weekend Television. These boundary-spanning initiatives continually raised questions about the relation between individuals as members of a business organization and as members of society as a whole. They also raised questions as to the influence of gender on collaboration and competition. Speculation is made here too about the roles of men and women, young and old in building the qualities necessary to collaborative and collective learning.

LIFT's first experiment in linking the Business Arts Forum with young people

LIFT's first steps in bringing business people to learn from a youth arts setting took place during the OUT of LIFT season in 1996. This brief, one-off session and subsequent research in the UK and US provided the foundations on which the Business Arts Forum's intergenerational dimension was subsequently built. It also sparked intergenerational engagement by other organizations.

The centrepiece of LIFT's 1996 season of productions made for, by and with young people was *Factory of Dreams*, the firework project with Stockwell Park School described in Chapter five. A small group of Forum members was invited to visit the Craft, Design and Technology Department of the school during the project's research and development phase.

We believed that a behind-the-scenes look at collaboration between artists, students and teachers on a project about fire with a group of 12- to 13-year-olds would offer insights into Forum members' efforts to encourage innovation and risk in their own organizations. In spite of appearances, there were many similarities between the two contexts. The school had embarked on the LIFT project at a time when pressure was acute to deliver the educational equivalent of 'bottom-line results', i.e. exam results and educational targets. Other challenges echoed organizational churn in the business world. Stockwell Park had just merged with another school. Over 40 languages were spoken among students and a high percentage of those without English as their first language had only been in the country for 18 months. Building a coherent culture of educational aspiration and motivation presented challenges in this context, just as it did in still larger commercial organizations.

There were doubts about allowing Business Arts Forum members into the classroom. The visit would put a spotlight on negotiations taking place between LIFT, the school and between different school departments. Contrary to expectations, it proved to be a vital staging post. The teachers were encouraged to be honest about the difficulties and challenges they faced. This was not a public relations or fundraising exercise. The strangers were bearing witness to the work involved and seeking to learn from it. It was at this meeting that, for the first time, teachers confidently voiced their belief in the educational value of *Factory of Dreams*. The group of young people spoke publicly about their hopes and aspirations. They taught the Forum members one of the design skills they had learned based on punched tin sheet, a traditional Pakistani decorative technique. Forum members made an image of their own dreams for incorporation into the final event. The simplicity of the invitation compelled business people to think as the children had about what it was that they wished from life in a much larger way than was usual in their day-to-day duties. After the meeting, school participants went forward with renewed enthusiasm. The Forum members provided a foretaste of the larger audience for whom the group would be performing in due course. A public performance was scheduled in nearby Brockwell Park for a London-wide audience. The date was published in the LIFT programme. There was a deadline to meet.

Forum member, Richard Elsner, found his visit to the school gave food for thought: 'I am more and more humbled by the experience of consulting across cultural barriers – the whole depth of cultural expectations, the limits of the ability of people of one culture to really feel they understand one another' (LIFT 1997).

Bobby Baker, an artist taking part in the Business Arts Forum, found it valuable to experience a project devised by other artists that took inspiration from different cultural traditions and scales of working. Several Forum members attended the public performances in Brockwell Park. Their experience was enriched by the earlier school visit.

LIFT's experiment sparks others

This initial experiment was a one-off, propelling the UK and US research described in the previous chapter.

On my return from the United States in 1997, I was eager to see ideas put into practice. A GBN conference in Windsor was the context for the next development in intergenerational learning. *The Futures of Europe* explored, among other issues, the impact of economic migration and the harmonization of immigration policies across Europe. The topic inevitably raised human rights issues and issues of racial and economic equity. Blair Gibb was one of the facilitators. Gibb had worked in the Port Authority of New York before coming to London to advise human rights organization, Amnesty International, on how the organization should respond to the increasing number of human rights abuses in which multinational corporations were implicated. Gibb was an adviser to the Business Arts Forum. Like us, she was preoccupied with questions of shifting relations between business and society and in rethinking corporate social responsibility. She had taken part in LIFT events involving young people during the previous Festival.[1] This experience informed facilitation of a session organized by Gibb at the conference.

In thinking about the future of London, particularly its economy, the place of diversity as a foundation stone could not be ignored. Between 1997 and 2000, the creative industries in the UK were reported as representing 7.9 per cent of GDP and had grown by an average of 9 per cent as compared to an average of 2.8 per cent for the rest of the economy (DCMS online). In this picture it was clear that diversity of imagination, worldview and cultural practice were the preconditions for London's creative economy. Within the performing arts, the vibrancy of the cultural industries is intimately connected to the presence of so many different cultures in the city. Where theatre, music, visual arts and, indirectly, advertising are concerned, cultural expression always takes place in civil society before its adoption by the commercial realm. This evolution always follows those who are simply finding a voice, often a minority voice, in a mainstream culture. In thinking about other aspects of Europe's cultural diversity such as harmonization of immigration procedures and so on, Gibb felt it essential for conference delegates to meet young people at the beginning of their search for a creative voice. These voices are often heard first in the civic realm, in other words through youth arts organizations, clubs and shared interest associations.

Members of the youth arts programme Project Phakama, who had just been on a first visit to South Africa, were invited to devise and facilitate this session at the conference. With guidance from Gibb and Phakama tutor Lucy Richardson, Kenny Guthrie, Chinh Hoang, Robert Hutchinson, Honza Noel and Anthony Oscyemi were encouraged to apply the skills they had learned in a youth arts setting to a new context: that of working with adults in business. Phakama called for a participatory process in which delegates were invited to talk about diversity in their own family histories. They were asked to offer different interpretations of a scene involving a racist incident, and then depict in mime their own views of Europe's futures.

This session offered tangible experience of the intimate connections between civil society and the foundations of the cultural
'industries'. To stimulate a lively and equal discussion among young
and adult participants, the form of this encounter needed subtle
consideration. It would not work if the expected path of a panel
discussion was taken. It would only come to life if the young people
shared creative responsibility for putting it together and did this on
their terms (with guidance). Indeed it would only work if this
session tested the leadership skills of Phakama members. This is
what happened. The occasion brought together two generations to
widen the cultural perspectives of both age groups. After the session,
Napier Collyns, a founder of GBN, commented: 'Now I get it. If
you invest in civil society, the rest comes from that.'

The ambience of the Phakama session was totally different from
other sessions that day. The energy and laughter spread to the neighbouring room, catching the attention of an international expert on
nuclear issues, Scilla Elworthy of the Oxford Research Group. She
realized that this quality of interaction was needed at a meeting she
was planning – the first international meeting ever of decision-
makers in the nuclear reprocessing industry. Some weeks later we
heard from Elworthy, the results of Phakama's intervention at the
conference.

> In no time at all, 25 hard-nosed executives were transformed into
> a laughing, boisterous bunch. It opened up a completely different,
> lively tone beyond their conventional exchanges. They were
> impressed by the young people's integrity and wanted to know their
> views. The session was a highlight for them.[2]
>
> (Elworthy conversation: 1998)

This intergenerational creative exchange helped participants
leave their vested interests and professional preoccupations at the
door, to concentrate on the risk of raising fundamental questions.
The young people had taken responsibility for shaping the sessions
and had been paid properly for their work. The experience contributed to their own professional development as arts leaders.

The quality of experience for the adults would not have been as
effective had it been delivered in a fully professionalized way. The

adults responded to the hope and energy of the young people at an instinctive level. Although the Phakama team were being paid, they offered something beyond a contractual relationship with the rest of the group. They were testing their skills and abilities in an unfamiliar setting and thus stretching their idea of who they were and what they themselves could offer to a wider world and issues of international import. Their youth and skills of facilitation gave 'permission' to the adults to behave differently. If this request had been put by people of the same age and by professional adult facilitators, there would probably have been more sceptics.

This experience showed that seeing the arts simply as a foundation of the so-called creative industries made it easy to ignore their ancient social role in sparking collective hope and adaptation.

London Weekend Television's Talent Challenge

Another youth arts initiative that drew on the experience of the Business Arts Forum and LIFT's *Factory of Dreams* project was organized by London Weekend Television (LWT). I gave freelance advice to the project in its initial stages prior to my visit to the US. The project was due to culminate in summer 1998. Preparations were well under way by the time of my return to the UK.

LWT and the Inner London Education Authority (ILEA) were partners in a Youth Festival before abolition of London's local government. The ILEA provided communication with schools and funding, LWT contributed other resources and provided television coverage. Faced with falling advertising revenues and no single channel of communication with London's schools following abolition of the ILEA, the company's only alternative source of collaboration was with other businesses and the LAB. The response of Regional Affairs Director, Emma Mandley, was the LWT Talent Challenge.

The aim of Talent Challenge was to harness human and financial resources within business to develop, manage and fundraise towards a youth arts event in London in summer 1998. Five businesses were enlisted: Halifax, Deloitte and Touche, IBM, Coca-Cola and Thames Water. Each company assigned a team of five managers to work for five hours a week on projects with young people in five

London boroughs, the boroughs in which the companies were based or had some other working link. The project was framed as a management development programme for participants rather than as commercial promotion. Each project was to involve around 200 young people aged 16–25 years, 1,000 in all. It was aimed at giving the young people an opportunity to explore their creative abilities and showcase their artistic talents in a site-specific large-scale event. A documentary team from LWT was assigned to film the process.

Of the five businesses involved, Halifax appeared to achieve the most successful partnership. A decision to base the project in the London Borough of Islington followed rigorous questioning by both parties (Halifax and the borough) about each other's aims and priorities. Much of the venture's success in Islington was attributed to the equity that was established during this initial contact. These early meetings determined expectations, balance of power, style and nature of the relationship and, indeed, the value all round of pursuing the relationship at all.

The other four business teams chose a different route and developed their projects in an area near their head offices. The strength of existing youth provision varied greatly and affected the scale and quality of each project. The partnerships were determined by a multitude of other factors too. For some of the businesses, the Chairman or Chief Executive had given an initial commitment to the Chairman of LWT that their company would take part, doubtless with little idea of what this would mean for individual staff members or line managers. Adverse perceptions of each company's culture by arts organizations determined the length of time it took to develop trust; the abilities and personal approach of individual team members varied greatly; the form of invitation issued to young people influenced the speed and success with which they were engaged.

It was interesting to witness that business participants faced difficulties parallel to arts organizations when making requests for sponsorship. Great effort was put into project launches and fundraising events that only ever dented the sums needed. Managers were surprised that they had little or no access to the sponsorship funds of their own companies. Only in the case of the Halifax was a business proposal put to Head Office to fund the overall project. Funding remained problematic for other teams and the arts co-ordinators they employed.

As to company culture, the Halifax was undergoing a dramatic change from a mutual society to the more competitive culture of a commercial bank. The company's approach to community partnership had a greater quality of mutuality to it than was observed in other businesses involved in Talent Challenge.

In contrast, there was initial suspicion of Coca-Cola. One manager from the company reflected after his first encounter with leaders of youth arts groups in Hammersmith, west London, that his company had a reputation for branding 'everything that moves' and that this was inappropriate when trying to build alliances.

This comment brought to the surface the personal layer between an individual as a private citizen and an individual as a corporate being. It was in this gap I sensed there was scope for reassertion of the public sphere.

Talent Challenge gave very real evidence of the value of learning across sectors and generations in the public sphere. It also brought other things to light. Contrary to common perception, it was the arts people who demonstrated the greatest continuity of engagement over the length of the project. The vast majority of business team members involved in the introductory session had moved on to other jobs part way through the project. Few had been able to sustain involvement following the job move. An image of arts practice is that it is a volatile world of shifting allegiances and jealously guarded professional practice. Two arts participants commented that the arts teams all wished to share information, whereas the businesses assumed they were in competition and were less willing to do so. It was assumed on the part of the business participants that the Challenge was a competition although this had never been explicitly stated or encouraged.

In attempting a project of this complexity, continuity and trust are essential ingredients. The mix of seniority, age and gender among the Halifax team members proved to be a good recipe for shared learning and collaboration. These observations pointed to the social learning resource that the arts in London represented in relation to other sectors. It also led me to probe more deeply why the public and civic sphere offers such richness of learning and why questions of gender and stage in life seem to be so important in facilitation of such schemes (Kelly 1998).

Drawing from evidence in the US, we could also expect that some of the young people engaged in the youth arts setting were likely to become leaders in their own communities, or beyond (Heath and Smyth 1999). Hence, the people that the adults were meeting represented a different leadership model from the one with which they most usually operated, pointing to a different future that would come to influence the long-term operating environment of their own businesses.

Theatre, for LIFT, emerges from society's need to reflect itself, to stretch ideas of what it thinks is possible and to engage in a common associative life that probes the boundaries of established communities. Society, and the idea of service in the interests of a society beyond one's own family and friends, is something that is real for many people in their daily working life. So, if the wish to connect and the richness of these forms of learning are so compelling, why might obstacles exist? Could answers lie in deeper human instincts more uncomfortable to name and be found in probing issues of gender?

Management styles of men and women

Witnessing how adults needed young people in order to learn in a playful way sparked reflection about the interdependent learning roles not only of generations but also of men and women. It felt somewhat countercultural to set off on this route of enquiry, after decades of arguing that men and women could achieve the same things and reach the same goals with the same rules. Once having recognized however that there were things to be learned from young people simply from who they were and their stage in life, it was interesting in the context of social and organizational adaptation to ask an additional question: what might men and women be for?

Observations led me to my own tentative hypotheses on a subject too huge and eternal to deal with in any depth here. Nevertheless, questions of gender were so often the subject of debate in organizational circles, among Business Arts Forum advisers and colleagues navigating across sectors, that the topic is worth touching on.

It is an unavoidable fact that the majority of people leading major corporations are men and that the hyper-competition and dominance of market values make for machismo language and military metaphors – driving profits forward, market dominance, target markets, the war for talent. These metaphors and this language influence profoundly the overall culture of organizations and the society on which they have an impact. The aggregate effect is one of a commercial arms race, a giant game defined by a dominant culture, a race for profit at all costs. No one dares sit it out for a moment in case someone else races ahead. To stop and think is to lose, or so it seems.

In the midst of these reflections, I met Nick Mayhew, an organizational anthropologist and environmental activist, similarly exercised by issues of gender. With a view to sparking debate about the behaviour of multinational corporations, he had devised a performance piece for presentation in corporate settings. Entitled *Tall, Dark, Handsome and No 1*, it was a mixture of pop music, images from advertising and corporate speak, aimed at exposing Western models of power and achievement and how these were contributing to environmental destruction in other parts of the world.

Blair Gibb, a poet and human rights champion, shared the view that men were seemingly losing sight of their own traditions of co-operation. Her concerns prompted this poem.

'The New Eunuchs'

My son was born whole.
In the first two seconds, I counted them all:
his fingers, toes, eyes and ears, his purple and engorged balls.
When he grew strong
and tall enough, he began moving daily
in and out of the temples of the unseen priests

who select young men for honour in our land.
Now, as each day ends, I join the women
waiting outside the sleek black walls –
mothers of sons, lovers of lovers, daughters of fathers,
friends of friends. We watch the smoke
seeping through the thin seams of their buildings
that stretch up toward the sky. We have heard
how they burn the hearts and hands
of the ones the priests choose. Listen,
lovers, sons, friends and fathers –
you read your women wrong.
We dare not say it, but we want you to be
passed over. Watch our eyes, counting every day
as you come through the doors.
Watch the women into whose arms
the men kissed by the priests' knives fall:
see how they weep, as they hold their deep-voiced
songless men, their heartless and handless men,
the gold-robed men, sent back to us
all head, all balls.

(Gibb 1998: 55)[3]

It was clear that if ideals of male achievement needed realigning, then this could not be done in isolation. They need somehow to be contrasted with what women had to offer. Recent research reveals that, 'Girls get competitive, but only if it's worth it' (*New Scientist* 2002).

Rosanne Roy and colleagues from McGill University in Montreal have found that boys will compete just for the sake of it, regardless of payoff. In one of the games devised as part of the research everyone won. The boys competed for the pure fun of competing, while the girls would spend more time watching the reactions of their competitors and responding to them, sometimes deciding not to compete, particularly if there was nothing to be gained.

A study by Aldo Rastuchini, Professor of Economics at the University of Minnesota, claims that women's inability to secure greater numbers of top corporate jobs has perhaps less to do with prejudice than the fact that women seem to be intrinsically less competitive than men (Greezy *et al.* 2003). The study reveals that, in test after test, women proved to be less competitive. Furthermore, one test revealed that, when men were pitted against women in a race, they became still more competitive than when running against men. Whether this is through 'hard wiring' or socialization remains to be established.

On a radio programme airing this research, Barbara Rheinhold, Director of Executive Development at Smith University, commented that these findings had profound lessons for corporations (Greezy *et al.* 2003: 1049–74). She reported that women were leaving in droves to start small businesses at which they had twice the success rate of men. This was the great price paid by corporations for expecting women to compete in ways that did not align with their values.

Progress for women has been argued on the basis of equality. But is equality equated with sameness? What if equality obliterates difference and in fact ends up undermining opportunities for women and men's different perspectives to come into play? Rightful insistence on gender equality has nevertheless made it extremely difficult to say that women and men might have different roles to play in balancing competition and collaboration. Yet these differences were only too evident in everyday experience and from an increasing number of studies, particularly in the realm of language. Linguistics professor Deborah Tannen's study of language revealed that men tend to speak to offer reports, women to establish rapport (Tannen 1992a).

Thinking back to the various organizations and projects encountered in Britain and the US, the leadership role of women was a constant theme. It was the subject of frequent comment that LIFT is an organization led by women. In Santa Fé, the youth mural project had been initiated by a woman and sanctioned by the city's female mayor in the face of exhortations to punish the young graffiti artists on the part of the local townspeople. The new manager in the Santa Fé garbage department who had the idea of painting the trucks was a woman. It was the say-so of all these individuals that overcame operational difficulties and resistant attitudes along the way. Positive change is very hard to effect unless sanctioned at the top and it was intriguing that all three of these leaders were women. Was this a coincidence? I did not deliberately seek out such examples. Nevertheless, the issue of gender relations seemed one of the critical questions raised by these boundary-spanning arts experiments.

Is the job of spanning boundaries easier for women? Added to personal experience that this is so, reinforcing evidence came to light through the experience of a LIFT colleague. During her time as a youth drama worker in Scotland in the 1980s Susan Maxwell was responsible for establishing youth theatre in a district council area outside Glasgow. Instead of one group, it was found necessary to set up four theatre groups in each area. The reason for this was that the boys could not travel across gang territories. Religious divisions compounded the territorial differences. It was only after two years of working within their own area and meeting on neutral territory – often on trips to Glasgow – that it was possible to start work with all four groups in a central area. Girls on the other hand were not the ones who established territory. They went out with boys from all areas and thus could travel between (email 2004).

This seems to indicate that women feel less threat and are seen as less of a threat in an uncertain situation, making it easier to span traditional boundaries, laying the foundations for new alliances. Does this mean that stereotypical female acculturation as providing hospitality is needed to make a safe space for new conversations to happen? Could it be that these skills are not simply decorative but essential to laying foundations for qualities of collaboration and change? Whether due to 'hard wiring' or socialization, might better understanding of these dynamics help to set different rules for a new game in which competition for different rewards is established? Does the ease of crossing boundaries even bring a responsibility for women leaders and for those men who find themselves outside the mainstream? Could it be that those jobs that are seen as the 'soft' roles in organizations – doling out charity to communities, as a luxury to be indulged in after the profits are made – are essential to defining the parameters for future competition? If this is so, it means these roles take on a new significance and imply different relationships and respect between men and women and different status for these roles within organizations.

In *Feminist Thought: A Comprehensive Introduction*, R. Tong writes:

> The condition of Otherness enables women to stand back and criticize norms, values, and practices that the dominant culture (patriarchy) seeks to impose on everyone, including those who live on its periphery – in this case, women. Thus, Otherness, for all of its associations with oppression and inferiority, is much more than an oppressed, inferior condition. Rather, it is a way of being, thinking, and speaking that allows for openness, plurality, diversity, and difference.
>
> (Tong 1989: 219)

To imply that men are all competitive and women are all nurturing, collaborative and community conscious is as silly as Margaret Thatcher's assertion that 'there is no such thing as society'. And clearly competition is not bad in itself. The important question is: what is the goal? When these goals are reaching their limits there is need for renegotiation and all have a part to play. Those with a view from outside the game are required to critique its quality. There are many routes to 'otherness', to finding oneself outside a dominant culture. If, as it would appear, outsiders are closer to the ground on which the game is fought, it would seem that, paradoxically, their power to do something about it is greater. But that takes a change of focus. It might be that, rather than focusing on the people who appear to have the greatest power, the best allies lie elsewhere, around the edge. To change the game, perhaps older men and younger women who perceive that they have nothing to lose, and have the spare capacity to look around, can create the best alliances to change the rules.

At a time when there is an emphasis on the professionalization of arts management, how strange to think that the channels of communication found in the arts between (largely) male patrons and those who find themselves securing funds for the arts (largely women) can be looked at in another way – as having a timeless role in social and cultural adaptation. In this context, professionalization may turn out to be counterproductive because generative conversations and high levels of trust are best forged in non-professionalized and non-specialized ways, beyond people's job titles, in a voluntary capacity in the public realm.

Men and women who find the norms and values of their organizations or professional practices have reached their limits might look at these seemingly marginalized arts spaces as a place in which to perceive new goals for which to aim.

Perhaps no other topic raises hackles as much as speaking about gender roles and patterns of response to societal challenges. To do so in the public fora of LIFT over the past would be to risk betrayal by revealing the fine texture of facilitation: how, for example, it has been necessary to avoid direct comparison between individual male speakers or to risk devaluing the contribution of individual women by favouring some over others. But the truth is that we have all needed one another and the varying roles of status, stage in life and gender are complementary and interdependent.

The fact remains within the social realm and particularly where the social joins with the business, women and men take different charge and adapt their work environments to considerably different degrees.

My consideration of these dynamics forced me to consider that we can never entirely escape who we are and where we come from, what we look like and what assumptions others make from this, but that, rather than ignore it, we can imagine what that role might bring to others, by asking the question of oneself – what am I for at this point in my life, being who I am or could be?

Consideration of these dynamics also helped throw light on theatre's role in social continuity and adaptation; namely that theatre-making and theatre-going are essentially social and collaborative acts at many levels, often between men and women, young and old, drawing on many different kinds of power, financial, creative, of hospitality, playfulness and welcome. It also made me look anew at the role of individuals stepping out to raise funds for the theatre. This inevitably involves making connections with those in power, for it is they who have the resources. This act is commonly thought of simply as a function, enabling the delivery of theatre to the public, rather than being seen as a foundation stone of social inventiveness and adaptation. This realization came to bring a new interpretation to the inventions, successes and failures of the Business Arts Forum.

TEN

CRAFTING A NEW DISCOURSE – EXPERIMENTS AND EVOLUTION

The theatre is a school for laughter and tears, an open forum where men may put old or misguided moralities to the test and embody in living examples the eternal truths of the human heart.
(Lorca 1935)[1]

This chapter describes both LIFT's evolution and that of the Forum's design. Alongside LIFT's internal changes, the Forum evolved in tune with external events, the changing priorities of large organizations, private and public, and those of the students and colleges with whom we worked. While wrestling with how to balance the interests of these groups, we needed to consider how to encourage business and public sector participants to sign up and pay for the Forum, thus resourcing everyone's connections with one another. This meant being constantly alert to what made the Forum distinct from other management development programmes, such as business school courses, team-building ventures and motivational speakers. Experiments and adaptations made from 1997 to 2004 are described. In the early years, the Forum took place over the period of the Festival. In 2001, LIFT as a whole abandoned its 20-year biennial Festival format to embark on a change of rhythm. The Forum was compelled to adapt in turn.

Is professionalization the route to follow?

Insights into Forum adaptation sometimes came from failure. Following the success of the first Fora in 1995 and 1996, the LIFT '97 Forum reached the limits of my expertise in design and facilitation. To this date, I designed the sessions with guidance from Tony Fegan, LIFT's Learning Director. The Business Arts Forum duties had not yet found their formal place within LIFT's wider learning activities, hence planning for each session was squeezed into already full work schedules. Different creative directors were employed to direct each individual session with little continuity. All were feeling their way on new ground, just as we were.

The Forum remained a bubble on the outside of LIFT, not fully integrated into LIFT's main activities or strategic direction. It was propelled largely through a wish on my part to prove that there was another way to connect with businesses and other organizations beyond the marketing or policy-delivery model. If it was to go anywhere, integration with LIFT's overall strategy was called for.

My situation recalled the doctoral thesis of a German friend, Peter Augsdorfer, on covert research in business organizations (Augsdorfer 1996). Covert research, popularly called 'bootleg research', is often described in the same breath as 'skunkworks'. While 'skunkworks' refers to an officially sanctioned unit detailed to address a particular organizational question, 'bootleg research' refers to work undertaken by individuals or unofficial groups preparing a case for integration into the main activities of the organization or research field. Elements of both could be perceived in the Forum and its relationship to LIFT as a whole. Only a limited number of LIFT staff participated in it so it was somewhat covert. Although sanctioned by the Festival Directors as a kind of skunkworks, a compulsion resembling that driving bootleg researchers was driving the Forum. An instinctive grasp of shape, pattern or inkling of a breakthrough discovery motivates bootleg researchers to work away for years before the rest of the organization is in the right place to incorporate their new ideas into its main trajectory. Our venture would not last if it continued to be just a bootleg activity or skunkworks. I could bring only a certain skill in sensing what was needed both in the business arena and from LIFT's point of view. In spite of the unstinting advice and support from outsiders, and additional workload it brought to colleagues, greater integration into LIFT's mainstream activities, resourcing and scheduling had to take place if it was to continue. If the Forum was too much for LIFT to encompass in its range of activities, then it should be abandoned.

It was time for a brainstorming meeting with LIFT colleagues and advisers. There were many questions to discuss including balancing priorities between LIFT's wider public purpose and demands for income generation via this route. Then there were Forum participants to think of. What is the appropriate balance between arts learning and rational analysis of people's experience in the Forum? How do we crystallize people's learning more effectively and translate this back to the workplace? How far do our responsibilities go in helping to make the transition from Forum to workplace? What is the role of the facilitators in this regard? What is the maximum number and correct balance of participants and how do we recruit them?

We had gone into the meeting thinking that answers to these questions lay in somehow professionalizing the Forum, making it more like a business school course. This would mean a further extension of our responsibilities and expertise. Having embarked on the Forum in the first place to escape from the exaggerated commercial emphasis of marketing sponsorship, if we followed that route we might just be swapping one kind of directly commercial relationship for another. One of our advisers, Charles Handy, said just as he was leaving: 'don't make it too professional'. This comment lingered, setting a different train of thought in motion and reminding me of Havel's words that 'so-called professionalism' is not enough (Havel 1992).

We nevertheless made several failed attempts to forge an alliance with a business school, offering the Forum as a dimension of their executive education. No school proved sufficiently motivated or flexible to link with LIFT's performance timetable and artistic priorities. In the end, we felt that this approach was not the right one for LIFT. One of our advisers, Arie de Geus, although keen for us to make such links, urged us at the same time to avoid a 'supply push' approach. By this he meant codifying what we had, predicting what the market wanted in our wish to draw on the Forum simply as a steady source of income. If we took this course, it would ultimately undermine an ability to draw others into ownership of it, thereby paradoxically reducing its adaptability and authenticity over time. For the LIFT Forum to evolve its special role it had to maintain a spirit of experiment and unpredictability with its feet firmly in the civic realm.

Focus on the art for inspiration

A redesign of the Forum, with longer sessions and more consistent artistic direction throughout, made for great improvements. What we needed was more art in the facilitation of conversations emerging from the theatre performances, not necessarily more professionalization. A leaflet was produced inviting people to take part. The invitation still emphasized those aspects with a ready appeal to business but had moved further than previous years in the direction of creative civic discourse. The fourth LIFT Business Arts Forum (in 1999) was announced as:

> An opportunity for forward-looking people from business and public sector to come together and develop new perspectives on the challenges we face in a fast-changing world. . . . The Forum offers a proven route to developing personal and organizational insights into: managing risk; leadership for innovation; second-guessing cultural shifts; corporate and team relationships that work.
>
> (LIFT 1999a)

The LIFT '99 Forum was the best yet. Integrating into the wider LIFT organizational plan its scheduling and budgeting, for the first time we were able to appoint ahead of time an artistic director to plan the Forum programme throughout. Ewan Marshall, Theatre Director, through his inclusive and improvisatory approach established equity among all participants. The sessions felt good as a result; the vitality of the conversation was going in the right direction with room for diverging views and dissent; the range of performances we had seen and the venues visited had led people on a journey across London and the world at the same time; the insights gained were significant; there had been practical outcomes.

Forum participants saw: *The Story I'm About to Tell* and *Ubu and the Truth Commission* from South Africa's Mehlo Players and the Khulumani Support Group at the Tricycle Theatre, Kilburn; *Concierto Barocco*, by Opera Transatlantica from Venezuela and Britain, at Three Mills Island Studios in east London; *Black on White* by Ensemble Modern from Germany, at the Barbican Centre; and *Project Phakama* at the Tricycle Theatre, Kilburn. Seminars had been held at *FT* headquarters, the Commonwealth Club and South Africa House. Participants had included people from oil company, Amerada Hess; the British Council; bankers, Coutts & Co.; financial publishers, the Economist Group; the National Health Service; and artists and members of Project Phakama.

What did participants say about the 1999 Forum?

'I found it wholly fascinating and a real stretch.'

'I've already horrified people at work by saying "why not?"'

'You have to give yourself experiences that add to the knowledge bank.'

'It made everyone step out of their comfort zone and led me to think differently about the process of change . . . .'

'We really explored the idea of a multicultural company – acknowledging that *everyone* sees things differently.'

'All my assumptions were challenged completely.'

'The valuing of difference, it was a reminder of that.'

'The idea that you can achieve something from nothing . . . and it comes from chaos.'

'Job descriptions and experience went out of the window.'

'It's worth going on a journey with people, rather than trying to convince them.'

What did participants get out of the Forum?

- 99 per cent had their assumptions challenged. (Out of a total of 40 people.)
- 100 per cent met people they would otherwise never have met.
- 100 per cent went to places in the city they would not otherwise have gone.
- 86 per cent had their expectations met or exceeded.
- 6 per cent dropped out (3 people out of 40).
- 50 per cent of arts and 33 per cent of National Health Service participants reported a rise in confidence in what they had to offer to others.
- 86 per cent reported a better understanding of the issues and emotions of working in diverse teams.
- 76 per cent reported improved understanding of how to effect change.
- 96 per cent said they wished to remain in contact.

What tangible results did the Forum inspire in the subsequent three months?

- Departments of the National Health Service and Home Office were brought together to address a particular mental health issue in a joint development programme.
- *The Story I'm About to Tell* (from South Africa) inspired inclusion of a cultural dimension to scenario planning in Kenya.[2]
- One business took a formalized look at the cultural obstacles to change in the company.
- The same company looked more acutely at the reality of running a multicultural business.
- A 'no blame' culture was applied to good effect among members of a youth arts group.
- A plan to develop co-learning links between arts organizations, businesses and communities grew in London's Docklands area.

(All quotations and data from LIFT 1999b)

Extending the discourse – The LIFT
Forum Network begins

So successful was the '99 Forum that a number of participants expressed a desire to continue meeting to exchange insights and working experience, and to delve further into particular questions. I had to decide whether this was something I wished to lead and, with colleagues, decide whether it felt consistent with LIFT's core mission and priorities. An extension of the Forum conversations was consistent with the wider organizational changes under way. It felt right as, by this time, we were beginning to question the historical biennial Festival format. Year-round programming was on the cards. We embarked on devising a Forum programme with our key advisers, led by de Geus, Heinzen, Fairtlough and Handy, the organizational members and colleagues at LIFT.

None of the preparations for the programme happened in a linear way and they took longer than hoped. Fearing my ability to pull it together before running out of funds, I arranged to meet Forum adviser, Fairtlough, and Sally Bibb of the Economist Group. I had calmly come to the view that, unless commitment to fund the Forum from one of the larger companies or government departments could be secured in the following two weeks, then plans to extend the Forum were unsustainable. Fairtlough and Bibb immediately agreed to fund the preparatory phase. The condition was that others contribute in due course.

With this added impetus, plans could begin although the path remained bumpy. Advisers and supporters were frequently not all available for the first meetings, so two had to be arranged. Artists and productions dropped out of the LIFT programme, making our artistic anchors uncertain. Speakers were not available on the date set months earlier with participants, venues were booked up and events intervened. In the midst of these uncertainties, a route map was nevertheless established making the link between LIFT performances and/or questions of potential interest to all participants. On occasions the Forum programme incorporated non-LIFT theatre productions appropriate to the theme in hand.

2000–1 Forum Network

Here is a flavour of the five sessions from the 2000–1 Forum Network programme. All focused on questions raised by Forum members and started from the assumption that insight could be gained from sharing experience across scales and forms of operation. Accounts of sessions were written up from the perspective of a young participant, Daisy Froud (LIFT Archive). Venues were found through Forum members or LIFT's civic networks.

The first session, in February 2000, was *Managing a Web of People with No Headquarters*, a question arising in the 1999 Forum. It took place in the pre-fabricated buildings of Weekend Arts College, a youth arts organization in Kilburn, north London. The session took as its starting point the experience of Project Phakama. Based in different provinces of South Africa and in London, Phakama facilitators were struggling to find equitable ways of communicating that transcended cultural preconceptions, historical language and race dominance and to come up with forms of management to match. Similar issues of communication across differences of geography, culture and technology faced other Forum members operating at very different scale: Tesco, a large retail chain, and Mars Information Services, part of the confectionery company. Speakers Maylene Catchpole of Phakama and Alison Grieve of Mars started the discussion.

In April 2000, Forum members convened at the Royal Court Theatre for a day-long session entitled *Continuity and Succession*. This topic had grown out of a LIFT production called *Departures* devised by artists Maya Krishna Rao, Gavin O'Shea, Abhilash Pillai and Bea Haut. Their starting point was the experience of a forced journey. What do you choose to take with you and what to leave behind? In the life of individuals and organizations, dynamics of continuity and succession were vital to address. It was a question hovering on the horizon at LIFT as the founders began to think about handing on the organization. Discussion after the show between Forum members Gerard Fairtlough and Richard Claughton became the starting point for the Forum session. It was the first time that two Forum members were invited to help shape the session in detail.

The evening before, Forum members attended a non-LIFT theatre performance: *Hard Fruit* by Jim Cartwright at the Royal Court Theatre. This performance and the theatre itself provided the backdrop for the session. Steve Tompkins, architect of the theatre's recent reconstruction, described how the building was 'marinated in history' and how intangible layers had shaped his transformation of a crumbling building into a modern theatre, respecting both continuity and change. The next speaker was James Macdonald, Director of *Hard Fruit*, seen the evening before. The play portrays a group of homosexual men reminiscing about an imagined golden age. The taciturn main character, Choke, is stuck in time, making a deliberate decision to turn his back on the present. The younger men refuse to acknowledge or understand the past or what it has given to them. There is little real communication between the two generations and Choke's refusal to change and lack of communication ends in tragedy.

The experience of continuity and change in a business setting came next. Participants heard how Richard Claughton of the Economist Intelligence Unit (EIU) was navigating through an intense period of change driven by new technologies. He described how, three years earlier, the EIU was an entirely print-based organization. Electronic media brought with it huge possibilities but also huge challenges to old ways of doing things. But the new could only be built on the old. There was a need to articulate the purpose and values of the company to inform the scope and form of future activities.

Fairtlough's story came next. He gave an account of how, when nearing retirement from the company he founded, he anointed his successor in an effort to influence the future of the company. The process of succession did not go well. He did not trust that the recruitment processes he had so carefully put in place for everyone else were applicable in his case. He admitted that this assumption was a hedge against his own mortality and was propelled by the vain idea that he knew best. He commented at the Forum session that 'the human truths of the theatre are more useful in such situations'. This caution would inform LIFT's own processes of succession some three years later.

In May 2000, a session took place in the tower headquarters of LWT: *The Artist as Sense-maker in the New Economy: Global, Wired and Largely Privatised*. Economist Diane Coyle set the scene, describing an economy no longer driven by moving 'lumpy' objects across geography but determined by increasing miniaturization and technological speed, limited only by imagination (Coyle 2001: 40). Bill Sharpe, ex-Director of Hewlett Packard Laboratories and now Director of design company, The Appliance Studio, also spoke of the speed and power of new technologies and the moral choices these present. Artist Sofie Leyton spoke of guiding primary school children in Stoke Newington to make aesthetic sense of the physical environment and history of the neighbourhood in which they lived. She described how the young people's experience informed a production by theatre company Theatre-Rites called *Cellarworks* and some months later was being built on further in *Style of our Lives*, a site-specific and participatory project based around their school. Opinions were aired in the ensuing discussion about the democratic accountability of technology strategy.

In June 2000 Forum members met at Union Chapel, Islington. They were joined in a day-long session by students from Kingsway College to focus on *Harnessing Potential – in Individuals, Organizations and Society*. The day began with a workshop devised by artist Peter Reder and aimed at revealing hidden potential in all involved. Participants brought personal objects to the session and were asked to gather other objects and impressions during an exploration of the neighbourhood surrounding the Chapel. Later in the day Forum member Victoria Ward spoke of how, as Chief Knowledge Officer of County Natwest, she had surfaced implicit knowledge of colleagues through storytelling and the co-creation of a book that came to be known as *The Rough Guide to Knowledge*. The final speaker, Shirley Brice Heath, spoke of the forms of learning needed to make the most of young people's potential in post-industrial societies. When there was no clear path to harnessing potential, she described the need to be continually learning and co-creating meaning across conventional boundaries.

The Business of Invention, in September 2000, was held at brand advisers Wolff Olins in their converted warehouse beside the Regent Canal. Three stories were told over dinner by the following: Bill Colquhoun of Shell Chemicals; Charles Handy, writer and broadcaster; and colleagues Fenton and Neal. Colquhoun had been struggling with how to reinvent his industry in the light of growing awareness of its environmental impact and finite raw materials. He related how difficult at a personal and organizational level it was to invent a new industry from within the old. Charles Handy spoke about the people he had interviewed for the book he had recently published with photographer, Elizabeth Handy. *The New Alchemists* gave an account of the personal motivations and life events that had propelled a group of innovators in business, social and creative enterprise (Handy and Handy 1999). Fenton and Neal gave an account of how they started the Festival and maintained its qualities of invention.

Mentoring

In October a new experiment began, building further on intergenerational connections. One of the LIFT Education Programmes was led by composer, Heiner Goebbels, with students from Guildhall School of Music and Weekend Arts College. LIFT suggested the students might benefit from being linked to Forum members as mentors. The principle was not to offer advice but to be a listening post beyond their institutions and LIFT. A shared workshop initiated the mentoring process followed by a series of conversations. Some of the mentoring relationships worked exceptionally well with exchange of insights and learning for both mentor and mentee. Others did not work at all. On balance, we decided to pursue a group conversation approach in the future.

The Forum sessions during 2000, a non-Festival year, experimented through an extended programme and deeper questioning of topics that had arisen during the previous Forum. It allowed us to test whether mentoring was something that LIFT should be facilitating. In the autumn of 2000 as the cycle came to a close, we met with the advisory team to discuss how to proceed. The occasional meetings based on participants' shared questions were deemed valuable and we were encouraged to build toward the 2001 Festival, gathering new participants on the way. As LIFT's biennial Festival format was left behind and plans laid for productions to be staged more consistently at different times of the year, the extended programme had prepared the Forum for this change of rhythm.

Forum sessions 2001

A first session, *The Business of Culture: the Local as Laboratory for the Global*, took place in January 2001. This coincided with LIFT's first out-of-Festival theatre presentation: Peter Brook's version of South African writer Can Themba's *The Suit*, in Brook's version presented in French and called *Le Costume*. The play is a tragic story of adultery and revenge, pride and lack of forgiveness. Can Themba's original story was first published in the 1950s in *Drum* magazine. Our view was that experience rooted in a particular place had greater lessons internationally than those things that were designed to be international. We had seen how *Death and the Maiden* presented in LIFT '89 had responded to the specifics of life in Chile and went on to become the most produced contemporary play in the world and how *Five Guys Named Moe*, developed through intimate links with audiences in Stratford East, went on to captivate the West End and Broadway.

The session inspired by *Le Costume* provided an opportunity to speak about specific experiences in South Africa; tragedy that transcends individual culture and challenges of working across cultures. Speakers included the South African High Commissioner, Cheryl Carolus; academic and writer, Charles Hampden-Turner; global executive coach, Karen Otazo; Unilever's Ralph Kugler; and LIFT's Lucy Neal. The session was held in the boardroom of Unilever. Discussion over dinner ranged from the injustices of globalization to personal experiences of working life.

The next session, entitled *The Business of Success: How Do You Choose to Measure It?*, was hosted by Forum adviser Paul Askew of SRU Group at two locations in Lincoln's Inn Fields, central London.

It involved around 50 people, some of whom were familiar with Forum sessions, and some of whom were new to it. Charles Handy began the evening at Sir John Soane's Museum, a house left to the public by one of London's great architects and collectors on condition that nothing was changed. The venue was chosen to provide tangible witness to the theme of Handy's talk: what people choose to leave behind them when they die as the ultimate measure of success.

We then moved on to public relations company, Brunswick, a few doors up the street. Over dinner, other speakers described measures of success in the arts, business and educational fields: Helen Alexander of the Economist Group; Tim Suter of QUEST[3]; Vivienne Cox of BP; and Sean Gregory of the Guildhall School of Music. All described the shortcomings of measurement systems applied in their particular field. In the arts world, visitor numbers were inadequate if it meant that a large number of visitors diminished the quality of experience for everyone. In business, the pressure of quarterly figures and short-term assessment of shareholder value was inhibiting the long-term process of change and cramping peoples' imaginations. In the educational field, exam results were frequently an inadequate indicator of future achievement – particularly in the creative arts. There was no ready solution, but a view emerged that the culture of measurement permeating many areas of life inhibited success in other ways.

The LIFT '01 Festival took place in June and July and new people joined the Forum for the Festival period from a range of private and public sector organizations. A group of students from Kingsway College also took part. Theatre director Gregory Thompson guided the Forum experience throughout, including the final session to crystallize what we had seen. After the summer break, a session to reflect on insights gained through the Festival experience was devised by artist Peter Reder. Taking the form of an installation in LIFT's rehearsal room in Clerkenwell, this session was called *Memento* and took people on a promenade through Peter's memories and impressions of the Festival and conversations he had had along the way. He memorably devised a 'Power Pointless' presentation depicting the number of tears he had shed at certain performances or the number of chips he had consumed on the way home.

One Forum participant, X, spoke of how he had truly understood, having seen *Voices*, a performance by Jeroen Willems of Dutch theatre company Hollandia, that *everyone* sees things differently. The performance was a devastating critique of power and morality. Willems transformed himself into five different characters, all 'pillars of society' around the remains of a dinner party. He laid bare the nature of corporate control and corruption through the writings of Italian iconoclast Pier Paolo Pasolini juxtaposed with archive speeches by Cor Herkstroter, Chairman of Royal Dutch Shell.

This Forum participant's work challenge at the time, as a civil servant was how to build consensus on pensions policy between civil servants and politicians. Two weeks before *Memento*, LIFT invited him to write up this challenge as a fairy story. Another Forum experiment in addressing challenges faced by individual participants, the tale provided the practical starting point for collective reflection. Each small group performed different versions of the tale. Some months later we heard that the session had provided a breakthrough for our Forum colleague to find a different approach to his work. Rather than striving to have a hard and fast solution at the ready, he sought to bring people together to build consensus across conventional lines.

Description of some of the Forum sessions gives an idea of how they were devised and the range of speakers and venues involved. We tried different session lengths from twilight discussions with a meal to day-long sessions; to creative workshops; to mentoring across generations; and to taking prompts from participants and calling on them to help devise the sessions. In September 2001 it was time to take stock.

September 2001 – a programme negotiated between all parties

As we met with advisers, the events of that month shaped our conversation and came to inform how we devised the next phase. There was much concern about slippery and bellicose language being used in the media. A need was felt to focus on language for the next phase of the Forum beginning in early 2002.

But before that, in October 2001 we were to present to the public *The Theft of Sita*, a collaboration of traditional Balinese Wayang Kulit shadow puppeteers and gamelan musicians, with Australian jazz musicians and British theatre designers. The show explored the relationship between tradition and modernity, exposing, among other issues, the pillaging of natural resources to serve the tourist industry in Bali.

This production was the starting point for a Forum session called *Sustainability: Balancing Organizational Values and Personal Beliefs*. This session explored how individuals frequently might wish to change working practice but are shackled by the sluggishness of their organizations, a lack of markets for more sustainable products or bad internal communication. When the gap between organizational values and personal beliefs becomes too great, the only choice is to take a personal risk: to face the truth or jump ship.

The ability to forge truthful language across professional disciplines and across cultures was seen as critical. This insight, together with concerns about language in the wider political and cultural context provided the stimulus for the next phase of the Business Arts Forum.

2002/3 programme: *An Exploration of Authenticity in Language, Work and Community*

The following list gives an idea of the programme sessions and performances they followed, the topics, venues and facilitators. Space allows for summaries only.

Language and Metaphor: How it Shapes our Actions and Views of Others

Performance: *The Mysteries*, adaptation directed by Mark Dornford-May at Lyric Theatre
Session venue: Soho Theatre
Facilitator: Fabio Santos

The Culture of Innovation: How Do You Keep it Going over Time?

Performance: *To you, the birdie!* Adaptation of Racine's Phèdre by
the Wooster Group at Riverside Studios
Session venue: Sadler's Wells
Facilitators: Wesley Enoch and Barbara Heinzen

Community: What Is it for You Now?
How Do We Plant a 1000 Year Old Tree?

An event for family and friends from an idea by Wesley Enoch
Session venue: National Children's Home
Facilitators: Forum Members, Jonathan Ives, Andrew Siddall, Sean
Gregory, Julian West, Cloth of Gold printmakers

Sensing for When to Say 'No' or 'Yes'

Performances in LIFT's Landscape of Childhood Season at various
venues
Session venue: National Children's Home
Facilitator: Mark Storer

Creative Conversation with Students from Lewisham College

Session venue: The Place Theatre
Led by Çaglar Kimyoncu

I Wanna Be Leader. . . . OK What Shall We Do?[4]

Performance: *Midnight's Children* at Barbican Centre
Session venue: Lewisham College
Facilitator: Thierry Lawson

Creative Conversation

BBC Digilab
Led by Euan Semple
With students from Lewisham College.

What Does 'Sustainability' Look Like?

Performances in LIFT's Family Friendly Season and Lecture by
Dr Vandana Shiva at various venues
Session venue: Royal Botanical Gardens, Kew
Facilitators: Barbara Heinzen and Jan Hendrickse

1000 Year Trees Planted

Venues: Southwark Park, London and Brisbane Australia
Ceremony with Young Friends of Southwark Park and Project
Phakama members
Facilitator: Fabio Santos, Phakama youth members and facilitators,
Reuben Hawkwood and Nick Lane

Session to prepare Lewisham Students for 2004 Forum

Performance: *Urban Afro-Saxons* by Talawa Theatre at Theatre
Royal Stratford East
Session venue: Lewisham College
Facilitators: Tony Fegan and Tim French

2004 programme: *Learning to Lead Through Relationships*

Overall creative direction: Gregory Thompson
Introductory session: *Who is 'we'?*
Venue: Toynbee Hall, E1
Facilitators: Gregory Thompson and Jan Fullerlove.

Global and Local Neighbours: Discomfort and Possibility

Performance: preceding *Tragedia Endogonidia* by Societas Raffaello
Sanzio at Laban Centre
Session venues: 999 Club and Laban Centre
Facilitators: Gregory Thompson and Gillian Clarke

Performances in 04 Enquiry season including *Tragedia Endogonidia
Episode IX*, Societas Raffaello Sanzio (Italy), Enquirer performances,
the Atlas Group (Beirut), Lecture by Lawrence Lessig, *Theatre of
Fire* by Groupe F.

Follow-up sessions:

What Did You See? What Did You Learn about
Yourself and Others?

Venue: Dragon Trust Hall, London WC2
Facilitator: Gregory Thompson

What Would You Do Differently in Your Work as a Result?
Tragedy or Comedy?

Venue: The Work Foundation, London SW1
Facilitator: Gregory Thompson

Conversations beyond the Forum

A number of Forum members tried to keep conversations going independently of LIFT but admitted that they found it difficult to sustain momentum without the shared structure of the Forum. Without participation in a joint, creative experiment and conversation, connections proved difficult to maintain. An online chat group was set up for Forum members, but in common with many such attempts, participants did not use it.[5] People seemed to need face-to-face encounter with the additional social and aesthetic frame provided by performances and Forum. The form of iterative encounter we had evolved was said to hold 'an authenticity difficult to find elsewhere'.[6]

The LIFT Teacher Forum

In the working world of schools, the demands of the National Curriculum and reduction in time allocated to the arts in the school week was stifling both students' access to arts teaching and the creativity of teachers. LIFT's response was to set up its first Teacher Forum in 1999, an experimental continuing professional development course for teachers and artists.

A programme of practice-based reflective learning, each year-long Teacher Forum cycle involved a residential weekend induction, exploration of teachers' and artists' own learning, motivation and values, observations of teacher and artist in the workplace and, as in the Business Arts Forum, reflection on the shared experience of LIFT shows and debates. By 2001/2, the Teacher Forum achieved accreditation towards the Advanced Diploma of Professional Studies from London University's Institute of Education. It also led to the development of arts projects within the schools of participating teachers.

Teacher Forum and Business Arts Forum share an evening

The practical workings of the Business Arts Forum contributed to thinking through aspects of how the Teacher Forum might work, particularly in the area of recruitment and how teachers would connect to LIFT performances. In turn, the Education Programme and Teacher Forum's findings about a methodology of shared learning between artists, teachers and communities came to inform how the Business Arts Forum could evolve forms of learning across conventional work, generation and social boundaries. Artists who had taken part in the Teacher Forum and other LIFT Education Programmes sometimes joined the Business Arts Forum and vice versa.

On occasions, although operating with different timetables, it made sense to bring the two groups together. Both groups attended Declan Donnellan's production of *Boris Godunov* by Pushkin, at Riverside Studios, Hammersmith. Donnellan was invited to speak to the LIFT groups before the performance. He described his fascination for one of Russia's best-loved epics and how he saw the play as a dissection of power and identity. The show was produced with 18 members of Moscow's leading theatre companies.[7]

Donnellan reminded the LIFT groups assembled on the terrace of the Riverside Studios that

> it's quite good to think that our identities are constructs that we believe in, like I believe that I am a theatre director, you believe whatever it is that you do. In fact, this really isn't the truth. Our identities . . . are completely provisional.
>
> (Donnellan 2001)

Donnellan cautioned that identities very soon become institutions with preservation of self as their sole objective. Institutions are an attempt to achieve certainty but, in that effort, too often take over and kill the things they were instituted for in the first place. To forget this is fatal. Donnellan called for 'the institution to take a permanent cold shower'.

Boris Godunov was presented in 2001. The rumblings of change at LIFT had begun two years earlier. The Festival had been submitting itself to a prolonged cold shower and was in the midst of its own institutional revolution. The Teacher and Business Arts Fora had as their context this far-reaching institutional revision.

The Festival itself changes form[8]

In spite of the Festival's success, in 1999 both the LIFT Board and staff acknowledged that there was a need for radical change. LIFT could not sit on its laurels. After almost 20 years of the Festival's existence, the landscape of theatre in London was opening up. Visits of international theatre and pioneering site-specific performances were more regularly visible. The Barbican Centre had embarked on a large-scale international programme with a budget far in excess of any LIFT could hope for. At the same time, LIFT sensed that the biennial theatre festival format restricted voyages of discovery around the nature of theatre and its transformative potential. It limited continuous and long-term collaboration with artists and audiences and the probing of more fundamental questions about theatre's role in society. In June 2000, Neal and Fenton realized that the LIFT format itself needed to be rethought if these questions were to make headway.

LIFT Strategy Review

Discussions and reflection within LIFT led to a formal Strategy Review and fundamental organizational renewal co-ordinated by Administrative Producer, Angela McSherry. Three key advisers to the Business Arts Forum undertook the Review: Heinzen, De Geus and Fairtlough, all experienced strategic planners. Consultations with staff, Board members, London's leading performance venues and arts colleagues followed. LIFT asked artists, academics and theatre programmers to join the debate about its future role and format.

During these discussions, the need to explore the boundaries of what theatre is and can be today came to shape LIFT's future direction. The decision was made to initiate a five-year Public Enquiry from 2001 to 2006.

The Enquiry is structured along three pathways, Performance, Learning and Evidence, each revealing to the public LIFT's different areas of work and the people LIFT engages. This format also opens the door to new collaborators. The Enquiry is a process operating through ever-widening circles of conversation.

Once again, LIFT started out on a path not knowing where it would lead. A number of questions guide the process: What can theatre be? Where can it take place? Who can be involved? Does theatre have a transformative power? What meaning can theatre have? Who is it for? Why? And how? Starting by not knowing allows points of entry for wider participation and new voices to be heard.

Performance

Performance is at the centre. This pathway embraces the presentation, production and commissioning of seasons and one-off performances of artists' work from Britain and around the world. LIFT encourages and supports artists to take their own experimentation, collaboration or research a step further than may have previously been possible, and finds ways to connect audiences with the ideas behind each performance.

Learning

If the LIFT Enquiry looks at the question 'What is theatre?' the Learning pathway asks: 'Who can be involved in making theatre? And what can be learnt in the process?' LIFT Learning invites all participants to draw on their imagination, creativity and experience in a process of reflection and action with others, valuing the contribution of each individual.

LIFT Learning includes activities such as Project Phakama, the LIFT Teacher Forum and Business Arts Forum, each involving participants of different ages, professions and cultural backgrounds. These programmes are autonomous with their own timetables and entry points for members. They are linked wherever possible. Other learning projects emerge from individual artists, productions or youth groups.

Evidence

The Evidence pathway is a completely new departure for LIFT, exploring the question of how theatre is received. It asks the question 'When the play ends, what begins?'[9] Artists, anthropologists, scientists and academics are asked to bear witness to the phenomenon of theatre, tracing the shifts of perception among artists and audiences, bringing their particular expertise and perspective to an investigation into the evidence of theatre and the traces it leaves.

As shown in Figure 10.1, three strands of Performance, Learning and Evidence are in continual interaction, responding and adapting to the external world and the internal worlds of artists and audiences. Like the double helix of DNA, the LIFT Enquiry is structured as a triple helix, opening up the conventional forms of Festival organization to a greater number of voices and imaginations: 'So, after 20 years, LIFT is dead. Long live LIFT!' (Robert Hewison, *Sunday Times*, 2001).

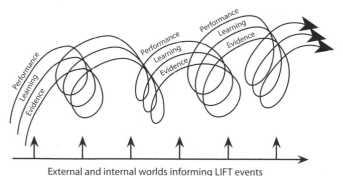

External and internal worlds informing LIFT events

Figure 10.1 Shape of the LIFT Enquiry

2004: the mid-point of the LIFT Enquiry

LIFT '04 marked the mid-point of LIFT's five-year Enquiry, staging year-round a public exploration of theatre worldwide: theatre as ritual, theatre as fire, theatre as ceremony, theatre as trespass, theatre as community and theatre simply as storytelling from the heart. One hundred people, over 50 days, were invited to tell others what theatre was to them.[10] As described by Angad Chowdhry, anthropologist and LIFT Enquirer:

> This is where the real strength of LIFT lies, in its capacity to restore and rescue from the fossilised grip of cultural common sense, everything that is held, reminding us of its event-ness. This restoration, this articulation as event, this call for celebration, is always a surprise.
>
> (LIFT 2005)

And what of the Forum?

Prior to the 2001 Festival Kate Owen, Head of Organizational Development at BP, approached LIFT to discuss formal participation in the Forum. I met Owen at a lunch organized by Charles and Elizabeth Handy seven years earlier when making steps towards changing LIFT's relations with business. Owen acknowledged an interest in the ideas we were exploring but at that time saw no place for them in the company. Seven years later, in early 2001, the world had changed and Owen felt different conversations were needed. She and her colleagues recognized that, if the company was to think about its future beyond oil, then a younger generation of leaders needed to embark on completely new forms of engagement and conversation from the ones their predecessors were used to having. If the company is to survive, then this will involve fundamental structural change never before experienced, either by the company or wider society. Different qualities of leadership and an ability to engage with and learn from people working in different spheres were required. Indeed, it was these concerns that Vivienne Cox of BP had touched on at the Forum session *The Business of Success:*

How Do We Choose to Measure It? Owen and colleague Ronnie Forbes took part in the 2001 Business Arts Forum. The creative and boundary-spanning conversations facilitated by LIFT held the open and imaginative qualities of shared learning sought by Owen and she agreed to resource the next phase of the Forum.

A meeting with advisers was set in September 2001 to devise the programme for the coming year. Cathy Dunn, a colleague of Owen in the Leadership Development department, was assigned to liaise with LIFT. Dunn invited other BP staff to take part in the Forum and join advisory sessions, from departments such as Strategy, Downstream Services and Diversity and Inclusion. During the September session, following discussion with key advisers in other sectors, we settled on the subject of authenticity of language as the focus for our own Forum Enquiry the ensuing year.

In taking the Forum forward, we attempt to move it towards a more self-organizing process in which regular participants take greater creative and curriculum responsibility for themselves and others. Whereas in the early years we faced more towards the businesses paying for the Forum, in later years we turned our gaze towards a space of public creative engagement in which business is just one participant alongside others. The focus is on ideas that transcend any one sector's direct self-interest, making for a new space of civic discourse and public collaboration, one that is resourced according to financial ability.

Box 10.1 The Forum process emerges from negotiation

1   Education, business and public sector participants and supporters are invited to meet to plan for the next and subsequent sessions. Urgent questions of common interest are elicited. The learning needs of everyone are borne in mind with a particular emphasis on those of young people.

2   LIFT internal discussions take place to establish a timetable and connections to the LIFT programme or

> other interesting theatre productions. Participants' questions from previous discussions are kept in mind.
> 3 An artist or arts educator to lead the next session or multiple sessions is then identified and briefed. Discussion with advisers and key participants is held to verify that we are going in the right direction. Speakers are identified and invited.
> 4 Venues are booked, appropriate to each session, and catering organized.
> 5 Forum participants and artist facilitator attend theatre performances, followed by the Forum session a few days later.
> 6 The session is written up, and initial reflections recorded.

How the money worked

During the period from 1995 to 2004 there were 32 seminars or day-long meetings involving a total of 195 people who attended 59 performances.

Income to LIFT above costs during this period was approximately £90,700. Fees for participants were on a sliding scale and ranged from £750 for business members in the first year to £2,000 in 2001. After 1997, greater investment was needed in the development and recruitment phase hence the larger company members and government departments were asked to invest from £5,000 to £20,000. These fees, once secured, enabled plans to be laid without exposing LIFT to financial risk: to commission creative facilitators, and book performances, workshop venues and catering, etc.

In 1999 we introduced a bursary for artists taking part. This programme offered professional development for artists too. The bursary was to acknowledge the differences between income levels in the group. Most artists are paid on a freelance basis and, if offers of paid work clashed with Forum sessions, they had a difficult choice. Such opportunities for professional development were rare and needed resourcing.[11]

Income to LIFT above costs was £3,247 in 1995; £10,946 in 1997. Income above costs for the two-year periods 1999/2001 and 2002/4 was £46,517 and £30,000 respectively.

This is an example of how the budget worked: there are 40 participants in the Forum from business, public sector, the arts and students from a central London college. Funds of £31,000 were secured at the beginning of the planning cycle, enabling the project to proceed and for LIFT's financial risk to be covered. This sum comes from a mix of private and public funding sources. For example: £15,000 from BP; £6,000 from Masterfoods; and bursaries for artists and a creative direction fee to a total of £10,000. Recruitment of other participants can then proceed. This generated at least an additional £8,000 in participant fees from public sector organizations such as the BBC, the Department of Health, the British Council, and the Qualifications and Curriculum Authority. An additional £15,000 was secured through a government scheme that matches funds to the arts from new areas of commercial activity[12]. Costs of running the Forum for one year are approximately £24,000. Thus the total income to the artistic programme of LIFT is, in this example, £30,000. Two tickets to four shows plus catering costs are included in participants' fees.

Financial certitude or act of faith?

To make the Forum work, paradoxically, we have to be prepared to give it up altogether. Every year we go back to the drawing board and say, 'Why are we doing this? Is it in tune with our core purpose? Who thinks it is worthwhile? How shall we proceed?' The cycle may begin again or it may not. But it is this avoidance of rigid codification that ensures the Forum's continuing authenticity and paradoxically lends it greater certainty. In the months at the end of each cycle, while we decided how to proceed, my work was resourced by LIFT, paid for from the previous cycle's surplus or sometimes undertaken speculatively until funds were found.

Discovery of new routes to funding the business of theatre echo a truth revealed by economist John Kay about other professions. Success is determined by constant attention to renewal of practice:

We live in a complex world which we only imperfectly understand. Our success in it depends crucially on our relationships with other people. In this environment, what has evolved will often outperform what has been designed, and purely instrumental motivation will often fail in its objectives. This gives rise to the paradox of obliquity whereby [in a study of the fishing industry] the crew which values the practice of fishing is more financially successful than the crew which is organised in pursuit of financial goals.

(Kay 2003: 350)

A new space for theatre

The Forum evolved to become a social and creative laboratory in which to engage in repeated collective imagining with fellow citizens, and, from these encounters, to re-imagine one's working role.

Through the experience of theatre, participants were moved to respond at a personal level beyond their professional categories, thereby given a starting point for communication across gender, culture and stage of life. In a context of structural change where the rules of engagement are impossible to discern, the only answer is to experiment in laboratories of intimate, manageable scale. Although we started out with an idea that we might be teaching business something from the arts, we came to understand that what we were doing was offering participants an opportunity to 'think through theatre in an age of globalization' (Bharucha 2001), which is subtly different and restores the theatre, in its relations with business, to a place of critique and reflection. This differed from other courses on offer in the crowded market of leadership and management development. It was through engagement with the theatre that a dimension of civic discourse was renewed.

While it was important to secure accreditation for teachers participating in the Teacher Forum, validation of the Business Arts Forum by an external authority was not seen as appropriate. There were two main reasons for this. First, I had in the back of my mind the comment of a business participant in the Paired Youth Adult Scheme in New York. She had cautioned us not to make any programme we evolved part of a formalized management development programme. Such schemes lose their authenticity if compulsion or deliberate career advancement is the motivation for taking part. In the context of the Business Arts Forum there was something wrong with being formally patted on the head for having a conversation with your neighbours. The rewards for such engagement are profoundly personal and cannot be prescribed by others.

The second reason that we avoided packaging and codifying the Forum was that it simply was ineffective in engaging participants. We tried several times to sell the Forum through producing a printed leaflet that we could mail out. This approach was largely a failure. In the end, each and every participant in the Forum got involved with LIFT through a personal conversation either with me, one of the advisers or facilitators, or one of the existing participants. I came to realize that this was no coincidence and was in fact consistent with the starting point for the Forum, i.e. that it had set out to question a directly commercial approach to business–arts relations. If a better conversation was to ensue, then it followed that any initial connection had to be through conversation rather than advertisement. This is detailed and long-term work but in reality no different from that of securing sponsorship via more conventional channels. We discovered the most productive route to engaging people from large organizations was to ensure that a link person was involved in the planning sessions and thus able to liaise with colleagues and a wider group within any individual organization. Indeed this shared ownership across organizations and sectors was the key.

Success in our efforts pointed towards a new place of engagement for the theatre to facilitate between business, government, formal and informal education, a space of creative, cultural and civic engagement over time.

Nevertheless, as the behaviour of multinational corporations and the complexities and assaults of globalization began to fracture cultural relations worldwide, LIFT felt compelled to add a further dimension to its questioning of relations between commerce and culture. These explorations prompted initiation of a lecture series. As a dimension of the LIFT Enquiry, the lectures set out to gain specialist knowledge of particular collisions between commerce and culture and to assess what the role of theatre might be as a place of engagement at these intersections.

ELEVEN

OVERSTEPPING THE MARKET

The spirit of interdependence binds culture and community until greed, commerce, and utilitarianism intrude. Then culture becomes commodity and community yet another market.

(Heath 2005)

The sponsors of LIFT's inaugural Education Programme claimed that the sponsorship had not represented 'value for money'. We had endeavoured to promote the sponsorship as agreed in the contract. The complexities of this effort exposed the limits of a marketing approach when applied to non-market issues, namely fostering the imaginations of young people and opening channels of communication across cultures in contemporary Britain. As the power of technology and effects of globalization grew through the 1990s, evidence accumulated of the limits of a market approach to other areas of common life.

Between then and today many commentators, including Beck, Klein, Stiglitz, Sen, Monbiot, Roy and Geldof, together with activists and popular movements, have responded to economic and social injustices of the late twentieth and early twenty-first centuries. LIFT too was compelled to gather evidence as to the growing primacy of the economic directly affecting LIFT artists public space for theatre's expression, or free cultural exchange.

Privatization of public space

As far back as 1989, a production staged at Broadgate, a large office development in the city, proved to be a barometer of the changing balance of public and private ownership in London.

The developers of Broadgate,[1] well-known patrons of the arts, understood that without animation the spaces between the new buildings could become soulless. They installed contemporary sculptures and an ice-rink in the style of New York's Rockefeller Center. A summer arts programme was introduced. A contemporary note was sought to convey the cosmopolitan character of the global commercial activities in the buildings around. Perceived by workers in the offices and members of the public as public space, this space was a key factor in the development gaining planning permission. LIFT was invited to present *Roman-Photo Tournage* by French spectacularists Royal de Luxe, depicting a zany photo-romance make-believe film played out for real with blood and tears, car chases a go-go, sound effects and music to match.

Once reassured the mock blood would not stain the white marble and (importantly as it turned out) that noise levels were acceptable, Broadgate managers welcomed the presentation and the attraction it offered for the public to visit the new space. At the first performance, people crowded on to every available inch of the balconies surrounding the arena, some travelling from out of London to gain a glimpse of French creative flair. Diplomatic officials and London's civic dignitaries attended this important aspect of Franco-British cultural relations that summer. The show lasted 50 minutes. The audience loved it. A second performance was to take place the following lunchtime.

That afternoon, the rumblings began. Bankers in top-floor dining rooms surrounding the public arena did not like the noise and insisted on cancellation. We remonstrated, we cajoled, we protested, arguing that it was 50 minutes out of 2 days in the year. The bankers ruled the day. After all, the logic went: they were paying a percentage of the management costs of the public space that subsidized the arts programme and thus use of the space was their deal to call. Although their employees had appreciated the first performance, their enjoyment did not enter the argument. It proved that this space had only limited public qualities. In reality, it was private and in the hands of a few powerful people who were not even fully aware of the impact of their decisions.

In the 1980s, widespread changes to the management of public space, often declining under local authority management, swept through the UK. A radio programme cataloguing privatization of the public realm reported that towns across Britain were falling into private hands that increasingly controlled what could and could not happen there (BBC 1994). For example, no preaching, selling of Women's Institute jam or attempts to canvass opinion other than on market issues was allowed in Basingstoke city centre's shopping area. In Luton it was decreed that older people should be discouraged from sitting on the benches. They were said to detract from a consumer ambience. These towns had given away control of their public space and thus the varied range of interactions possible. The cost was invisible in the thrust for greater efficiency and wide-ranging reductions in the local authority's responsibilities.

The importance of such spaces goes well beyond their visible public function. The centre of any community, public spaces provide places of deliberate and chance encounter, negotiation, celebration, ritual, protest, play, display and experiment. They are also part of a city people's intimate life with parks and open spaces being important components in building and maintaining identity, in marking major moments in the development of friendships, responsibility and collective self-respect (Bianchini and Landry 1995). Public space in cities is always in short supply, heavily contested and set about with rules. Common land and the village green never existed without rules either. Nevertheless, when enclosed by single interests, neglected by those with resources or colonized for single use, diversity and common usage of public space go too, together with the fine texture of human relationships for which they provide the context.

Extensive privatization, corporate scandal, and environmental and human rights violations contributed to deepening suspicion or outrage at business behaviour worldwide. Artists expressed their views.

In LIFT '95, Neelam Chowdhry and The Company from Chandigarh in Punjab, presented *The Madwoman of our City*[2] in response to the world's worst industrial disaster, the explosion of Union Carbide's factory in Bhopal. Chowdhry's production set in India depicted a power-crazed businessman finding gold beneath a city and his determination to blow up the buildings and reap the profits. The play was a comic fantasy about a world where dreamers not money-makers have the upper hand and a mad woman turns out to be more than a match for even the largest corporation.

Performances of *Things Fall Apart* presented in LIFT '97 had as their backdrop contemporary Nigeria, falling apart under Abacha's military regime and the environmental degradations of the oil industry. The execution of writer and activist, Ken Saro-Wiwa, brought business's relations with wider society into sharp focus for artists, producers and audiences.

As globalization bit and the growing speed of communications redrew boundaries in ways we could barely grasp, other artists reflected on these seismic shifts.

In LIFT '01, Australian and Balinese artists portrayed the aggregate effects of the tourist industry in *The Theft of Sita*. Such was the demand for white-water rafting in Bali that resources for irrigation were diverted from farmers' fields to local rapids ensuring these were high enough to fulfil the desires of holidaymakers.

Performance companies **moti**roti, based in London, and the Builders' Association from New York, together with artists from India, explored global connections and cultural confusions in their show and associated web site, *Alladeen*.[3] A dimension of the show is based on interviews with call-centre operators in Bangalore where many young Indian graduates manage the supermarket shopping, debt collection, transcription of doctors' notes, car hire, airline ticketing and loan selling for callers from Europe and the US.

I set out to visit Bangalore, said to be the fastest growing city in India, to witness for myself this aspect of globalization. My path was smoothed by earlier connections forged by **moti**roti.[4] In contrast to such centres in Britain, it is now well publicized that staff in India take on American or UK aliases so that people they are calling in downtown Detroit or the suburbs of Leeds never guess that they are talking to someone in India. Call operators switch fluently and easily from their Indian identities into their American aliases, displaying mastery of American accents and knowledge of current television soaps and the weather Stateside. Once on line they are discouraged from revealing their true location. Prejudice demands they disguise their true identity. Trainees receive rigorous phonetic induction to perfect their accents and are said to suffer from 'mother tongue interference' when this training is incomplete. Time zone differences require night-time working with adverse effects on health, family and social life.

While economists and business people simply say that the work has gone to the location charging the most favourable fees, cultural and political commentators say relocation of call centres to India is simply crass exploitation of the 'third' by the 'first' world with racism driving the need for disguise of true identity and location.

Neither completely tally with the sophisticated atmosphere and vitality of the company I visited. There was good career progression in the company and a seemingly infinite expansion of their business. Without this possibility of work at home, graduates were faced with having to work abroad.

What struck me far more strongly was an image from Beaumarchais' biting satire of pre-Revolutionary France, *The Marriage of Figaro*. This savage portrayal of the *Ancien Régime* depicted the aristocracy as isolated, unable to complete basic tasks for themselves or even to communicate with one other. Figaro and Susanna do all the work and know every intimate detail of the lives of their masters, the licentious Count and depressed Countess of Almaviva. Duke Almaviva relied on Figaro for all his practical requirements. Likewise, more and more intimate information about customers in the West is held in call centres half a world away. Call operators were in command of the information and knew very well what part they were playing. Customers making the calls were the ones living without all the facts.

International artists arriving as LIFT's guests in Britain come from parts of the world often affected by corporate behaviour overlaying a history of European colonialism. LIFT cannot ignore the tensions and dilemmas this provokes in shaping principles of

cultural practice. Evidence was mounting that the inequities of globalization were driving an insuperable wedge between peoples. In the
words of Stuart Hall, cultural critic: 'The impulse of 'difference'
operating in and across the world is as powerful and as unintended
a consequence of capitalist globalisation and modernity as the
impulse towards the McDonaldsisation of the world' (Hall and
Maharaj 2001: 21).

Businesses are increasingly forced by a rising tide of public
opinion to reflect on cultural questions and on the long-term nature
of their corporate responsibilities and relations to wider society,
including principles of fair trade and social justice. Many businesses
are picking up on local cultures as the source of inspiration for
widening the product range to match market preferences. But this
is culture as consumer choice. How do individuals think about how
business and culture can meet for deeper discussion?

When thinking about this, I found helpful a simple diagram by
scenario planner, Kees van der Heijden, depicting business's relation with society as the generic business idea.

We see in Figure 11.1 how entrepreneurial invention comes
from understanding evolving needs in society, leading to a business's distinctive competencies and in turn to results and additional
resources with which to invest in further invention. It goes without
saying that the impulse of 'understanding evolving needs in society'
is not straightforward. The needs of society are so great and various
that choices have to be made – particularly in societies already saturated with goods – and 'evolving needs' are too easy to invent and
exploit. On what basis are those choices made? How does one learn
about the choices to *be* made? And 'society', who is included in
society, who excluded, and who chooses? With what values are those
choices made?

Figure 11.1, drafted in the early to mid-1990s, suggests a purely
observational stance on the part of business. Like a butterfly, society
is there to be caught, dissected, assessed and analysed by the collec-
tor setting out with a net and magnifying glass. It is as though the
person doing the observing is not a member of the society observed.
Perhaps in a slow-moving world this stance was sufficient, but not
any longer. The economy is not out there, to be observed. According

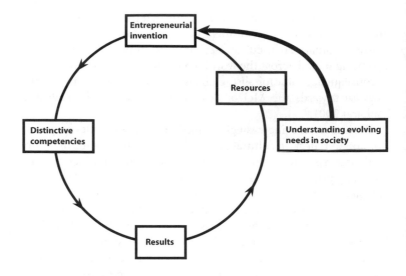

Figure 11.1 The generic business idea

Source: reproduced courtesy of Kees van der Heijden

to economist Coyle: 'Growth is in a sense, more or less what we imagine it to be' (Coyle 1997: 218).

In this context, it is as well to bear in mind: 'In dreams begins responsibility' (Yeats 1914). What is more, Indian bio-activist Dr Vandana Shiva would point out to us that the idea of a post-industrial society is a lie. Polluting heavy industry still exists, it is just relocated to somewhere out of sight in the South (Shiva, LIFT lecture).

What is the social responsibility of business or indeed each one of us in these circumstances? Is it doling out charity to communities, or does it become a responsibility to reflect on one's own dreaming and constantly to question the relationship between observer and observed, giver and receiver, buyer and seller? Making responsible consumer or strategic choices in the so-called 'weight-less' post-industrial economies of the West is like wrestling with cobwebs. An ability to answer these questions satisfactorily and to build this long-term questioning into the generation of business ideas and consumer choice will determine, not the responsibility, but the *viability* of business in society, indeed of society itself.

We began to speculate about the role LIFT might play in addressing such issues more directly in the context of the LIFT Enquiry and alongside the Business Arts Forum. The sense of injustice demanded a position be taken. In the words of writer Arundhati Roy, conditions in relation to the inequities and iniquities of business today call for 'an art which can make the impalpable palpable, the intangible tangible, the invisible visible, the inevitable evitable. An art that can draw out the incorporeal adversary and make it real. Bring it to book' (Roy 2002: 215).

Platform, a UK-based interdisciplinary group of artists, economists, social scientists and environmental activists, had been commissioned to present *Homeland* in LIFT '93. Through the history of a common light bulb, Platform investigated Londoners' direct links to producers through international trade systems, identifying sources of sand for glass, copper for fuse wire and so on. The geography of production and consumption were made visible, links made to our own daily lives. Platform's long-term enquiry into the culture and impact of transnational corporations, with particular reference to the oil industry, was documented through projects, performances and events such as *Killing Us Softly* and *90% Crude*. *Unravelling the Carbon Web*, a detailed study of the nature of multinational corporations, revealed organizational boundaries so diffuse and multiple that changes of direction demanded consideration by every citizen as to their own role and responsibility in the picture.

The question for LIFT was how to go about making sense of the diverse, wide-ranging and enormous questions posed by the contemporary relationship of business to the arts and wider society. We felt this had something to do with a re-assertion of the traditional public space of the theatre: a cultural commons on which to bring together players from both the commercial and arts worlds to reflect on dreams and responsibilities.

A way needed to be found to bring the cultural and commercial worlds together in a non-competitive way, opening up a wide horizon to which both worlds would need to respond. Indirectly and sometimes directly, we had been addressing such issues in the Forum. Some few members of the Business Arts Forum had been frustrated by the reluctance of colleagues to make the long-term commitment needed for participation. They were convinced that colleagues should be having similar conversations and looking at horizons beyond their in-trays. A shorter and more conventional provocation through a public lecture series alongside the Forum would be a way of bringing business, artists, policy-makers and public together to stimulate debate and discussion across conventional lines.

Research for how we might go about devising the lecture series led me to public-interest activist David Bollier, who reminded me of an English folk poem still powerful in its lessons:

> They hang the man and flog the woman
> That steal the goose from off the common,
> But let the greater villain loose
> That steals the common from the goose . . .
> . . .
> The law locks up the man or woman
> Who steals the goose from off the common,
> And geese will still a common lack,
> Til they go and steal it back.
>
> (Folk poem c.1764)

The benefits of goods held in common result from 'a distinct community, managing a resource through specific rules and traditions' (Bollier 2002). This raised the question of how, when goods held in common are now global in scope and inevitably defined by processes of intercultural engagement and negotiation, is a distinct community to be forged both globally and locally? What forms might these cultural commons take in relation to the all-pervading thrust of the market and how are specific rules and traditions to be imagined and established? Does theatre and face-to-face encounter have a role? What role might such intimate interaction have in stealing back the commons?

In 2003, LIFT initiated *Imagining a Cultural Commons*, a series of lectures with speakers chosen who were making practical and imaginative responses to the contemporary excesses of business, or in some way illuminating the key role in social adaptation of the free exchange of culture.

Lectures were deliberately and specifically promoted to audiences from public, private and arts sectors. Topics included the privatization of genetic material and water, developments in copyright and the role of culture in enabling us to move beyond oil. Recognizing that the lecture series brought to the fore constitutional and human rights issues, LIFT asked advocate of the theatre and South African constitutional lawyer Albie Sachs to act as a guide.

Prior to each lecture, groups with specialist knowledge in each field were invited to help LIFT prepare the speaker's brief, frame questions and ensure news of the forthcoming visit reached potential audiences. Funding for the first lecture was provided by Counterpoint, the British Council's cultural relations think tank. Subsequent lectures were sponsored by bankers Morgan Stanley, provoking discussion between colleagues, clients, artists, policymakers and academics. The GLA supported our investigation of the link between culture and alternative energy.

Physicist and bio-activist, Dr Vandana Shiva, gave the first lecture in the central hall of the Natural History Museum. Entitled *Biodiversity, Cultural Diversity and Celebration: Intimate Links and Matters of Survival*, the lecture formed part of the LIFT May '03 Family Friendly season of performance for young audiences and their families.

In her lecture, Shiva described how seed is under threat of private ownership and how multinational monopoly regimes are undermining biodiversity and thus resilience of crops and communities in India. Interrupting her job as a physicist, her response had been to take action and initiate a seed bank and seed-sharing scheme across India. Shiva brought to life the inseparable link between culture and agriculture as embodied in the traditional celebrations of Chattishgarh where there are approximately 200,000 varieties of rice grown, each with its own special qualities. Knowledge of plant and animal diversity is inseparable from culture and memory of specific life forms passed down the generations, their properties and adaptation to specific places. Shiva described how every farmer's family brings its rice to the local divinity, mixing the seed to perform a ritual symbolizing the year, planting, sowing, ploughing, harvesting. At every step, the powers of nature are invoked and in exchange commitment is made to act rightly, not damaging the earth or denying neighbours their rights. This celebration is an annual reassertion of seed held in common, a reminder that it belongs to all and needs all to care for it.

This picture contrasts starkly with the failed promise of higher yields from seed genetically modified to be pest-resistant. Shiva described how multinational corporations are locking farmers unwittingly into a cycle of debt and dependence on seeds that rely on chemicals to succeed. Some 20,000 farmers are reported to have committed suicide because the seeds are failing. The price paid by farmers for the promise of higher crop yields is that the seed does not regenerate. It is modified with a 'terminator' gene so that it can no longer be collected for growing the subsequent year. Neither can it be shared in celebration and reassertion of a common culture and resource.[5]

We learned that moves to patent and modify biological material offer at least a double assault: first, the assumption that seed is an invention to be owned rather than being the result of millennia of co-operation between humans and the natural world; and, second, that in peddling seed that cannot be replanted, the agricultural and cultural life – and thus resilience – of communities is destroyed. Shiva's lecture brought these issues before a wider public, gave confidence to those artists working in urban settings attempting to reconnect with the natural world and reminded LIFT about the role of theatre and celebration in a common associative life. Her lecture also informed audiences of agribusiness's attempts to control the food chain and the threats to long-term biological resilience this potentially presented. Shiva's visit to London coincided with the UK's debate on genetic modification (GM) of crops and added to voices in this discussion.

The second LIFT lecture was held at the Royal Geographical Society in May 2004. Entitled *The Creative Commons in a Connected*

World, this lecture by US attorney Lawrence Lessig laid out how the collision of the two worlds of IP and IP – intellectual property and Internet protocols – is eroding cultural freedoms (Lessig 2002). Creeping control of the Internet by commercial interests, punitive copyright extension and digital rights management are combining to proscribe true generativity of ideas. When these effects coincide with the concentration of a smaller and smaller number of media corporations, Lessig asserts that democratic rights are under threat.

Lessig gave the background to copyright law, established in 1710 in England to provide authors with incentives in their lifetime. Copyright was limited to enable the spread of culture and to prevent all published works falling into the hands of a tight monopoly of publishers. In 1774, length of copyright was set at 14 years following the death of the author or creator, with the right to renew for another term. Since then copyright has been progressively extended not only in length but also in forms of expression covered. Dramatic change came about in 1978 when copyright, now grown to 75 years, was extended automatically to all published works for the full term of the copyright. Published works include film, music and photographs. Works already in the public domain, freely accessible to anyone to build upon, were removed from that free use.

The impact of this change on authors, filmmakers and other creators is significant. All innovation builds on its forebears. Copyright legislation now means that anyone setting out to build on the work of others needs permission.[6] But, Lessig asked, what if your chosen art form uses images from television to critique a political culture that manipulates similar images for its own ends and uses a small number of media publishers to promote its views? Lessig related the experience of Robert Greenwald, producer of *Uncovered*, a film about the Iraq War and President Bush. When preparing to release the film on a DVD, Greenwald, wished to include a one-minute clip from a long interview made with the President on NBC's *Meet the Press*. Permission was denied for fear the clip did not 'make the President look good'. In a world where networks must curry favour with a political elite in order to gain access, such copyright refusals deny political critique.

Lessig also pointed out that the number of permissions needed for the creation of new works is now so burdensome that many ignore it. This makes criminals of those makers. To counter this trend, Lessig and colleagues have devised a new form of copyright, the Creative Commons licence, by which artists can reserve some rights but announce clearly that their work is adaptable by others without the need to seek permission. During Lessig's visit to London he was able to contribute to efforts to give away the BBC archive under a Creative Commons licence and add to debates about copyright implications of participatory theatre practice.

The task of reclaiming the commons in the face of commercial intrusions is daunting to say the least. Nevertheless, commentators such as Naomi Klein remind us that all is not gloom and that revivals of 'deep democracy' are bubbling up in many parts of the world (Klein 2002). Activists in biodiversity, water rights, environment and cyberspace are marshalling their arguments and, thanks to popular mobilization, progress is being made in the realm of legislation. Dr Vandana Shiva and colleagues have succeeded in overturning the right of Corporations RiceTec and Syngenta to patent rice genes. Patenting of the neem gene, a tree with natural antiseptic qualities, has been forbidden. Enclosure of a river for private use has been overturned (Shiva, LIFT lecture 2003).

The arts sponsorship dynamics of the last decades have brought the arts into close contact with individuals working in mining, oil, retailing, entertainment, advertising and public services increasingly managed like businesses, such as health, education and care of the aged. Neighbours are confused and muzzled in surprising ways, acknowledging a need to get to grips with issues they hardly know how to name and shrugging helplessly at the all-pervading ideology of the bottom line. Such a feeling brings reminders of another era and political regime when theatre companies arrived from former Soviet countries with political overseers literally or metaphorically sitting in on every conversation. The ideological straitjacket of the market has begun to take on eerie resemblance to the totalitarian socialist regimes it triumphed in overthrowing.

The negotiation of more humane systems demands structural change so profound, that no individual, business leader or politician can do it alone. Since the commercial world is part of the problem, then it must also be part of the solution. But not *the* solution, taking everything into its embrace, washed clean as the thinly disguised successor to a nineteenth-century colonialist.

Vaclav Havel, through his years as a playwright and his work with colleagues in Civic Forum, led former socialist republic Czechoslovakia to a post-totalitarian era. He even foresaw the subtle and sophisticated effects of the triumph of capitalism and has pointers to offer:

> If a better economic and political model is to be created, then perhaps more than ever before it must derive from profound existential and moral changes in society. This is not something that can be designed and introduced like a new car. If it is to be more than just a new variation on the old degeneration, it must above all be an expression of life in the process of transforming itself. A better system will not automatically ensure a better life. In fact the opposite is true: only by creating a better life can a better system be developed.
>
> (Havel 1986: 70)

When we embarked on the Business Arts Forum in 1995, it was first of all an attempt to establish that business had things to learn from the arts and then to assert more confidently that the arts have a part to play in building a common associative life beyond simply serving the direct interests of the market. In simpler political times, those in the arts concerned about business behaviour could simply turn away from the corporate dollar. The world is different now. We exist in a mixed economy and it appears the ideologies of socialism and capitalism have more or less merged worldwide.

The only conversation left is what culture of capitalism are we responsible for enacting in our various roles? Are we left with a place of escape for reflection and critique? Do we have the power to temper the culture of capitalism in which we are implicated beyond reaching for fair-trade items on the supermarket shelves, choosing ethical investments or participating in radical actions? How do we cross the street to gain access to a larger horizon? We are all responsible now. The speed of change and power of technologies has left a gap in our governance and accountability. The consequences of strategic and management decisions made every day have unimagined impacts. A view of the aggregate effect of our actions and intentions demands places of collective reflection, critique, negotiation and imagination from which to look back at the daily round. There has to be a reinvention of the public realm, not as the denigrated provider of public services nor new territory for the market, but as a place of engagement, reflection and invention, a place of escape from the pressures to deliver in our various roles – a cultural commons on which to meet and to rehearse 'life in the process of transforming itself' (Havel 1986: 70).

The Business Arts Forum has attempted to support LIFT's mission of illuminating the role of theatre for our times by creating a space for individuals to think about what they and their organizations are for. The Forum has done this by eliciting the personal and civic dimensions of participants' identities, rather than their organizational ones, for it is from here that a different view of organizational behaviour can be imagined. All participants, regardless of gender, culture and stage in life, have a part to play in imagining the road ahead in different ways, perhaps in potential disagreement, but ultimately as fellow citizens and neighbours, not shouting but listening.

People working in businesses and other large organizations can attempt to change the organization for which they work by changing their own performance.

During my 1997 US trip to gauge the shifting relationships between arts, commerce and communities, I asked John Seely Brown, Director of Xerox's Palo Alto Research Centre, to identify the biggest challenge facing him. He responded with one word: 'meaning'. He proceeded to explain that, following a discussion we had had that morning, he had left to attend a meeting with Xerox clients about renewal of their contract. Seely Brown arrived with a formal presentation but, putting it aside, he moved away from the podium to sit with his clients at the same level. He spoke frankly about the need for business *not* as usual and the need for a return to first principles, to imagine how Xerox might improve qualities of communication and how the company and their clients might aim to make a difference in response to contemporary needs. People in the meeting moved forward, alert to a new departure.

Seely Brown reported later that he would have been unlikely to change his stance and tone at the meeting had he not had the earlier discussion about art and business, about young people and their futures, about homogenizing tendencies and adverse effects of Western corporate values.

Significantly, Seely Brown's stance had changed from standing at a podium to one of a shared conversation, sitting among the group, starting with an admittance that the way ahead was unknown. This change brought to mind that, in the early years of the Forum, our business advisers delivered expert perspectives from a podium in classic lecture mode. This was necessary at the time to validate the Forum to those preoccupied with operational responsibilities in their organizations, sometimes sceptical that engagement with contemporary performance had much to offer. In later years, Fairtlough, Geus and Handy simply had to be participants in the room for the space to be made 'safe' for others needing their validation.

It seems that a change in direction demands a change of performance quite literally in the way one relates to others, the stance one takes, where one chooses to walk, to whom one chooses to listen, the constituencies with whom one chooses to engage. Seely Brown later reflected that: 'Paradoxically, the way ahead is to look not forward, but to look around.'

Economist Coyle was asked: just as a land-based economy had its rituals to renew ties of interdependence, shared humanity and connections to the natural world – even to critique and subvert power, how will those shared rituals and ties of interdependence be celebrated now? And what is the role of theatre? Coyle responded that she did not know but that she considered it a phenomenally important question. We, in our own fashion, have been attempting to answer it. But why should anyone beyond those directly involved find interest in our efforts?

TWELVE

INVENTIVE SOCIETIES BEGIN ON OUR DOORSTEP

It is precisely this space between diversities and differences wherein the intracultural is most sharply, and productively negotiated.

(Bharucha 2001: 84)

We need art to show how courage grows ... creating equal conversations is now the supreme art.

(Zeldin 1998: 18–19)[1]

So how will empathy be created and homage to the natural world be renewed in a weightless economy where trade relations are instantaneous and span the globe? And what can an examination through the experience of and engagement with theatre contribute to huge questions such as these? In this final chapter will be explored ways in which the Business Arts Forum offers a response to these questions. The Forum is a small-scale initiative. Here you will find ideas as to its wider significance beyond those directly involved. At the close of the book, a return is made to questions of generation and succession.

Experience at LIFT reveals that cultural exchange truly happens only at the level of personal engagement, thus with empathy. Neither can be forced or prescribed. Empathy might or might not result from witnessing and apprehending the experience of others, and, when it does, arises spontaneously involving a change in oneself. The *Oxford English Dictionary* definition of empathy is 'the power of projecting one's personality into (and so fully comprehending) the object of contemplation'. Full comprehension is rarely possible however, merely an approximate apprehension of something that changes one's own outlook.

It is 1997 and a group of mathematicians, management consultants and software designers gather in a Stanford University seminar room.[2] Keith Devlin, a teacher and popularizer of mathematics, has invited me to speak about the theatre and its powers to strengthen communities and communication across cultures. Gazing at the palm trees outside I wonder what interest this group has in what I have to say.[3]

The idea that mathematicians might be interested in empathy and theatre-making, let alone that there might be a maths of empathy creation, is puzzling. Such a thing could unite or divide in equal measure. What if such processes are built into how we communicate thus denying an ability to question the qualities and objects of empathy encouraged? What if the computer coders got it slightly wrong and empathy turned to its close cousins, pity or sympathy? Extrapolating from there and in accordance with the fears of a creeping corporate desire to copyright, is empathy ripe for patenting accessible only on someone else's terms? Could it become just another product for sale in the increasing commercialization of intimate life?

Building empathy across boundaries of power and culture demands equity of communication on neutral ground with openness and generosity, leaving one's job title, status in life or immediate self-interest at the door. Imagining such interactions inevitably involves questions of scale, culture, location, form, participation and time. Engagement of this quality cannot be forced. I believe it can only be small-scale, intimate and voluntary.

As soon as small numbers come into play, the arts world faces accusations of elitism. But what if small numbers are required to build the intimacy needed for negotiation of trust and empathy across cultures, generations and levels of power and that such dynamics are impossible to build on a mass scale for eternity but must be made and remade and remade and remade in every life for life? What does this mean for assessing the effectiveness and relevance of practices such as LIFT's Business Arts Forum?

Complexity and emergence

Leaving the mathematicians in California, I continued my journey to New Mexico to visit the Santa Fé Institute established to undertake research into complex systems. I hoped to find there ways to improve understanding of arts sector dynamics in London, particularly how small-scale activities in one place can grow to have large effects beyond the boundaries of any one institution.

Researchers at the Institute were drawn together by a desire to research deep commonalities linking artificial, human and natural systems.[4] The Institute's questioning of the reductionist principles of Western science followed pioneers in holistic and systems thinking of the 1920s and 1930s, who believed that the reduction of systems to their component parts was inadequate for full understanding of their workings. Such complex systems could only be understood if considered as a whole. Assumptions that order and disorder are fixed and eternal opposites was rejected in favour of the conception that chaos and order are stages in a process of ever-changing emergence and dynamic transformation over time.

Complexity theory illuminates how small changes can have huge effects. More recently ideas have begun to circulate that the spread of natural phenomena such as epidemic disease might illuminate the development of social phenomena (Gladwell 2000; Ball 2004). Although social systems, subject as they are to powers of reflection, are never subject to the immutable laws of nature, parallels are useful. For example, just as only a small number of vectors are necessary to the spread of disease, ideas spread by a small number of people can rapidly reach a critical tipping point at which point they enter the mainstream. But just as with disease, the spread of implicit knowledge involves transmission via the body. Geography and face-to-face encounter are critical to the perception and transmission of embodied knowledge.

Two primary points of learning emerged from a glimpse of complexity theories. One was why intensive experience in small numbers is a more effective route to the spread of ideas than projects of shallower experience rolled out universally. I will come on later to this question. The other concerned a practical question of how the Forum might further diversify sources of income to LIFT.

We speculated in the early years about franchising out the Forum, suggesting that other arts organizations might pay a fee for replication. There was much interest in the US and the UK about how to scale out successful social innovations and franchising was one route to go, but that implied, among other things, a continuing responsibility for training and quality control. We ultimately decided that any of these would take energy beyond our organizational capacity, interests and priorities. Some years on a useful study was made on this topic by the Center for the Advancement of Social Entrepreneurship at Duke University (Dees *et al.* 2002). In this study, Dees and colleagues offer a matrix of strategic choices between dissemination, affiliation or branching of either programme, organization or principles, singly or in combination.

LIFT took on board that the Forum itself was not precisely replicable anywhere else. What was replicable elsewhere was a sense of felt need that relations between arts and business were worth questioning and, furthermore, that art has the power to bring people together as human beings across the boundaries of arts, business and civic life to address the big questions facing society. In the end, we thought that giving away the ideas would lead more rapidly to the change in business–arts relations we sought and that we would even have things to learn if such efforts were pursued elsewhere as they would develop differently. Some asked if we were troubled by the threat of competition. We responded that we had to have faith that the vitality and relevance of LIFT productions would continue to inspire the relatively small number of participants needed to make it a success in its prime location – London. Although eager to engage new participants, LIFT needed a relatively small number to make a significant difference to LIFT's organizational life, confidence and income.

Participation and knowledge construction

Coming back to the question of whether depth or spread of experience is more effective in the dissemination of ideas, it was interesting to note that the need for participation in diverse, inclusive learning communities was growing in the world of business learning. In a room in London in 2003, a gathering of scenario planners speculated about the future of their practice. Responding to a sense that the butterfly collection approach to 'understanding evolving needs in society' was reaching its limits, here too forms of interaction were changing in the search for future learning, action and organizational renewal.

The nature of knowledge as depicted by biologist and philosopher, Brian Goodwin, and colleagues at Schumacher College, was brought to their attention.[5]

Two forms of knowledge construction are seen in Figure 12.1: one 'knowing by gaining control', leading to disappointment and despair and 'knowing by participation' where, through participation, inclusion and diversity of perspectives, hope and play ensue. Control assumes certain answers are to be found, whereas knowing by participation allows for uncertainty to be the starting point for mutually negotiated insights to emerge.

Learning is shown not to be a simple matter of cognitive processes in individual minds but a commitment to collectively negotiated knowledge. This looked like the congregations with which we had been experimenting at LIFT.

From the scientific field, the place of participation and intergenerational learning in professional development is described as follows:

> To learn means to change one's 'identity' (i.e. to develop a new or different sense of self) as a consequence of active participation in a social practice. The measures of learning become new ways of being – new ways of talking, acting, describing oneself, or relating to others. These new ways of being develop when for example, one changes from novice to expert, newcomer to old-timer, or naive to mature practitioner in a social practice such as the activities of a

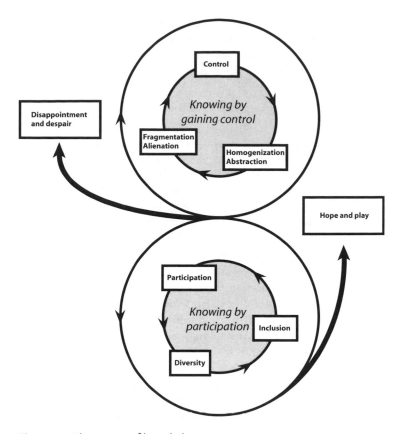

Figure 12.1 The nature of knowledge
Source: Courtesy of Schumacher College

science curriculum or an engineering workplace. From this perspective, the most important condition for learning to be a scientist (or any expert) is participating in the relevant social practices.

(Eisenhart and Finkel 1998: 8)

Hence, in many fields of learning and personal development there is no substitute for participation in small-scale collective practice, through apprenticeship to others, of different generations and diverse backgrounds, transforming the identity and performance of those involved. It is this kind of knowledge that is portable, allowing for action and invention elsewhere to be shaped by previous immersive experience. The people who have had this experience become the carriers.

Modernity, tradition and difference

A book called *Invented Here: Maximizing your Organization's Internal Growth and Profitability, a Practical Guide to Transforming Work* (Victor and Boynton 1998) describes how invention comes from the painstaking process of making explicit the often hidden expertise of those with craft knowledge and traditions. Essentially aesthetic – perception of shape, feeling, emotions and values, skills of hand, eye, ear and body – such craft skills and traditions can only be revealed in real places in real time in painstaking and detailed fashion. Intimate scale of social interaction is a precondition for such revelations. This instinct had informed LIFT's transformation from Festival to Enquiry providing a place of renewal for our own theatrical craft skills and traditions: of celebration, subversion, critique and creation.

When inclusion and play across differences of culture, gender, working perspective and generation are essential to social invention such as this, few assumptions can be made about the terms on which one meets, but they are likely to require painstaking attention to both tradition and invention. Ever aware of the problematic relation between observer and observed, contemporary artists continually seek to disturb relationships between artist and audience, questioning perceptions of modernity and tradition.

At a conference held in London in 2002, Stuart Hall asserted that artists intent on engaging with issues of their own cultural heritage have three choices in response. They can:

1 set out on an exploration of traditional culture, resisting modernity and defending tradition against change of any

kind, guaranteeing authenticity by not moving. This route Hall claims results in a frozen and dangerous sentimentality.

2 adhere to a utopian cosmopolitanism, connected globally by the Internet and talking to everyone all the time – somewhat nightmarish and difficult to maintain in Hall's view.

3 practise what Hall calls vernacular cosmopolitanism, meaning that artists do not lose touch with traditions, but are willing to move and speak across boundaries. It means that artists are not prepared to lose themselves in homogenised culture or to become frozen in tradition. Artists learn to speak in translation whilst accepting that no translation is perfect. It means that they hold on to the particular without being lost in 'a featureless global conversation'.

(see Ings 2003: 14)

Frozen tradition allows for no adaptation and few points of entry and participation for others. Contemporary reinterpretation of tradition offers points of conversation, debate and connection, opening more easily channels of communication between traditions. Wider survival and inventiveness may just depend on these cultural qualities.

Social inventiveness

As the world's scientists arrive at overwhelming consensus about the evidence for climate change, artists are being called upon to offer leadership in the challenges that face us.

In the third LIFT lecture, *The Hydrogen Economy: a Question of Culture?*, US economist and futures thinker Jeremy Rifkin spoke of the challenge of moving beyond a dependency on oil and the promise held out by hydrogen technologies and micro-generation of power from alternative energy sources. The profound revolution this will take is just beginning to be grasped. For certain it will demand advances and breakthroughs in technology, but it will also require the building of micro-connections at neighbourhood level between residents, institutions, schools, businesses and hospitals. It will demand new inspiration for the painstaking task of engaging with neighbours, drawing on an infinity of cultural traditions in the search for invention. Rifkin called for a new metaphysics to guide this new energy era, based 'on deep play and making a bond with the planet' (third LIFT lecture). David King, Chief Scientific Adviser to the UK government, made a similar plea to a meeting of artists at the Royal Society of Arts in May 2005, calling on them for leadership in the search for a way forward.[6]

Many years earlier, in her own search for how we might solve the contemporary puzzle of fuel and invent an economy in which nature is included in political agreements, Barbara Heinzen had engaged with the cultural explorations of LIFT. At the same time she delved into English history for the foundations of the industrial era. She found three drivers: extremity, engagement and experiment.

A lack of fuel in the seventeenth and eighteenth centuries and the social disruptions of recurrent epidemic disease created opportunities for people to engage across conventional boundaries of class and working skill in practical experiments to meet everyday needs. She illustrates this with the image of a seventeenth-century windmill, built on the outskirts of Grantham, where Newton was a schoolboy. In order to build the windmill – a novel source of energy at that time – a neighbourly project was required. She imagines local gentlemen, merchants and yeomen provided funds and brought knowledge from the Netherlands where windmills were common; craftsmen offered skills in joinery and sail-making; shipwrights and coopers brought knowledge of the properties of cloth, wood, stone and metal, craft skills and local knowledge of wind and water; others provided drafting skills; children reminded people to keep things simple and playful; and men and women laid on food and drink. Everyone's skill and perspective were needed to solve the puzzle of a lack of fuel. On Sundays, neighbours went out beyond the village boundaries to inspect construction, young Newton among them. An ability to engage and co-operate across levels of wealth, expertise and generation turns out to be a vital dimension of social inventiveness. As for Newton, still just a boy, he built a scale model of the windmill, increasing his own knowledge on the back of a neighbourhood project (Westfall 1993).

Survival and adaptation depends on neighbourliness

A knowledge of people's skills and resources and the trust and knowledge needed in order to draw on them emerges first and foremost from neighbourliness, a phenomenon that comes about through intimate contact over time across a diverse range of people, working together project by project. It would have been known in Grantham who had the necessary skills, resources and crafts needed for the task in hand. Neighbourliness is not only required for inventiveness, but is also the result of an inventive approach and a willingness to engage in the daily life of the place in which you live. Neighbourliness is based on exchange of skills, expertise and resources in the acknowledgement of a common curiosity or need and in a spirit of reciprocity. Active neighbourliness reinforces itself. It is critical to laying the social foundations of major structural change in society. It is not a professional, transactional, contractual exchange. It is not first and foremost about money. It is essentially an iterative and evolving conversation based on emerging need – a culture of giving with no hope of immediate return where the starting point is shared curiosity or uncertainty, not a deal for mutual benefit or a conversation for unilateral extraction. This may at times be for a specific purpose, but at other times it is for no purpose at all, other than to keep the conversation going in case of future extremity. Celebration and festivity play their part in interrupting the daily round, in fostering creativity, in forging communication across levels of power and in renewing connections to the seasons and the specifics of place.

Today, just as in Newton's time, the skills and perspectives of many will be needed to solve the puzzle of fuel. This demands both technological but also neighbourly invention on an unknown scale. In making the transition from one system to another, links need to be established between the current way of doing things and the concepts, technologies and social foundations of an emerging system. An emerging system is, by definition, unknown and no respecter of traditional boundaries and definitions. It requires ways and people from diverse starting points to span them.

Spanning cultural boundaries means collaborating with people whose ideas, activities and cultural assumptions are vastly different from one's own. It is precisely in this encounter and engagement on common ground that the greatest learning and invention is likely to take place. Such learning accelerates and diffuses even more quickly when collaboration involves all parties working together around practical experiments in a spirit of equity and enquiry. It is likely that those individuals and institutions participating in and learning from such experiments often taking place at the boundaries may well have a disproportionate impact on the future. They may also enable themselves and their neighbours to survive the crises that are without doubt on the horizon – or already upon us or on our neighbours on the other side of the globe.

Public interest advocate, David Bollier, writes 'the renaissance of the commons is a quiet insurgency with diverse manifestations . . . not just about policy, it is about a cultural rediscovery of public collaboration' (Bollier 2002). Forms of interaction called for cannot be devised on the terms of one constituency alone and will involve the creation of multiple 'cultural commons' on which to meet, imagine, negotiate and speak in translation.

All the people who came together to make the Grantham windmill doubtless regularly went to church together, or attended other local festivities and rituals, reinforcing social relationships, giving opportunities for experiment to proceed and trust to be developed at its own pace, co-operation to be rehearsed and inevitable neighbourly tensions renegotiated around a transcendent interest. If people are to connect and negotiate, a common project is needed around which to do this and, in a city such as London with its many co-existing cultures, new rituals of connection are required.

Such considerations have informed the make-up, timetable and focus of the LIFT Business Arts Forum as seen in Figure 12.2.

Imagined as a place in which to build a 'new neighbourliness in a global performing space' participants include people of different working backgrounds, of different generations; people based in Britain and internationally; people with financial resources and operational responsibilities in the commercial realm; and people with other kinds of power and expertise in the creative, environ-

A new neighbourliness in a global performing space

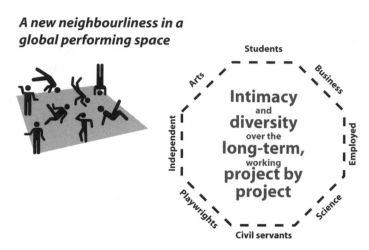

Figure 12.2 The LIFT Forum – experiment and engagement

Source: © B.J. Heinzen 1999

mental, cultural dialogue, broadcasting and government fields. The performances and projects of LIFT spark iterative connections, building neighbourliness on neutral ground over time, through shared aesthetic exploration mediated by a shared experience of theatre. LIFT productions practise, for the main, vernacular cosmopolitanism, building on traditions and reflecting specific experience through contemporary perspectives, offering critique of power and reminders of shared humanity. Finally the Forum has fluid form, hovering on the edge of chaos and order, metamorphosing to fit need, based not only on rational analysis or prescription, but on people's latent craft and aesthetic skills alongside the talk. For the most part people are on their feet during Forum sessions. There is little passive consumption of prepared information. People attend as themselves, not as representatives of this or that organization, working discipline or college but as citizens. In the midst of action, when these sessions work at their best, people become indifferent to surface difference but flourish amid the specific different stories and imaginations of those involved. Participant

Sally Bibb credits the Forum with giving her the confidence to challenge the status quo in a world where, she believes, trust matters.

The challenge of moving beyond a dependency on fossil fuels requires us to reconnect with aesthetic sensibilities and to relearn the craft of neighbourhood in order to feel for the path ahead. It means being on one's feet to rehearse connection with the natural world that sustains us in ways we have forgotten and that lie in traditions familiar or unfamiliar. In cities of London's scale it is obvious neither who our neighbours are, nor where lines of collaboration might lie. Theatre in all its forms is one superb rallying point around which one can discover these strands and, in the discovery, negotiate neighbourliness in new ways. Visual art and dance too, ceramics and music all can offer ways to meet the neighbours but theatre has a particular role to play because of its essentially collective nature. Simply crossing the street to embark on familiar conversations is not sufficient however. Commons are needed on which to meet strangers and to discover directions that are as yet unknown. Celebration and aesthetic elaboration have a key part to play in forging channels of communication across these lines.

Sociologist Scott Lash's describes in 'Reflexive Anthropology' his response to the primacy of the economic. It fits closely with the role that arts organizations might play in this context:

> Everyday activities in the 'we' are about the routine achievement of meaning: about the production of substantive goods, and guided by an understanding of . . . what is regarded as substantively good by that community. The substantively good is not encountered by communal beings as an 'imperative' divorced from the mundane and the everyday. . . . The meanings and practices incorporating the substantive good are learnt, but then become unconscious as if inscribed on the body.
>
> (Beck *et al.* 1994: 157)

If we are to adapt and respond to our contemporary challenges, cultural institutions need to integrate far more actively a participatory, intercultural and intergenerational flow into their core artistic programme and organizational structure, going well beyond delivering on the periphery a number of education projects. Rather, it means integration of such considerations into the heart of how cultural organizations think and act, not seeing culture as product but remembering culture as survival. The style of connection needed now is very different from the conventional sponsorship or patronage approach or the conventional stance of many arts organizations. In Heinzen's words:

> Most of our institutions focus on the politics of delivery which provide us with the services we want. LIFT is experimenting with the politics of invention and the skills of agreement needed to survive an unpredictable future.
>
> (Heinzen, LIFT Communication 2003)

At the Arts Council's inception, it was taken for granted that the arts were part of Britain's reconstruction effort after the Second World War. The management of arts organizations in recent years has taken a professionalizing approach based largely on business models. But now I believe the arts sector needs to consider that the most effective routes to adaptation are to be found in connecting with one another in non-specialized and non-professionalized ways. We need to rediscover who we are to one another in simple ways.

For those in search of business traditions of connection at human scale need not look far. One such in England is Crittall Windows, an Essex company that went on to influence modern architecture and design all over the world through the manufacture of metal window frames (Blake and Crittall 2004). In 1926, the company employed 10,000 people from backgrounds across the UK, Polish refugees and men injured in the war. The company provided houses and healthcare for its employees and supported many creative and sporting activities, building social and community connections across the different groups brought together through work. Walter Francis Crittall was visionary in his integration of arts, architecture and design into every aspect of the company's activities, commissioning portraits of retiring employees from young painters and compiling *The Metal Window Dictionary*. In this he offered to the public domain technical terms and craft knowledge his company had developed over many years.

Some may view such corporate culture and relationships as self-interested paternalism and the relic of an industrial age. Nevertheless, for our own post-paternalist age questions remain as to appropriate qualities of connection, responsibility and respect across levels of power in society, across distances of geography and culture and across the lines of commerce and communities.

Connections across levels of power

The arts have always had a relationship with power, but not just as supplicant to patron. The theatre in particular has also illuminated the paradoxes, ambiguities and responsibilities of power through harking to little-heard voices. Fundraising fits into this picture not simply as a way to find resources for what it is that an organization already does or wishes to deliver. In the search for money, by definition fundraisers forge channels of communication with those in power with financial resources.

This brings implications for fundraisers: a need to be alert to the responsibilities that come with their boundary-spanning role and the politics of connection facilitated as a result. It will take as much, if not more, effort to connect and build trust with those with few financial resources as it does to those with plenty. This means paying equal, if not more, attention to the field commonly thought of as arts education as it does to building channels of communication to the wealthy.

Implications also follow in relation to arts policies vis-à-vis business. For business to have access to spaces of equal participation at micro-level, on what terms are these to be encouraged? Such forms of connection bring with them ethical questions of continuity and commitment, in particular in relation to younger participants. Too often young people are seen simply as crowded territory for consumer competition, not as social resource for adaptation, learning and renewal.

The power of government has not melted away with the growth of multinational corporations; it has however become more intertwined. There is still much that can be done to encourage business to engage with the arts at one remove from its own direct self-interest to point out a space in which it can in fact rehearse its own disinterest, and even have contact with its own critics. It is this ability that will enable business to imagine a changed future role, a space in which to imagine its own evolving long-term future. In supporting such 'cultural commons', there is thus a need in Britain to push back the commercial relationships encouraged in past decades. An arm's length relationship between arts, communities and business needs to be reasserted just as, in the reconstruction of Britain in the post-Second World War years, the ACE enshrined the principle of arts funding at arm's length from political influence. Business is now so diffuse, however, that this will demand not legislation necessarily, but new social and cultural agreements that set the norms of behaviour.

Creating continuity and capacity for renewal

Over the last 25 years, LIFT has changed views of what theatre is, who can be involved, and where it can take place. Over the last 10 years, the Business Arts Forum has laid the foundations for a new relationship between LIFT and the commercial world, forging a new space for reflection, creative civic discourse and engagement. These changes have come about by starting conversations on the doorstep, and by learning how to cross the street to walk in other worlds. They have come too from a felt sense of need interacting with personal stories, external events and organizational experimentation. Starting out with an acknowledgement of ignorance and uncertainty, it has been long and detailed work, founded at every stage on developing points of entry for individuals to participate in collective reflection and action.

At the very start was a personal change of performance. Sociologist Richard Sennett describes the struggle at a personal and philosophical level. His picture, in tune with how it felt to embark on a renegotiation of LIFT's relationship with the commercial world, gives a glimpse of the process:

> when one recognises in the distress the lord and servant within oneself and then the lord and servant within others, the upheavals

alter the way one acts with other human beings. In the latter two phases, the old lord loses his power over the bondsman, not because the bondsman overthrows him or takes his place, but because the unhappy bondsman becomes a different human being, one who deals with the lord non-competitively; this forces the lord to modulate his own behaviour.

(Sennett 1980: 129)

These changes involve a taking of responsibility, an intention to take action even if the road ahead is unclear. In so doing, the first steps are made in a new direction.

Before closing this book, I return to the importance of connection across generations. The revolution required to invent new ways of living with the planet will take more than one working lifetime and constant engagement, experiment balancing a tradition with innovation, competition with collaboration, commerce with culture.

LIFT and the Forum are in the midst of their own journey in this regard. To the best of its ability LIFT has involved young people in the making of the Festival through the many different aspects of LIFT Learning from performances to student placements, and from aspects of curating to commissioning. At every moment leaders must be thinking: How do we make ourselves obsolete? How do we pass things on? How do we encourage a spirit of public collaboration in a younger generation?

As regards the Festival as a whole and the Forum – just one learning programme amid others at LIFT – the things created are both ours and not ours. LIFT and the Forum are not copyrightable brands synonymous with the people that lead them. They are sets of ideas, values, processes and relationships, a set of questions and congregations sparked by the work of artists, laying paths to the future.

In 2003 Neal and Fenton announced their intention to hand the Festival on to a new generation. It would take two years to make this transition. One important staging post turned out to be the Business Arts Forum session three years earlier entitled *Continuity and Succession*. This afforded timely insights into the process of passing LIFT to others.[7] Fairtlough, Forum adviser, admitted publicly for the first time that he should have trusted the values he had fostered among both company staff and his own Board to carry the organization forward, appointing the right person for the right time in the organization's evolution – without his direct interference. The leadership lesson was to create the frame but keep out of the centre of the picture.

Fenton, Neal and colleagues at LIFT kept these lessons in mind as they laid the foundations for handing the Festival to a new Artistic Director. The LIFT Board was well prepared and enthusiastically embraced the task of appointing LIFT's next leader. In 2005, Angharad Wynne-Jones took up her role to guide LIFT into the coming era.

By stepping away myself as Forum Director, the space for adaptation is freed up for a new phase of the Forum too. The Forum processes, relationships and values are moving from the periphery of the Festival to the centre enabling participants to have still more direct engagement with the artists at the heart of LIFT. The forum has contributed in fundamental ways to LIFT's future artistic trajectory, its adaptation and survival. In the words of Wynne-Jones (2005): 'It is through the making of the change that we will be changed in the making.'

APPENDIX ONE

TIMELINE OF LIFT, THE BUSINESS ARTS FORUM AND WORLD EVENTS

FESTIVAL	FORUM EVOLUTION	THE WORLD AND LONDON
1980s		Deregulation of financial services.
Biennial Festivals.		Privatization of state monopolies.
1986	Commercial sponsorship begins at LIFT.	Abolition of the GLC. Tiananmen Square massacre.
1989		Perestroika and fall of Berlin Wall. Nelson Mandela released from prison.
1991	Civic partnerships developed.	States' role discredited, business models prevail.
1993 LIFT Education begins.	BT sponsorship of Education Programme.	
1994	BT sponsorship ends.	Baring's Bank crashes.
1995	First Forum during Festival period.	Shell's Brent Spar rig occupied.
Four-week festival.	Testing if business had something to learn from the arts. Forum income to LIFT after costs: £3,247.	Ken Saro-Wiwa executed. Business exposed to non-business, non-governmental groups.

1996	Forum meetings year round.	
Out of LIFT Season for, by, with young people.	Public arts project with 120 13-year-olds. First intergenerational session connecting business people to young people and teachers in school.	Dot.com economy booms.
Start of Project Phakama.	Testing lessons to be learned by business about risk, innovation, intercultural and cross-departmental collaboration. Deficit of £6,750 carried forward to 1997.	
1997 Four-week Festival.	Second Forum during Festival period. Public sector participants join Forum. Income to LIFT after costs: £10,946. Forum reaches limits of expertise – return to the drawing board.	New Labour wins election. Expectation that 'society' would matter again.
1999 Four-week Festival.	Third Forum during Festival period. Private and public sector participants. Young members of Phakama lead part of session and participate in Forum throughout. Bursaries for artists taking part. First LIFT Teacher Forum held.	World Trade Organisation provokes demonstrations in Seattle and other capital cities. Market model being questioned.
1999–2000	Plans laid for Forum Network. Visits to non-LIFT theatre performances. Youth mentoring and year-round seminars and evening sessions at different locations across London.	Dot.com bubble bursts. New economic model discredited.

2001 Four-week Festival.	Fourth Forum during Festival period. Artistic Director of Forum throughout. First informal link with London arts college. Students participate throughout. Net income for 1999–2001 combined: £46,517.	September 11 attacks.
2002 LIFT begins Enquiry.	Plans laid for continuation of Forum. Business funding for Forum to embark on a conversation rather than look to direct business outcomes. Link with Lewisham College and participation of one student year group throughout the year. Forum session on long-term thinking with public outcome involving young people in Southwark and young refugees. Planting of a tree to last 1,000 years.	Afghanistan bombed. Highlights tensions, American imperialism and need for dialogue.
2003–4	LIFT lecture series: *Imagining a Cultural Commons.* Forum during LIFT seasons. Income £15,000.	War declared on Iraq.
2005	New LIFT Artistic leadership.	G8 nations meet. World poverty and climate change on the agenda.

APPENDIX TWO

SUMMARY OF PRODUCTIONS SEEN BY BUSINESS ARTS FORUM MEMBERS IN LIFT '95

This is a list of some of the productions from LIFT '95. It is not a complete list of all productions and events, simply the ones seen by Business Arts Forum members to give an idea of the range experienced. It is a fraction of total productions seen by members in subsequent Festivals and seasons.

Birds of Fire, Groupe F, France, directed by Christophe Berthonneau.

Famed for his large-scale civic celebrations, Berthonneau had two giant burning birds converge on the Thames to light up the centre of the city.

Noiject, by Company Karas from Japan, directed by Saburo Teshigawara.

The stage dominated by a huge iron set, banks of speakers and bare light bulbs, Teshigawara led his company in a performance reflecting the speed and frenetic pulse of urban life.

Zumbi, by Black Theatre Co-op, a collaboration of Brazilian and British artists directed by Marcio Meirelles from Salvador.

A fast-paced music-drama depicted the story of Zumbi, a runaway slave leader whose legacy of resistance lasted a hundred years, and combined stories of struggle and resistance from contemporary Britain's black community.

Jozi Jozi and The Suit, the Market Theatre and Theatre Connections, Johannesburg, South Africa.

Jozi Jozi – the familiar name for Johannesburg – brought to life in a satirical a cappella musical the joys and trials of downtown life in the 'not-so-new South Africa'. The Suit, by writer Can Themba, directed by Barney Simon, is one of South Africa's greatest love stories made tragic through adultery and revenge.

Murx den Europäer! – Ein patriotischer Abend (Kill the European! – A Patriotic Evening), the Volksbühne Theatre, Berlin.

Set on a colossal stage in a specially constructed theatre in east London, this piece from former East Berlin offered an absurd critique of the German nation and the unreality of a unified Europe.

Toiles, Cirque Plume, France.

A combination of theatre, music and magic, this groundbreaking contemporary circus took ensemble working and risk to new heights.

Take a Peek! Bobby Baker, UK.

Artist Bobby Baker took a behind-the-scenes look at life in a health centre. An excursion through body and mind, a visit to the doctor took on the surreal qualities of the circus.

The St Pancras Project, Deborah Warner.

The secrets of the abandoned Midland Grand Hotel at St Pancras were brought to life in a fantastical walk above and below stairs in one of London's best loved landmarks.

The Madwoman of our City, The Company, India, directed by Neelam Mansingh Chowdhry.

A comic fantasy about a world where dreamers, not money-makers, have the upper hand, this production from Chandigarh retold Giraudoux's The Madwoman of Chaillot set in India.

Phaedra, National Theatre of Craiova, Romania, directed by Silviu Purcarete.

A darkly atmospheric adaptation of the original Greek plays by Euripides and Seneca about the tragic consequences of forbidden love.

The Tale of Teeka, Les Deux Mondes, Canada.

Especially designed for nine-year-olds and up, *The Tale of Teeka* was set in 1950s rural Quebec, simply and movingly portraying the life of a mistreated boy and his pet goose.

File O, Xi Ju Che Jian Theatre, China, directed by Mou Sen.

Highly visual in style, *File O* told of the experiences of two young men in contemporary China. One story is told in the official files, but their emotions and thoughts remain theirs alone.

Sadness, William Yang, Australia.

Through photographs, *Sadness* documented the rediscovery of William Yang's Chinese heritage and coming to terms with the deaths of his friends through Aids.

Super-per, Bak-truppen, Norway.

Performance company Bak-truppen retold the story of Peer Gynt as a speed trip around the world, with cabaret and bafflement.

Seka Barong of Singapadu, Bali.

A spectacular dance drama of ravishing beauty, this production by a company from Bali depicted the struggle between the black magic of Rangda and the spirits of the Barong.

KEY LIFT ADAPTATIONS RE SPONSORSHIP AND BUSINESS ARTS FORUM

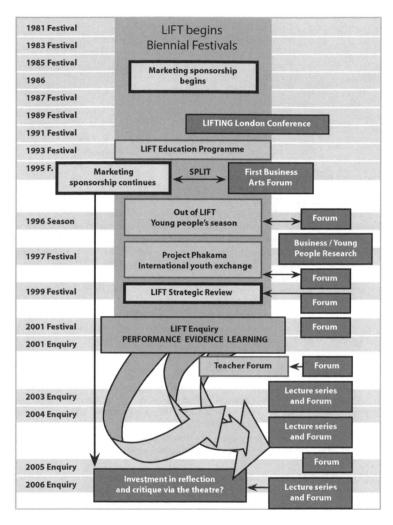

Figure A3.1 Timeline of key LIFT adaptations in relation to sponsorship and the Business Arts Forum

NOTES

ONE: STARTING BY NOT KNOWING

1   Peter Daubeny's World Theatre Season ended in 1976. Theatre producer Thelma Holt brought productions on an occasional basis.
2   Information from the 2001 Census and analysis commissioned by the GLA reveals that London is one of the most ethnically diverse cities in the world. There are 42 communities of over 10,000 born outside the UK and now living in London (*London – The World in a City*, Marian Storkey, DMAG Briefing 2005–6). There are more than 300 languages spoken by London's school-children (*Multilingual Capital: The Languages of London*, ed. Phillip Baker and John Eversley, Battlebridge Publications, 2000).
3   GLAA became Greater London Arts (GLA); London Arts Board (LAB); London Arts (LA); and, currently, reabsorbed into the Arts Council, is now Arts Council, London (ACE London).

TWO: LIFT LEARNS THE LANGUAGE OF BUSINESS

1   Richard Adams and Nigel Coke were LIFT's graphic designers at that time.
2   The British Council receives government funding via the Foreign and Commonwealth Office. It is the United Kingdom's international organization for educational opportunities and cultural relations.
3   Opening nights are less costly as ticket sales build towards the end of a run. If members chose to go on another night, they were asked to pay.

THREE: FINESSING THE RULES OF ENGAGEMENT

1   *Aimer, ce n'est pas se regarder l'un l'autre; c'est regarder ensemble dans la même direction.*

FOUR: REDISCOVERING THE CIVIL SOCIETY AMIDST THE MARKET AND THE STATE

1   Frequently cited quotation of Margaret Mead, attributed to an informal source. Reference web site www.mead2001.org/faq.
2   *Oxford English Dictionary.*

3 Changed to Arts and Business (A&B) in 1999.
4 For example, Lloyd, T. (2004).
5 No official figures exist.
6 A scheme administered by ABSA matching first-time business sponsors' support pound for pound.
7 www.commonpurpose.org.uk.
8 This section adapted from Yu, R. *LIFTING London Report*, (1992), LIFT Archive.
9 LIFT was introduced to Angell Town by architects Burrell Foley Fischer.
10 Following LIFTING London, the Islington access and mentoring schemes won a Queen's Award for Education.

FIVE: ENTER YOUNG THEATRE-MAKERS

1 Freelance arts educationalists, Polona Baloh Brown and Michael MacMillan, led the pilot phase.
2 'There is no such thing as society. There are individual men and women and there are families' (Thatcher 1987 in *Women's Own*).
3 Southern African Development Community.
4 This section to p. 99 taken from writing by Anna Ledgard (Ledgard 2006).
5 On 14 May 1991, Winnie Mandela, the former wife of Nelson Mandela, was found guilty of taking part in the kidnapping of four youths suspected of being police informers, 14-year-old Stompie Moeketsi among them. Mandela's chief bodyguard, Jerry Richardson, was later sentenced for the boy's murder.

SIX: BLEACHED BONES AND STARTING AGAIN

1 *La vie humaine commence de l'autre côté du désespoir.*
2 Baring became Chairman of the Foundation in 1998.
3 Baring was at that time Chairman of Commercial Union Assurance.
4 This work was based on research of the Statistical Unit at the United Nations Research Institute for Social Development (UNRISD), Geneva. From 1960 to the 1990s, the Unit collected and tested statistical indicators of development, looking for reliable and comparable data for its database that at one point included 120 countries. Discontinued in the 1990s, the work contributed to the Human Development Index now used by the United Nations.
5 Prince of Wales Business Leaders' Forum.

SEVEN: GIVING BIRTH TO THE LIFT BUSINESS ARTS FORUM

1 See Appendix two for descriptions.

EIGHT: TAKING STEPS INTO THE WORLD OF ORGANISATIONS

1 Cited by Karen Otazo, Forum Adviser.
2 Tooting Bec, south London.

3 Research commissioned by the LAB in 1996.
4 LIFT Adviser Arie de Geus introduced me to Lynda Gratton, Professor of Organizational Development at London Business School, and hence to members of the Leading Edge Research Consortium.
5 For comprehensive organizational analysis of companies participating in the Leading Edge Research Consortium see Gratton, L. *et al.* (1999).
6 I was directed to Santa Fé by Adelma Roach whose *The Work of Youth Arts* describes in greater detail the learning outcomes of the mural project.

NINE: COLLECTIVE LEARNING

1 See Gibb with Schwartz (1999).
2 Source: conversation with Scilla Elworthy, Oxford Research Group. Team member Gemma Emmanuel-Waterton joined previously named Phakama facilitators at this session.
3 By kind permission of Gibb's son, Devlin Barrett. Gibb died in 1999.

TEN: CRAFTING A NEW DISCOURSE – EXPERIMENTS AND EVOLUTION

1 Spoken to an audience of actors in Madrid at a special performance of *Yerma*, David Johnston (1989).
2 Heinzen facilitated East Africa scenarios at the invitation of the Society for International Development.
3 QUEST stands for Quality, Efficiency and Standards. The organization offers independent advice to the Secretary of State for Culture, Media and Sport on best practice in the delivery of the government's cultural and sporting objectives.
4 From a poem by Rogel McGough, *The Header.*
5 No official figures exist, but Internet research indicates 80 per cent of chat groups fail in the first three months.
6 Euan Semple, Head of Knowledge Management, BBC, Forum planning meeting 2001.
7 Declan Donnellan is founding Director of UK theatre company, Cheek by Jowl.
8 Adapted from 'The Story of the LIFT Enquiry', LIFT internal paper (2005), LIFT Archive.
9 Rustom Bharucha, LIFT lecture.
10 Video recordings in LIFT Archive.
11 Bursaries funded through ACE London and the Jerwood Charity.
12 AEB's New Partners' Scheme

ELEVEN: OVERSTEPPING THE MARKET

1 Rosehaugh Stanhope.
2 A musical adaptation of Giraudoux's *The Mad Woman of Chaillot.*
3 www.motiroti.com and www.alladeen.com.

4 The author is a Board member of **moti**roti.
5 Lecture given by Dr Vandana Shiva in May 2003, www.liftfest.org.uk/lectures.
6 Permissions have been sought for all quotations in copyright used in this book. One was dropped because fees charged by publishers were too great.

TWELVE: INVENTIVE SOCIETIES BEGIN ON OUR DOORSTEP

1 From *Conversation: How Talk Can Change Your Life* by Theodore Zeldin, published by Harvill Press. Reprinted by permission of The Random House Group Ltd.
2 The Centre for the Study of the Language of Information.
3 Devlin (1997) describes the Cartesian foundations of mathematics as crumbling, no longer the repository of unquestionable truths.
4 www.santafe.edu.
5 *Where is the Practice of Scenarios Going?* Presentation by Kees van der Heijden, 7 November 2002.
6 RSA, ACE Arts and Ecology Programme.
7 Described in Chapter ten.

BIBLIOGRAPHY

ACGB (Arts Council of Great Britain) (1946) *Royal Charter*, Oxford: Oxford University Press.

Adams, J. (ed.) (1998) *A New Paradigm for Developing Organizations, Transforming Work*, Arlington, VA: Miles River Press.

Allan, J., Fairtlough, G. and Heinzen, B. (2002) *The Power of the Tale*, Chichester: John Wiley & Sons Inc.

Augsdorfer, P. (1996) *Forbidden Fruit, An Analysis of Bootlegging, Uncertainty and Learning in Corporate R&D*, Aldershot: Avebury.

Baker, P. and Eversley, J. (eds) (2000) *Multilingual Capital: The Languages of London*, London: Battlebridge Publications.

Baldwin, J. (1970) *Notes of a Native Son*, London: Penguin.

Ball, P. (2004) *Critical Mass*, London: Arrow Books.

BBC (1994) *File on Four*, Radio 4.

Beck, U. (2000) *What is Globalization?*, Cambridge: Polity Press.

Beck, U., Giddens, A. and Lash, S. (1994) *Reflexive Modernization: Politics, Tradition and Aesthetics in the Modern Social Order*, Stanford, CA: Stanford University Press.

Bentley, E. (1952) *New Republic*, 29 December.

Benyus, J.M. (2002) *Biomimicry: Innovation Inspired by Nature*, New York: HarperCollins.

Bharucha, R. (2001) *The Politics of Cultural Practice: Thinking Through Theatre in an Age of Globalization*, New Delhi: Oxford University Press.

Bianchini, F. and Landry, C. (1995) *The Creative City*, London: Demos in association with Comedia.

Bibb, S. and Kourdi, J. (2004) *Trust Matters*, Basingstoke: Palgrave Macmillan.

Blake, D.J. and Crittall, A. (2004) *Window Vision*, Essex: Crittall Windows.

Bollier, D. (2002) 'Commons Sense', *Multinational Monitor*, Vol. 23 No. 7/8.

Browning, R. (1864) 'Abt Vogler', st. 2. in A. Roberts (ed.) (1997) *Oxford Authors: Robert Browning*, Oxford: Oxford University Press.

Conry, J.C. (1998) 'Women as Fundraisers: Their Experience in and Influence on an Emerging Profession', *New Directions for Philanthropic Fundraising* 19, San Francisco: Jossey-Bass.

Coyle, D. (1997) *The Weightless World: Thriving in the Digital Age*, Oxford: Capstone.

Coyle, D. (2001) *Paradoxes of Prosperity*, London: Texere.

Dees, G., Battle Anderson, B. and Wei-Skillern, J. (2002) 'Pathways to Social Impact: Strategies for Scaling Out Successful Social Innovations', *CASE Working Paper Series 3*.

Devlin, K. (1997) *Goodbye Descartes: The End of Logic and the Search for a New Cosmology of the Mind*, Chichester: John Wiley and Sons.

Donnellan, D. and Handy, C. (2001) Talk prior to *Boris Godunov*, LIFT Archive.

Ebron, P.A. (2002) *Performing Africa*, Princeton, NJ: Princeton University Press.

Edwards, B. (1979) *Drawing on the Right Side of the Brain*, Los Angeles: J.P. Tarcher.

Edwards, B. (1987) *Drawing on the Artist Within*, Glasgow: William Collins.

Eisenhart, M.A. and Finkel, E. (1998) *Women's Science: Learning and Succeeding from the Margins*, Chicago, IL: University of Chicago Press.

Eisner, E. (2000) 'Ten Lessons the Arts Teach', in *Learning and the Arts: Crossing Boundaries*. Proceedings of a meeting for education, arts and youth funders, January, Los Angeles.

Eliot, T.S. [1940] (1963), 'East Coker', Four Quartets, *Collected Poems*, London: Faber and Faber.

Fairtlough, G. (1994) *Creative Compartments*, London: Adamantine Press.

Fairtlough, G. (2005) *The Three Ways of Getting Things Done: Hierarchy, Heterarchy and Responsible Autonomy*, Bridport: Triarchy Press.

Fischman, W., Solomon, B., Greenspan, D. and Gardner, H. (2004) *Making Good: How Young People Cope with Moral Dilemmas at Work*, Boston, MA: Harvard University Press.

Geus, A. de (1997) *The Living Company; Growth, Learning and Longevity in Business*, London: Nicholas Brealey Publishing.

Gibb, B. (1998) 'The New Eunuchs', *Anchoring the Light*, London: The Poets.

Gibb, B. with Schwartz, P. (1999) *When Good Companies Do Bad Things: Responsibility and Risk in an Age of Globalization*, Chichester: John Wiley & Sons Inc.

Gladwell, M. (2000) *The Tipping Point: How Little Things Can Make a Big Difference*, New York: Little, Brown and Company.

Gordon, B. (1998) *Bazaars and Fair Ladies: The History of the American Fundraising Fair*, Knoxville, TN: University of Tennessee Press.

Gratton, L., Hope-Hailey, V., Stiles, P. and Truss, C. (1999) *Strategic Human Resource Management, Corporate Rhetoric and Human Reality*, Oxford: Oxford University Press.

Greezy, U., Niederle, M. and Rustichini, A. (2003) 'Performance in Competitive Environments: Gender Differences,' *Quarterly Journal of Economics*, Vol. 118 No. 3 (August).

Grigson, J. (1993) *Jane Grigson's Fish Book*, London: Penguin.

Hall, S. (2001) *Museums of Modern Art and the End of History*, London: inIVA.

Hall, S. and Maharaj, S. (2001) 'Modernity and Difference', *Annotations* 6, London: inIVA.

Hampden-Turner, C.M. and Trompenaars, A. (1993) *The Seven Cultures of Capitalism*, New York: Doubleday.

Hampden-Turner, C.M. and Trompenaars, A. (2000) *Building Cross-cultural Competence: How to Create Wealth from Conflicting Values*, Chichester: John Wiley & Sons Inc.

Handy, C. (1994) *The Empty Raincoat: Making Sense of the Future*, London: Hutchinson.

Handy, C. (1997) *The Hungry Spirit*, London: Hutchinson.

Handy, C. (1998) *The Search for Meaning*, London: Lemos and Crane.

Handy, C. (2001) *The Elephant and the Flea*, London: Hutchinson.

Handy, C. and Handy, E. (1999) *The New Alchemists*, London: Hutchinson.

Harcourt, W., Muliro, A. and Heinzen, B. (eds) (2004) 'Development: Surviving Uncertainty', *Journal of the Society for International Development*, Vol. 47 No 4.

Harding, F. (ed.) (2002) *The Performance Arts in Africa*, London: Routledge.

Havel, V. (1986) [1978] 'The Power of the Powerless', *Living in Truth*, J. Vladislav (ed.), London: Faber and Faber.

Havel, V. [1991] (1992) *Summer Meditations on Politics, Morality and Civility in a Time of Transition*, trans. Paul Wilson, London: Faber and Faber.

Heath, S.B. (2005) Cross-London Lecture, King's College, 28 June.

Heath, S.B. and Smyth, L. (1999) *Artshow: Youth and Community Development, A Resource Guide*, Washington, DC: Partners for Livable Communities.

Heinzen, B. (1984) 'Social Foundations of Economic Development', unpublished paper, November.

Heinzen, B. (forthcoming) *Feeling for Stones: Learning and Invention When Facing the Unknown*, awaiting publication, available from eburke@dircon.co.uk.

Her Majesty's Stationery Office (1991) *London: World City*, London: HMSO.

Hutton, W. (1995) *The State We're In*, London: Jonathan Cape.

Hutton, W. (2002) *The World We're In*, London: Little Brown.

Ings, R. (2003) *Connecting Flights: New Cultures of the Diaspora*, London: British Council.

Ingvar, D. (1985) 'Memory of the Future: an Essay on the Temporal Organization of Conscious Awareness', *Human Neurobiology*, Vol. 4.

Jeyasingh, S. (2002) 'For Art's Sake!', *Connections*, Commission for Racial Equality, online.

Johnston, D. (1989) Introduction to Lorca, F.G. *Blood Wedding*, London: Hodder and Stoughton.

Jordan, W.R. (2003) *The Sunflower Forest: Ecological Restoration and the New Communion with Nature*, London: University of California Press.

Kay, J. (2003) *The Truth About Markets*, London: Allen Lane.

Kelly, K. (1998) *The Development of Dreamwork, a Youth Arts Project. A Partnership between the Halifax plc and Islington Council Established in Collaboration with the LWT Talent Challenge*, report.

Klein, N. (2000) *No Logo: Taking Aim at the Brand Bullies*, London: Flamingo.

Klein, N. (2002) *Fences and Windows: Dispatches from the Front Lines of the Globalisation Debate*, London: Flamingo.

Knell, J. (2004) *The Art of Dying*, www.missionmoneymodels.og.uk.

Kundera, M. (1984) *The Unbearable Lightness of Being*, trans. Michael Henry Heim, London: Faber and Faber.

Lave, J. and Wenger, E. (1991) *Situated Learning: Legitimate Peripheral Participation*, Cambridge: Cambridge University Press.

Ledgard, A. (2006) 'Fair Exchange: Shared Professional Development', in Burnard, P. and Hennessy, S. (eds) *Reflective Practices in Arts Education*, Dordrecht, NL: Kluwer Academic Publishers and writings in LIFT Archive.

Lessig, L. (2002) *The Future of Ideas: the Fate of the Commons in a Connected World*, New York: First Vintage Books.

LIFT (1992) *LIFTING London Report*, Ros Yu, LIFT Archive.

LIFT (1994) LIFT Brainstorm Meeting Transcription, LIFT Archive, 7 February.

LIFT (1995) LIFT '95 Business Arts Forum Report, Krishna Guha, LIFT Archive.

LIFT (1997) LIFT Learning Document (1997), LIFT Archive.

LIFT (1999a) LIFT '99 Forum (promotional) leaflet, LIFT Archive.

LIFT (1999b) LIFT '99 Forum Report, LIFT Archive.

LIFT (2005) LIFT internal paper 'The Story of the LIFT Enquiry', LIFT Archive.

Lloyd, T. (2004) *Why Rich People Give*, London: Philanthropy UK.

Locke, J. [1690] (2004) 'Dedicatory Epistle', *An Essay Concerning Human Understanding*, R. Woolhouse (ed.), London: Penguin, p. 3.

Lohmann, R.A. (2003) 'The Commons: Our Mission If We Choose to Accept It', *The Nonprofit Quarterly*, Summer.

Maturana, H. and Varela, F. (1987) *The Tree of Knowledge*, Boston, MA: New Science Library.

Meadows, D.H. (1997) 'Places to Intervene in a System', *Whole Earth*, Winter: 78–84.

Mistry, R. (1995) *A Fine Balance*, London: Faber and Faber.

Monbiot, G. (2003) *The Age of Consent*, London: Flamingo.

New Scientist (2002) 'Girls Get Competitive, But Only If It's Worth It', 24 August.

Pepys, S. [1665] (1890) *Diary and Correspondence of Samuel Pepys, F.R.S.*, London: George Allen and Unwin. Vol 2, p. 259, 9 November 1665.

Prabhu, G. and Heap, S. (2001) 'Zurich Financial Services' Partnerships with Indian NGOs', *Journal of Corporate Citizenship*, Sheffield: Greenleaf.

Putnam, R.D. (1993) 'The Prosperous Community: Social Capital and Public Life', *The American Prospect*, Online (30 November 2002).

Pye, D. (1978) *The Nature and Aesthetics of Design*, London: Herbert Press.

Reynolds, J. [1774] (1975) *Discourses on Art*, R. Wark (ed.), London: Yale University Press, p. 99.

Rifkin, J. (2000) *The Age of Access: How the Shift from Ownership to Access is Transforming Modern Life*, London: Penguin.

Rowntree, J. (1996) *Learning through the Arts: Professional Development Needs and Implications for Arts and Education in London*, LIFT Archive.

Roy, A. (2002) *The Algebra of Infinite Justice*, New Delhi: Penguin India.

Royal Society for Arts, Manufactures and Commerce (1994) *Tomorrow's Company Report*.

Saint-Exupéry, A. de (1939) *(Terre des Hommes)*; (2000) *Wind, Sand and Stars*, London: Penguin Classics.

Sartre, J.-P. [1943] (1960) *Les Mouches*, London: Penguin.

Seely Brown, J. and Duguid, P. (2000) *The Social Life of Information*, Boston, MA: Harvard Business School Press.

Sellars, P. (1990) *Los Angeles Festival Programme*, Los Angeles, CA: LA Festival.

Semler, R. (1993) *Maverick*, London: Arrow Business Books.

Sen, A. (1999) *Development as Freedom*, Oxford: Oxford University Press.

Senge, P.M. (1990) *The Fifth Discipline: the Art and Practice of the Learning Organization*, London: Century Business.

Sennett, R. (1980) *Authority*, London: Secker and Warburg.

Shah, K. (2001) 'Depressed in the US? Just Call India for Solace', *The Economic Times*, November.

Shakespeare, W. (1994) *Complete Works of Shakespeare*, Glasgow: HarperCollins, p. 237.

Shiva, V. (2000) *Tomorrow's Biodiversity*, London: Thames and Hudson.

Smit, T. (2001) *Eden*, London: Bantam Press.

Smith, A. (1776) *Wealth of Nations*, bk 1, ch. 2.

Stiglitz, J. (2003) *Globalization and its Discontents*, New York: W.W. Norton and Company.

Storkey, M. (1994) *London's Ethnic Minorities – One City, Many Communities*, London: London Research Centre.

Tan, E. (2001) *PIDGIN Interrupted Transmission*, London: Film and Video Umbrella.

Tannen, D. (1992a) *You Just Don't Understand: Women and Men in Conversation*, London: Virago.

Tannen, D. (1992b) *That's Not What I Meant! How Conversational Style Makes or Breaks Your Relations With Others*, London: Virago.

Tong, R. (1989) *Feminist Thought: a Comprehensive Introduction*, Boulder, CO: Westview Press.

Varela, F.J., Thompson, E. and Rosch, E. (1993) *The Embodied Mind: Cognitive Science and Human Experience*, Boston, MA: MIT Press.

Victor, B. and Boynton, A.C. (1998) *Invented Here: Maximising Your Organization's Internal Growth and Profitability, a Practical Guide to Transforming Work*, Boston, MA: Harvard Business School Press.

Waldrop, M.M. (1992) *Complexity: the Emerging Science at the Edge of Order and Chaos*, New York: Simon and Schuster.

Wa Thiong'o, N. (1993) *Moving the Centre, the Struggle for Cultural Freedoms*, London: Heinemann.

Wend Fenton, R. de and Neal, L. (2005) *The Turning World, Stories from the London International Festival of Theatre*, London: Gulbenkian.

Wenger, E., McDermott, R. and Snyder, W.M. (2002) *Cultivating Communities of Practice*, Boston, MA: Harvard Business School Press.

Wertheim, M. (1997) *Pythagoras' Trousers; God, Physics and the Gender Wars*, London: Fourth Estate.

Westfall, R. (1993) *The Life of Isaac Newton*, Cambridge: Cambridge University Press.

Women's Own (1987) Interview with Margaret Thatcher, 31 October.

Wu, C.T. (2002) *Privatising Culture, Corporate Art Intervention since the 1980s*, London: Verso.

Wynne-Jones, A. (2005) 'Exploring Internationalism', *London 2012 Report*, in preparation. Extract from keynote address at '2012 Exploring Internationalism Forum', held at East London University, July 2005, published in *LIFT News*, Autumn 2005, LIFT Archive.

Yeats, W.B. [1914] (1990) Epigraph 'responsibilities', *The Poems*, D. Albright (ed.), London: Dent, p. 148.

Zadek, S. (2001) *The Civil Corporation, the New Economy of Corporate Citizenship*, London: Earthscan.

Zeldin, T. (1994) *An Intimate History of Humanity*, London: Sinclair Stevenson.

Zeldin, T. (1998) *Conversation: How Talk Can Change Your Life*, London: Harvill Press, reprinted by permission of The Random House Group Ltd.

Web references consulted in 2004 and 2005

Bollier, D., www.bollier.org

Commission for Racial Equality, www.cre.gov.uk

Common Purpose, www.commonpurpose.org.uk

Crittall Windows, www.crittall-windows.co.uk

Department for Culture, Media and Sport, www.culture.gov.uk

Institute of International Visual Arts, www.iniva.org

Lessig, L., www.lessig.org

London International Festival of Theatre, www.liftfest.org.uk

London School of Economics, Centre for Civil Society, www.lse.ac.uk/collections/ CCS

Mission, Money, Models Project, www.missionmodelsmoney.org.uk

motiroti and *Alladeen*, www.motiroti.com and www.alladeen.com

Longplayer, www.longplayer.org

Rifkin, J., Foundation on Economic Trends, www.foet.org

Royal Society for Arts, Manufactures and Commerce, www.rsa.org.uk

Shiva, V., www.navdanya.org

Society for International Development, www.sidint.org

INDEX